Enterprise Series: Downsizing to UNIX

Steve Glines

NEW RIDERS PUBLISHING

New Riders Publishing, Carmel, Indiana

Enterprise Series: Downsizing to UNIX

By Steve Glines

Published by:
New Riders Publishing
11711 N. College Ave., Suite 140
Carmel, IN 46032 USA

Printed in the United States of America 1 2 3 4 5 6 7 8 9 0

Library of Congress Cataloging-in-Publication Data

Glines, Steve, 1952-
Downsizing to UNIX/Steve Glines.
       p.   cm.
Includes index.
ISBN 1-56205-074-5 : $49.95
1. Operating systems (Computers) 2. UNIX (Computer file) I.
Title.
QA76.76.063G588   1992
005.4'3—dc20 92-28883
       CIP

Publisher

David P. Ewing

Associate Publisher

Tim Huddleston

Acquisitions Editor

Brad Koch

Managing Editor

Cheri Robinson

Product Director

Michael Groh

Developmental Editor

Nancy E. Sixsmith

Editors

Rob Lawson
Nora Loechel
Lisa D. Wagner

Technical Editors

Karla Kitalong
Rita Lewis
Joe Wade

Editorial Secretary

Karen Opal

Acquisitions Assistant

Geneil Breeze

Book Design and Production

William Hartman
Hartman Publishing

Proofreaders

Rob Lawson
Nancy E. Sixsmith

Indexed by

Sharon Hilgenberg

About the Author

Steve Glines is an authority in Management Information Systems and Open Systems computing. Over the last ten years he has written extensively for Patty Seybold's "UNIX in the Office" and for *Unix Review*, and has been profiled in UNIX Today (Open Systems Today). His consulting clientele span four continents ranging from Moscow to San Francisco. Mr. Glines is the subject of biographies in *Marquis Who's Who in Emerging Leaders in America* and *Who's Who in the World*, among others, and was nominated by *Inc. Magazine* as Entrepreneur of the Year in 1990.

Over the past twenty five years, Mr. Glines has been a programmer, technical writer, software porting manager, product manager for systems software, and an information systems architect. For the past two years, he has devoted himself to lecturing on the topic of UNIX and Open Systems integration, writing (this is his second book for New Riders Publishing) and advising his international clientele. Mr. Glines serves as Senior Technical Editor for the New Riders series of books in UNIX.

Acknowledgments

New Riders Publishing expresses sincere thanks to the following individuals for their contributions:

Michael Groh, for developing and nurturing the project, and for his excellent authoring skill.

Nancy Sixsmith, for managing the project through its many stages.

Rob Lawson, Nora Loechel, and Lisa D. Wagner, for their cheerful demeanors and accurate editing.

Karla Kitalong and Rita Lewis, for their invaluable help at the author-review stage.

Karen Opal and Geneil Breeze, for acquisitions and editorial help wherever needed.

Bill Hartman, as always, for his excellent layout and artistic skills.

Trademark Acknowledgments

New Riders Publishing has made every attempt to supply trademark information about company names, products, and services mentioned in this book. Trademarks indicated below were derived from various sources. New Riders Publishing cannot attest to the accuracy of this information.

Warning and Disclaimer

This book is designed to provide information about the UNIX computer program. Every effort has been made to make this book as complete and as accurate as possible, but no warranty or fitness is implied.

The information is provided on an "as is" basis. The author and New Riders Publishing shall have neither liability nor responsibility to any person or entity with respect to any loss or damages arising from the information contained in this book or from the use of the disks or programs that may accompany it.

Contents at a Glance

Table of Contents

Part Two: The Design of a Management Information System

Part Three: UNIX Enhancements for Management Information Systems

9 Designing a Management Information System with UNIX 287

Introduction

The MIS (management information system) departments of most mid- to large-size companies in the 1990's are caught between a number of inexorable forces: increasing costs of personnel, decreasing costs of computing hardware, and an ever-increasing workload. As a result, many thousands of companies are engaged in "downsizing" activity; that is, moving traditional MIS tasks from large scale mainframe systems to lower-cost distributed networks of PCs and UNIX workstations.

The reasons for downsizing are compelling. Rather than the millions of dollars that a full-size mainframe systems costs to install and support, a distributed UNIX system can be implemented for a few tens of thousands of dollars. UNIX is a perfectly scalable operating system; the smallest system possible consists of a single workstation while the largest UNIX installations involve literally thousands of workstations networked together.

1

Modern UNIX systems include graphical user interfaces similar to those found in DOS and Macintosh environments. Most UNIX installations include large file servers storing gigabytes of data and automated backup systems to provide a high level of data security. With a modicum of attention from the administrator, UNIX system security and data integrity are insured.

UNIX provides advanced features that can change the way people use computers on their desktops. Rather than being limited to a single-tasking, single-threaded operating system like DOS, the users attached to a UNIX system enjoy the productivity and enhanced throughput possible from a true multitasking operating system. UNIX has emerged as a platform on which tightly integrated applications dynamically exchange data in a seamless fashion.

In spite of its inherent power, UNIX has not yet been widely adopted in MIS environments. The typical UNIX operating system is not easy to learn or use. Although the underlying architecture of UNIX is easy to understand, the UNIX command line can appear hostile and forbidding to the unprepared user. The learning curve for UNIX can be steep. *Downsizing to UNIX* has been designed to reduce the learning curve required to become proficient with UNIX as an MIS environment.

Downsizing to UNIX was specifically written to aid MIS managers, systems-support people, and others involved or interested in downsizing full-scale mainframe data processing to a distributed UNIX network. Without adequate preparation, the process of moving a traditional MIS to UNIX could be a frustrating, difficult endeavor. Rather than replicate information available in introductory UNIX books, the topics discussed in *Downsizing to UNIX* are tailored to the concerns of an MIS department. Within these covers you will find suggestions, hints, and tips on all aspects of data processing, including data and system security, backup, process management, and hardware selection.

UNIX is arguably the least "standardized" of popular operating systems. At the same time that UNIX's flexibility and extensibility are its strongest advantages, the ability to modify the internals of UNIX have led to a number of UNIX variants. Essentially every vendor of UNIX hardware and software has "enhanced" the core utilities and applications found in every UNIX system. Usually these enhancements include new commands, a larger number of command-line switches, and customized procedures for common tasks like backups and user-account management.

The topics and information contained in *Downsizing to UNIX* are applicable to *all* commonly available version of UNIX. Rather than focus on a single version of UNIX, the author presents solutions that are appropriate for essentially *any* implementation of UNIX.

Downsizing to UNIX prepares the experienced MIS professional to take full advantage of the advanced features provided by UNIX. Although a certain amount of technical jargon is unavoidable, *Downsizing to UNIX* assumes no prior knowledge of UNIX.

Although proprietary mainframes have dominated the MIS (management information system) world for decades, UNIX is a mature and flexible platform for MIS development. *Downsizing to UNIX* will help you to use the tools and concepts that are available in UNIX and to apply them to the unique requirements of your management information system.

You learn to develop these management information systems under client-server architecture, open systems architecture, or (more specifically) under an environment that consists of UNIX and networks.

For the advanced MIS professional, UNIX represents freedom from many of the constraints imposed by mainframe environments. *Downsizing to UNIX* provides all of the detailed information required to embark on downsizing projects of any size. The bonus disk included with *Downsizing to UNIX* provides many of the tools required for successful implementation of a UNIX-hosted MIS.

Who Should Read this Book?

Downsizing to UNIX is written for the data-processing professional who knows little about UNIX, but who needs to learn this complex operating system quickly.

Written by a well-known UNIX authority, the confusing and difficult nature of UNIX is presented in a non-technical, non-intimidating manner. Thus, *Downsizing to UNIX* is perfectly suited for the first-time UNIX user.

How this Book is Different from Most Computer Books

Downsizing to UNIX is designed and written to accommodate the way you work. The author of *Downsizing to UNIX* and the editors at New Riders Publishing know that you probably do not have a great deal of time to learn the principals and techniques presented in this book, and that you are anxious to begin using this information to help you become more productive in your daily work.

This book, therefore, does not lead you through endless exercises for every concept and does not waste your time by repeating clearly obvious information. Each chapter introduces you to an important group of related concepts and quickly shows you how these techniques can be applied to your particular situation.

The chapters of this book also lead you through the basic steps you must follow to incorporate each new concept and capability into your own environment. The information is presented in a fast-paced manner to help you become productive in the shortest time possible once you understand the concepts and techniques involved.

Later in this introduction you will find descriptions of each of this book's sections and chapters.

How this Book is Organized

Downsizing to UNIX is divided into four parts. In the first three parts, the material flows from background information, to fundamental design concepts of the MIS, to special UNIX enhancements.

Part Four presents documentation of the utilities contained on the disk that accompanies *Downsizing to UNIX*.

Part One: UNIX and the UNIX Philosophy

Part One is a thorough overview of the UNIX philosophy. It specifically deals with developing an MIS under UNIX.

Chapter One, "Why UNIX?" deals with the economical advantages of UNIX over other systems. Also discussed are the minimal differences between UNIX standards and the minimal headaches of retraining users. There is also advice given on ways to migrate from mainframes and PC-based networks.

Chapter Two, "How UNIX Works" explores the inner workings of UNIX, showing its maturity and flexibility. The chapter also shows what a UNIX system looks like to the user who uses one of many shells (and that almost any interactive program can be used as a shell). There is also an exploration of the major UNIX subsystems, including file and access security, printing, communication, time-dependent processing, and user interfaces.

Chapter Three, "Organization and Structure of the UNIX File System" explores the way the UNIX file system is structured, examines conventions for file-naming, and discusses the physical ordering of files, directories, and network connections.

Chapter Four, "The UNIX Programmer's Toolkit" examines the tools and conventions in the UNIX toolkit. These tools include individual commands as well as pipes, daemons, and local and remote connections and communications.

Chapter Five, "Limitations of UNIX Resources" is an honest evaluation of the limitations and flaws of UNIX and its resources. The chapter shows that, although the standard resources may not always be ideal, new tools and concepts have been introduced to mitigate and/or remove these obstacles.

Part Two: The Design of a Management Information System

Part Two discusses work and data flow in an MIS, resource management, and migration strategies.

Chapter Six, "Work and Data Flow in an MIS," establishes a common ground for MIS and UNIX users. The chapter discusses collecting and verifying data and ways to use this data. A typical MIS system is also described.

Chapter Seven, "Resource Management," explores the management of system resources, the management of users, and the limitations of standard UNIX.

Chapter Eight, "Migration Strategies," explores some migration scenarios and case studies. The chapter also discusses migrating from a mainframe, migrating up from a network of personal computers, making room for the heterogeneous network, and migrating databases.

Part Three: UNIX Enhancements for Management Information Systems

This section is devoted to programs and techniques that address the problems of database-oriented information systems running under UNIX.

Chapter Nine, "Designing a Management Information System with UNIX," discusses tactics and strategies for designing an MIS under UNIX.

Chapter Ten, "Menus for Security and Simplicity," presents the concept behind (and the source code for) the menu shell. The chapter discusses conventions, how to install the menu shell, using the shell archive, and building a menu.

Chapter Eleven, "Data-Entry Screens—Mimicking the Mainframes," discusses data-entry screens and stand-alone data-entry screen programs. The SCREEN program is also introduced.

Chapter Twelve, "Program Spooling (Batch Spooling)," discusses the process of spooling jobs to the printer. The chapter also analyzes the EBATCH and BATCHQ batch-spooling systems.

Chapter Thirteen, "Useful System Administration Commands and Utilities," explains how to kill aberrant users, how to use private cryptography in UNIX, and describes the PCRYPT package in detail.

Part Four: Downsizing to UNIX Disk

The contents of the disk are as follows:

- ❖ **BATCHQ.** A batch-queue management program, BATCHQ provides an automatic method of preventing more than five background tasks from running simultaneously on a system (prevents overhead overload).

- ❖ **DPS.** Removes a user process and all related processes from memory. It provides appropriate housekeeping tasks to make sure that all references to the user are removed from memory and all processes begun by the user are terminated.

- ❖ **EBATCH.** Provides greater control of job tasks launched into the background on a UNIX system.

- ❖ **MSH.** Forms the basis of a menuing system for UNIX systems. Complete source code is included for several menu front-ends to control access to the operating system.

- ❖ **PCRYPT.** A data encryption/decryption application that converts ASCII text to a binary format.

- ❖ **SCREEN.** A data-entry screen generator, it makes it easy to design new data-entry screens to serve as part of the menuing system that restricts access to the operating system.

New Riders' Enterprise Series

Downsizing to UNIX is the second volume of the Enterprise Series by New Riders Publishing. This series explores the many facets of enterprise computing, which is a field that is far too vast to fit into a single volume.

The first volume of the series, *Connectivity: Local Area Networks*, was published in the summer of 1992. It provides solutions for accomplishing the enterprise-connectivity goals of any organization.

Operating Systems: Workstations and LANs, available in the fall of 1992, will explore the characteristics of the most common workstation and local area network operating systems.

Applications: Local Area Networks, also available in the fall of 1992, will discuss advanced application topics: electronic mail, downsizing, and client-server applications.

Conventions Used in this Book

As you work through this book, you will notice special typeface conventions that show you at a glance what actions to take.

❖ All UNIX command names, file names, directory names, shell variable names, and screen messages appear in this `special typeface`.

❖ Information that you type appears in this **`bold special typeface`**.

❖ All variable elements appear in this *italic typeface*.

This book also uses three special icons, which help you identify certain parts of the text:

 A **note** presents brief, additional information relating to the current topic. A note can also be used as a reminder or to clarify a point.

 A **tip** is an added insight for your benefit.

 A **warning** serves as a caution. It points to the careful use of a procedure or to and event that can cause a loss of data or work.

New Riders Publishing

The staff of New Riders Publishing is committed to bringing you the very best in computer reference material. Each New Riders book is the result of months of work by authors and staff, who research and refine the information contained within its covers.

As part of this commitment to you, the NRP reader, New Riders invites your input. Please let us know if you enjoy this book, if you have trouble with the information and examples presented, or if you have a suggestion for the next edition.

Please note, however, that the New Riders staff cannot serve as a technical resource for UNIX or UNIX application-related questions, including hardware or software problems.

If you have a question or comment about any New Riders book, please write to NRP at the following address. We will respond to as many readers as we can. Your name, address, or phone number will never become part of a mailing list or be used for any other purpose than to help us continue to bring you the best books possible.

New Riders Publishing
Prentice Hall Computer Publishing
Attn: Managing Editor
11711 N. College Avenue
Carmel, IN 46032

If you prefer, you can FAX New Riders Publishing at the following number:

(317) 571-3484

Thank you for selecting *Downsizing to UNIX*!

Part One: UNIX and the UNIX Philosophy

Why UNIX?

How UNIX Works

The Organization and Structure of the UNIX File System

The UNIX Programmer's Toolkit

Limitations of UNIX Resources

Topics covered in this chapter:

Understanding the Economics of UNIX

Defining UNIX Standards

Using Applications

Retraining: Fears and Reality

Migrating to UNIX

Chapter 1

Why UNIX?

In the good old days of data processing, the MIS (Management Information Systems) manager had few choices. If the organization was large enough, an IBM mainframe was the obvious choice. If the organization was too small to justify the expense of a mainframe computer, he (or she) could choose one of the smaller, mid-range systems from IBM, such as the System 36 or 38. If the MIS manager was adventurous, or if the best software in the industry only ran on a particular minicomputer, he bought a Prime, a Burroughs, a DEC, a DG, or a Hewlett-Packard system.

NOTE Many mid-range computer manufacturers produced equipment that was specialized for particular applications. For example, Prime found its niche in transportation, Burroughs specialized in banking, and DEC built scientific and engineering machines.

15

If the company grew or diversified, the MIS manager faced some serious and expensive problems. To migrate from a minicomputer or an IBM mid-range computer to a 4341, the low end of the 370 series required a change in operating systems, as well as a software rewrite. In general, applications could not be migrated between operating systems, even within a manufacturer's product line. If the company grew still more, the MIS manager faced the prospect of migrating from one mainframe operating system to another (for example, from DOS to DOS/VS to DOS/VSE, or from DOS to MVS or CMS). Standards in the mainframe world were (and are) as easy to come by as good advice.

There have been attempts, over the years, to create an operating system that spans the range from a single user to a mainframe.

 An operating system that is available on many different sized computers (single user to mainframe) is *scaleable*.

Most of these attempts were made with proprietary operating systems, in which the hardware manufacturers, especially the minicomputer manufacturers, offered a greater and greater range of hardware platforms. Unfortunately, because of the proprietary nature of their systems, these operating systems never achieved generic status.

The first real breakthrough in "open systems" came from the IBM PC. The PC's generic architecture made it easy to clone; mass-production made it inexpensive. Many applications were cheaper to run on stand-alone PCs than on expensive mainframes. Still-independent PCs, or even networked PCs, could not replace the mainframe. What was needed was a generic multi-user and multitasking operating system that could run on everything from a PC to a mainframe. Enter UNIX!

UNIX was developed by a several programmers at Bell Laboratories who wanted to create a portable "Star Wars" game. Because they did not know how long they would have use of a particular piece of hardware, they developed a portable operating system that was capable of supporting their game. They called it *UNIX*, which was a play on the name Multics—a complex operating system designed by Honeywell.

Because Bell Laboratories did not consider UNIX to be commercially viable, it gave UNIX to colleges and universities. As a result, much of the development work on UNIX was carried out as university research projects. This research gave rise to a number of products and companies. Sun Microsystems was founded by a team of researchers and graduate students from the University of California at Berkeley; the MACH multiprocessor UNIX kernel was a product of from Carnegie-Mellon University in Pittsburgh.

In 1980, AT&T began selling unsupported source-code licenses to anyone who could spend $50,000. Microsoft and others bought source licenses and began remarketing UNIX under names like XENIX, VENIX, and AIX. In its early stages of development, UNIX was resold, primarily on the PDP-11 and VAX series of computers. While this was taking place, a revolution occurred in the development of microprocessors with the introduction of the Intel 80X86 series and the Motorola 680X0 series of chips. Operating systems were needed to take advantage of these chips—UNIX fit the bill by being in the right place at the right time.

With UNIX and inexpensive microprocessors, dozens of small computer-hardware manufacturers were created, all offering UNIX with price/performance ratio orders of a magnitude less than those of minicomputers and mainframes. Because none of these micro-and super-micro computers rivaled the mainframe or minicomputer in performance, UNIX was slow to catch on in the business world, except in the smallest enterprises.

While nobody in the MIS world was looking, these super-micro-computers became extremely powerful, and they now rival all but the most powerful mainframes in terms of raw computing power. These advances have come in the form of very fast Intel 486 chips (soon 586 chips), SCSI II disks, mature network products such as Ethernet and FDDI, and symmetric multiprocessing versions of UNIX.

Given that the hardware will support mainframe kinds of applications, what are the reasons for, and the problems with, migrating to UNIX? The following sections discuss these issues.

Understanding the Economics of UNIX

UNIX is a mature operating system. At the time of this writing, four million UNIX licenses have sold worldwide, which is far more than any other multi-user operating system. As a result, the development and maintenance cost of UNIX (per system) is far lower than any other multi-user operating system. Even if the cost were not spread over many systems, the design of UNIX lends itself to portability and ease of maintenance. The following are some case studies:

❖ One major computer hardware manufacturer fully supports both UNIX and its proprietary operating system. In fact, UNIX now accounts for over 40% of sales, yet this manufacturer maintains a programming staff of more than 3000 to maintain the proprietary operating system and fewer than 100 to maintain its version of UNIX.

❖ Another computer hardware manufacturer dropped its proprietary operating system entirely because it cost less to port UNIX with its proprietary applications than it did to port his operating system alone. Although the proprietary operating system for existing customers will be supported, all new systems will be shipped with UNIX (with a resulting savings in the tens of millions of dollars over the next five years).

❖ A mainframe user (a Fortune 1000 company) realized that the annual cost of simply maintaining its network of mainframes exceeded the cost of replacement every two years. As a result, the company began a five year plan to move to UNIX Open Systems. As each mainframe was retired, it was replaced with a network of super-minicomputers running UNIX.

❖ One of the Bell Telephone operating companies was faced with the obsolescence of its network of 20 aging minicomputers used for recording and billing telephone calls. The choice had been made to move to UNIX-based systems and to consolidate billing to one site, but at the time the decision was made, there were no conventional UNIX-based systems capable of handling the load.

In a move contrary to conventional wisdom, the company chose to use UNIX on an existing mainframe—specifically, Amdahl's UTS (a version of UNIX) on an Amdahl mainframe. The managers chose to face the migration costs early in the cycle and thus to extend the useful life of their mainframes by migrating to UNIX. Originally, the mainframe had been partitioned into four logical computers, each running the mainframe operating system MVS. One by one, each of the applications was converted to run under UNIX and the logical computer was converted to UTS. At the time of this writing, the system consists of three UTS-based logical computers and one that continues to run MVS. Each of the UTS-based logical computers supports roughly 1500 terminals.

UNIX is a mature operating system and its development costs have more than been paid for. UNIX is designed to be portable, so the cost of moving it to a new hardware platform is minimal. Because UNIX runs on every hardware platform, from an IBM PC to an IBM mainframe, your costs of migrating up are minimized.

Most colleges and universities teach UNIX, so most new graduates already are familiar with it; few students are knowledgeable about mainframe operations. Finally, most of the important mainframe, mini-, and micro-based applications programs are available on UNIX and most new software development is written on and for UNIX. UNIX has given rise to a passionate love/hate relationship in the data processing community—but UNIX is here to stay.

Defining UNIX Standards

Today there is a UNIX standard. This was not always the case, however. At one time, there were three different standards because AT&T did not consider UNIX to be valuable except as a trade name. As a result, Microsoft's XENIX evolved into the standard for the business sector. The Berkeley version of UNIX evolved in a different direction and became the standard in the engineering sector; AT&T's own version evolved into UNIX System V.

Through a series of negotiations, the differences between XENIX and AT&T UNIX were resolved after the release of UNIX System V Release 3. The differences were minor, but most versions of UNIX System V/386 now execute programs written under XENIX. Both programs that are compiled and linked under XENIX, as well as shell scripts written for XENIX, execute properly. (These UNIX terms are explained thoroughly in the following chapters.)

System V versus Berkeley

The differences between UNIX System V and the Berkeley variant were more serious and fundamental. The Berkeley version of UNIX incorporated networking capabilities as services supported by the UNIX kernel. This philosophy was at variance with the AT&T belief that the kernel should be the smallest possible program—it should be just large enough to support the hardware (and all "services" should be performed by external programs). The Berkeley concept of internal kernel "sockets" gave the device drivers in the system provide direct access to other systems on a network. In this scheme, the UNIX kernel was responsible for data communications and integrity throughout all nodes of a network. Thus, the SUN Microsystems Network File Service relied on the UNIX kernel for external file-system support, as well as for the communications that this entailed.

This approach contrasted sharply with the AT&T streams approach, in which device drivers provided direct, uncorrected access to the network.

 A *stream* acts like a device driver, but it is really a bidirectional pipeline program.

The AT&T Remote File System relied heavily on the streams concept. The streams program handles all communications issues the same way the kernel does in the Berkeley version. The major difference between the two versions is that, although streams may be installed or removed at will, the Berkeley sockets are a permanent part of the Berkeley kernel and they use system resources, even if they are not used.

UNIX System V Release 4

The compromise between the Berkeley version and the standard AT&T UNIX was a completely rewritten UNIX that embodied the best of both systems. Sockets were abandoned in favor of streams and both the NFS (network file service) and RFS (remote file system) were retained. The NFS was rewritten to take advantage of streams and is now the favored choice for cross network files.

The new version, called UNIX System V Release 4, incorporates the standard Berkeley file definitions, as well as UNIX and XENIX. The result is a system that is far larger than any previous versions of UNIX, but it is also a version of UNIX that is more amenable to the MIS manager.

The Open Software Foundation (OSF)

The Open Software Foundation was created by a group of companies who did not want to pay royalties for UNIX to AT&T. This organization has had some good ideas, and it will play an important role in the future of UNIX. Chief among these good ideas is the concept of Application Binary Interface (ABI). To explain this concept, you must understand the way UNIX software is delivered and supported.

Traditionally, a software developer has to compile his software on dozens of different hardware and software platforms. This process can be very expensive, and only a few large developers can afford it. If UNIX is to succeed as well as MS-DOS, there must be a mechanism that enables compiled software created on one machine to be recompiled on any other, without the use of the original source code.

This concept has been around for a long time. One of the original ideas behind the Pascal language is that compilations take place in two steps. The first step is to compile Pascal code into a universal intermediate language called *p-code*. The second step is to use a compiler to create native executable binary code from the universal p-code. Thus, only p-code has to be distributed and a native p-code compiler or interpreter on the target machine performs the task of creating executable code.

Ryan-McFarlan, Informix, and other software vendors use this concept except that, rather than use a native compiler for the p-code, they provide *interpreters*. Interpreters are far slower for executing programs than are identical programs executing as native code.

Application Binary Interface (ABI) takes binary code that is compiled on a number of target machines and translates the code into the native binary code of the host machine. In essence, a program compiled on an SCO UNIX machine can be "recompiled" to run on any other machine, as long as the other machine has an ABI interface program.

If and when ABI becomes a reality, generic UNIX software will become feasible and as widely available as is software for the PC. The Open Software Foundation has designated a number of UNIX systems as primary ABI-interface machines. These systems include SCO UNIX and 88-Open UNIX, which is UNIX that is designed to run on the Intel 88000 chip. The IBM RISC chip, as well as DEC's new RISC, will probably be included in the ABI standard because IBM and DEC are the Open Software Foundation's prime benefactors.

The Free Software Foundation

The Free Software Foundation should not be confused with the Open Software Foundation, even though both are located in Cambridge, Massachusetts. The Free Software Foundation is a clearinghouse for top-quality, public-domain software. Most of the software offered by the Free Software Foundation is UNIX-oriented, and the stated object of the Free Software Foundation is to provide a public-domain version of UNIX in source code form. Because "UNIX" is a trade name of AT&T, the Free Software Foundation calls its operating system Gnu, which stands for "Gnu is not UNIX."

Gnu is an ongoing project, but many of the best UNIX utility programs have been completed and are available in source code (Ansi Standard C). These programs have been incorporated into several "real" versions of UNIX. For example, the Gnu "bison" program is a superset of the UNIX "yacc" utility. The best known product of the Free Software Foundation is EMACS, which is an excellent text editor. Products are available for the cost of the media. To obtain more information, contact:

The Free Software Foundation
675 Massachusetts Avenue
Cambridge Massachusetts 02139
(617)876-3296

Posix, X/Open, and SVID

A number of standards and standard bodies have evolved. The first standards definition was the System V Interface Definition (SVID). SVID was created by AT&T to define UNIX and its clones. Concurrent to the development of SVID, and in compliance with it, is Posix, which is a standard developed by the IEEE and adopted by the U.S. government. Posix is a subset of the SVID; all versions of UNIX System V, and several other operating systems, are compliant with the Posix standard. For example, Digital Equipment Corporation offers an add-on product to its proprietary VMS operating system that enables it to conform to the Posix standard.

If Posix is a minimum requirement in the United States, the same can be said of the requirements of the X/Open committee in Europe. As with Posix, all versions of UNIX System V are compliant with the X/Open standards.

To understand how small the differences are between competing versions of UNIX, consider the UNIX, non-UNIX, and "almost-UNIX" operating systems that pass all three tests: Posix, X/Open, and SVID. These systems include UNIX System V Release 4, SunOS, SCO UNIX, OSF/1, and Lynx (a real-time clone of UNIX). There are differences between these operating systems, and some of these differences are quite dramatic (these differences are discussed where appropriate).

X Windows

The topic of X Windows always arouses interest, but in most MIS environments, X Windows is irrelevant. The MIS environment consists of the following three functions:

❖ Simple data entry and retrieval

❖ Posting programs that summarize and transfer data from one file to another

❖ Reports

None of these functions requires X Windows or anything more than dumb terminals. The object of this book is to show the MIS manager how to replace block mode IBM 3270 terminals (or the equivalent mid-range terminals) with the more responsive dumb ASCII terminals.

Using Applications

For years, UNIX had a reputation for a conspicuous lack of application programs. This reputation was justified until 1985. Today there is no major application that has not been ported to UNIX, and most new software development efforts are done on UNIX systems. There are some well-known applications that cannot be ported to UNIX because their architecture does not allow it, at least not in their present form (for example, COPIX and MAPIX, which are Material Requirements Planning programs).

There are a growing number of full accounting and MRP programs, some written in COBOL and others in fourth-generation languages that have run under UNIX for years. In fact, most of the programs written in fourth-generation languages were initially developed under UNIX. There are also thousands of vertical software packages available for UNIX. This book, however, is intended for those who build and maintain their own MIS systems or design them for others.

All standard application programs are available under UNIX. For example, almost every word processing program, from Microsoft Word to WordPerfect, are available on UNIX.

 Many of the most popular MS-DOS word processing programs work on UNIX but they often work awkwardly. For example, WordPerfect is heavily dependent on the use of function keys. On a PC there are ten function keys that can be used with the Shift key, the Control key, and the Alt key (a total of forty function keys). Most "dumb" terminals used with UNIX have, at most, 16 function keys that can be used with the standard Shift key, (a total of 32 function keys). Thus, programs like WordPerfect almost require terminals that emulate the IBM PC console and have the "standard" PC keyboard layout, which makes standard UNIX applications that expect sixteen function keys hard to use. The only solution is to try to match applications to the terminals in use.

In addition to most of the popular word processing programs, UNIX supports a wide variety of spreadsheets, including Lotus 1-2-3 and others that are written specifically to take advantage of the features of UNIX. More important to the MIS manager than conventional applications are the database managers and languages that the system will support. In this area, UNIX is rich.

The list of conventional languages is a long one. It includes at least half a dozen versions of COBOL, FORTRAN, BASIC, and RPG. Of course, the native language of UNIX is C, which has a unique trait. There are times when even the most dedicated COBOL programmer on a mainframe needs to use assembly language for one reason or another. Under UNIX, C serves the purpose as a transportable low-level language.

The C language has been described as the lowest of the high-level languages or as a high-level assembly language. In either case, a knowledge of C is not a prerequisite for using UNIX.

Perhaps the greatest contribution UNIX brings its number and variety of database-management systems (DBMSs). Under UNIX, the DBMS serves two purposes. First, it provides indexes for the data, a data dictionary, as well as some form of query language that is usually based on the industry standard Structured Query Language (SQL).

Second, and more important for the MIS manager, the DBMS acts as a transaction-processing monitor (TP), serving the same purpose under UNIX that TP monitors, such as CICS, do on a mainframe. If you are migrating from a PC or network of PCs to UNIX, you should know that there are several versions of dBASE available for UNIX as well. All in all, UNIX offers a rich set of applications and application-development tools, in a stable environment, that is suitable for MIS development.

Retraining: Fears and Reality

UNIX is just another operating system, as far as training is concerned. As will be seen shortly, however, there are aspects of UNIX that actually make it easier to learn than many other systems. For example, unlike mainframe operating systems that often offer a smorgasbord of features and capabilities, UNIX has a philosophy that dictates where programs, devices, and data are stored, as well as a standard set of commands. Once this philosophy is mastered, UNIX becomes conceptually simple (at least from the structural point of view).

What often overwhelms novice UNIX users is the number and diversity of UNIX commands. Many of the commands fall into families of commands, however, and once one member of the family is mastered, the other commands are easy to use.

Many aspects of UNIX have been incorporated into other operating systems. If you are comfortable with MS-DOS, for instance, UNIX will not seem quite as difficult. Many of the concepts (and commands) that are used in DOS were taken directly from UNIX. For example, the concept of directory trees is used in both UNIX and DOS, as is the command used to create directories, `mkdir`. Other commands that appear cryptic are in fact mnemonic (such as `mv` for move and `rm` for remove). Other commands are acronyms (for example, `grep` stands for *g*eneralized *r*egular *e*xpression *p*arser, and `sed` is short for *s*tream *ed*itor). A last group of commands are simply the initials of the authors (for example, the language `awk` stands for the initials of creators Aho, Weinberger, and Kernighan).

UNIX training falls into three categories: training for users, programmers, and system administrators. For end users, UNIX training consists of little more than logging onto the system. Of course, users must also be trained in the use of new applications which, under UNIX, are often easier to use and are generally more interactive than their mainframe equivalents.

Programmer training is a little more involved. To the programmer who is accustomed to working with PCs, UNIX will seem familiar and the transition will be easy. The programmer that is used to mainframes will find it a little more difficult because efficient UNIX programming requires a fundamental shift in program design.

The system administrator will find a system that, although complex at first blush, is easy to maintain and relatively easy to learn.

Becoming an expert at anything, including UNIX administration, takes time, but the time to become proficient with UNIX takes years less than with the typical mainframe.

The reality of UNIX is that it is a relatively simple system that can be mastered in a short period of time. After mastering UNIX, you will find that the knowledge is transportable from a humble PC to a mighty mainframe.

Chapters 2 through 5 are designed to help the MIS professional learn what the "UNIX philosophy" is and what tools are available for system design and management.

Migrating to UNIX

Application migration to UNIX is usually simple and straightforward. The only major consideration is the fact that most IBM systems are EBCDIC (Extended Binary Coded Decimal Interchange Code) oriented; most UNIX systems are ASCII (American Standard Code for Information Interchange) oriented. Normally this does not present any problems because UNIX has the capability to translate from EBCDIC to ASCII through the dd (disk-to-disk copy) command. Most UNIX systems are capable of reading and writing a nine-track tape (with additional hardware and software), although the technology used in most UNIX systems tends toward high-density cartridge tape systems.

The problems of translating EBCDIC to ASCII involve matters of discrete programming. That is, if the programs used on the mainframe use the binary equivalent of a particular character or sequence of characters, that program has to be rewritten. For example, uppercase letter "A" is stored as the decimal number 65 in ASCII; the same letter is represented as the decimal number 193 in EBCDIC.

Problems can occur if the mainframe programmers have used "clever" techniques to speed up their programs, and you intend to recompile the same programs used on the mainframe on the UNIX system.

It is unlikely that you will be able to use much of your mainframe (or mid-range) programs on UNIX because none of the TP monitors on those platforms work on UNIX. The chances are that, rather than porting thousands of lines of COBOL or RPG code to UNIX, you will use one of the database managers as a programming language and as a TP manager, at least as far as on-line transaction processing is concerned.

The case for batch-oriented programs is a little different. In some cases, you may still be able to use your original code by using one of the database "front ends" to your language. For example, Micro Focus and LPI COBOL are standard ANSI compilers, so much of your original COBOL source code can be compiled.

To access the database, however, you may need a database interface kit for your compiler, available from the DBMS publisher. If you have chosen Informix as your database engine, you may use your original COBOL source code with the Informix product ISQL/COBOL (*I*mbedded *SQL* for *COBOL*). Other DBMS vendors have equivalent products. Moving your data is relatively straightforward: most of the current crop of DBMSs enable you to import ASCII files straight into their databases.

Realistically, migration strategies vary from site to site. A migration from a network of PCs, from an IBM mid-range system, or from some other minicomputer is easiest if completed all at once. First translate the programs, then transfer the data and resume operations on the UNIX system. Obviously, programs that are written for an IBM System 38 or AS/400 cannot be converted overnight, but once the program conversion has taken place, the data can easily be converted and migrated over a weekend.

A migration from a mainframe to UNIX is more involved. The company has to continue operating while the migration takes place. Considering the volume of data, programs, and personnel associated with a mainframe, it is unlikely that a migration can be accomplished overnight or on a weekend.

Mainframe-to-UNIX Migration Strategy

Given the worst of circumstances or the largest of mainframe installations, what follows is a relatively painless and orderly migration plan. It is painless because it replaces mainframe components with UNIX-based components at a rate that enables personnel to become used to the UNIX environment while the migration takes place.

At the start of a migration, a mainframe system resembles that shown in figure 1.1. At the center of activity is the mainframe. Connected to the mainframe are 3270 cluster controllers, which in turn are connected to 3270 style terminals.

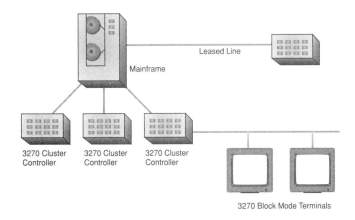

Figure 1.1:
Typical mainframe system architecture.

The first step in the migration process is to replace the 3270 cluster controllers and 3270 block-mode terminals with small UNIX-based systems and ASCII terminals. A typical IBM PC clone, with a 80386 processor that uses SCO UNIX can adequately support as many terminals and printers as a typical 3270 cluster controller can.

To handle the communications with the mainframe is a 3270 emulation package, consisting of both hardware and software. In the first stage of migration, the UNIX system merely acts as a replacement for the 3270 cluster controllers. Multi-dropped leased lines are replaced with X.25 wide area communications. After the first stage of migration, the system looks like that shown in figure 1.2.

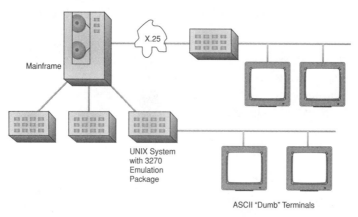

Figure 1.2:
Typical mainframe with UNIX systems at the periphery.

The second stage of migration adds local programs, such as word processors, spreadsheets, and electronic mail, to the UNIX systems, while connecting the UNIX-based systems in local or wide area networks. At this point, any stand-alone programs can be migrated to the appropriate UNIX systems; any PCs that should be integrated into the network can also be integrated. The goal of this step in the process is to create an independent data path from any UNIX-based system to all others and to offload any small programs from the mainframe.

At the end of this stage, the mainframe is still used for data entry, database maintenance, and reporting functions. Most (if not all) peripheral programs are now running under UNIX and users should be familiar with UNIX and networking. At this point in the migration, the system looks like that shown in figure 1.3.

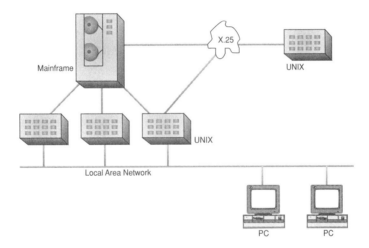

Figure 1.3:
UNIX, thoroughly integrated into the mainframe environment.

The third step in the migration is to bring data entry into the UNIX environment. By this point, a UNIX DBMS has been chosen. Programs may be divided into functional groups—such as order entry or shipping and receiving. Only those portions of the mainframe database that are required for data entry are moved to the UNIX system while data-entry screens are written.

When this is implemented, the mainframe is no longer used for direct data entry, and 3270 terminal emulation can be discarded. The mainframe is still used for what it does best, batch processing, so data entered into the UNIX DBMS is now transferred to and retrieved from the mainframe by periodically using RJE (Remote Job Entry). Architecturally, the system still resembles figure 1.3, but the chore of transaction processing has been transferred to the UNIX systems.

The fourth and final stage of the migration to UNIX is to port the remaining mainframe database and batch programs to one or more UNIX-based "file servers". Because no transaction-processing monitor is required at this stage, the mainframe programs can be recompiled on the UNIX systems or translated into a language that is appropriate for the chosen database. This last stage can be accomplished incrementally because it is really a continuation of the previous step. Because the eventual goal is the elimination of the mainframe, the system architecture will gradually resemble that of figure 1.4. (at which point the mainframe can be turned off).

This migration strategy is expensive in time and materials, but it is designed to enable the smooth transition from one system to the other while giving management, programmers, and end users time to learn and adjust.

Is this migration worth it? In the long term, yes it is. A migration from a proprietary system to UNIX, although difficult, need only occur once because the migration from one make and model of UNIX-based hardware to another can be made almost overnight and with relative ease.

Is today's UNIX really the last word in operating systems? The answer is no, but new innovations in operating-system technology will probably be added to UNIX, rather than be implemented as a whole new system. You can expect UNIX to evolve rather than remain stagnant, and it will remain backwardly-compatible with previous versions.

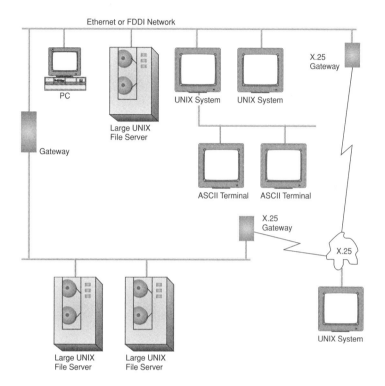

Figure 1.4:
The architecture of a pure UNIX-based MIS system.

In the next chapters, the basic design of UNIX is discussed, which includes a frank discussion of the virtues and vices of UNIX as a platform for management-information systems.

Chapter 2

How UNIX Works

This chapter is not intended to replace any of the UNIX manuals, rather it will act as a guide and supplement to those manuals. Learning UNIX has always been a "Catch 22"—if you already know how UNIX works, the manuals make sense to you; if you do not already know UNIX, the manuals are just a lot of paper that grow with each release. At the moment, there are over 30 volumes in the full set, but only a subset of the volumes is really necessary (the remainder are highly technical references for the programmer).

The volumes of the UNIX manual that are helpful for you as you use this book as a reference are the following:

- ❖ *Product Overview and Master Index*
- ❖ *System Administrator's Guide*
- ❖ *System Administrator's Reference Manual*
- ❖ *User's Guide*
- ❖ *User's Reference Manual*

❖ *Network User's and Administrator's Guide*

❖ *Programmer's Guide: ANSI C and Programming Support Tools*

❖ *Programmer's Reference Manual*

Most of the commands in this book are listed in the *User's Reference Manual*, which, in combination with the *User's Guide*, contains the bulk of the knowledge required to use UNIX. The *Administrator's Guide and Reference Manual* are extensions of these books. They enable the ordinary user to become a *superuser* (what the system administrator is called in UNIX). Most UNIX vendors ship at least one copy of these volumes with their hardware or software.

One of the easiest ways to start learning UNIX is as a user. The following sections explore UNIX as an ordinary user sees it.

Discovering UNIX as a User

Typically, your first experience with UNIX consists of logging in. If you are logging in remotely (with a modem over a telephone line), you may have some difficulty.

 Most modems, when they receive a call, adjust quickly to whatever parameters the calling modem has set. These parameters include the speed of transmission, known as the *baud rate*, parity settings, and modem type.

Older modems (Bell 103) enabled you to communicate at any baud rate, as long as it was below 300 baud. Newer modems (Bell 212) recognize Bell 103 signals and adjust to the lower baud rate, to 1200 baud, or to 2400 baud. When these modems receive a call, they automatically adjust their baud rate to whatever the incoming call is set. This means that UNIX must also adjust.

The superuser (system administrator) has set a default baud rate and a series of alternate baud rates. If you are logging in at a baud rate that is different from the default, UNIX needs to know it. You can signal UNIX to try the first alternate by sending a *break* signal.

Normal ASCII terminals contain a break key that sends the break signal. If you are logging in remotely from a PC or from some other computer, there is usually a software break signal that is activated by a combination of control or function keys. Each receipt of the break signal causes UNIX to try the next alternate set of baud rates.

The newest modems, those that communicate at 9600 baud or higher, are somewhat easier to use. These modems detect the baud rate of the incoming call and adjust to the call while maintaining a constant baud rate to the computer. If the superuser defines a speed of 9600 baud for the modem, the modem maintains that rate to the computer, regardless of the speed of the incoming call. For example, the modem communicates with the computer at 9600 baud, while communicating with the remote system at 1200 baud.

A carriage return usually notifies UNIX that the baud rate is set correctly, after which the `login:` is displayed. If the UNIX system has a site name, the login prompt is displayed as `sitename login:`.

When you see the login prompt, enter your login ID, which was assigned for you by the system administrator. You may have chosen your login ID, but the system administrator has to make it available. As soon as you enter it and press Enter, the system prompts you for a password.

Passwords on UNIX Systems

On older systems, a password was not necessary, but the system prompted you for it anyway. On these systems, a carriage return registered a "null" password, and you were then in the system. Newer versions of UNIX require a password. In fact, the newest releases of UNIX require passwords that contain letters and at least one punctuation character, and these passwords must be at least three characters long. The minimum length of a password can be set by the superuser and it is usually five or six characters long. (This change in the rules for passwords is the result of several well-publicized computer break-ins.)

On older versions of UNIX, the password was kept in encrypted form in an accessible file called /etc/passwd.

The *encryption* program is relatively well known and is a derivative of the German Enigma cipher. The password, as entered, is "salted" to generate one of many possible encryptions. This "salted" encryption is what used to be stored in the passwd file. To decipher passwords, a "hacker" merely compared all the possible encryptions of common words in a dictionary against the encrypted passwords.

To thwart hackers, the encrypted password has been moved from the /etc/passwd file to a file that is readable only by the superuser, called /etc/shadow. The ordinary password file still contains information needed by programs run by the ordinary user, but it no longer contains the encrypted password.

Most users, if left to their own devices, use ordinary words for passwords—usually representing someone or something they know. To prevent this, the new password scheme requires at least one punctuation character in the password. This scheme does not prevent hackers from breaking into a system, but it slows them down.

The system administrator can also require that users change their passwords after a predetermined number of weeks. Any new password must differ from the old password by at least three characters.

 You cannot just rotate characters in your password. For example, if your old password was "123bingo," the system rejects "bingo123" as a new password. It must differ from the old password by at least three characters—"456bingo," for example, would be accepted.

The Home Directory

After you log in successfully, the system places you in your *home directory*. On versions of UNIX previous to Release 4, the normal location for users' home directories was in /usr. For example, if a users' login ID was joe, his home directory would be /usr/joe. This is pure convention—the system administrator can actually place a user's home directory anywhere on the system.

The /usr directory also contains several other system-related directories, so in Release 4 all users are placed in a /home directory. The new convention is to place joe in /home/joe. This removal of users from the /usr directory to /home has one distinct advantage: it is easier to back up all of the users' files without also backing up part of the operating system.

After placing you in your home directory, the system executes a shell. A *shell*, in UNIX terminology, is your interface to the system. UNIX comes equipped with at least two and often three different shells. The original (and usually standard) shell is called the Bourne shell, which signals its presence with the $ prompt.

An alternate shell is the C shell, which is normally considered the standard shell for programmers. The C shell was developed at the University of California at Berkeley and is now delivered with almost every version of UNIX. The C shell signals its presence with the % prompt.

The third standard shell is a superset of the Bourne shell, which embodies all the attributes of the Bourne shell, as well as some of the best features of the C shell. This shell is called the Korn shell, which also uses the dollar sign prompt. The Korn shell is delivered as a standard part of Release 4 and as an add-on product for other releases of UNIX.

 The standard shell prompts can be changed at will. The C shell offers the greatest variety of prompts.

These three shells are the standard UNIX shells but, as will be seen in later chapters, almost any executable program that interacts with a user can be defined as a shell.

Startup Scripts

As the shell begins operation (and before you see the prompt), the shell has read and executed any customized instructions set by the system administrator or by you. In the case of the standard or Bourne shell, the first commands executed are in the system-wide *shell script*, /etc/profile, followed by the local commands found in a file named .profile that is located in your home directory. Other shells use other initialization scripts (discussed in a later section).

After logging in, the shell displays its prompt and you can execute any commands for which you have permission. In this respect, UNIX is like many other operating systems, except that UNIX is more easily extensible than are many others.

 You can create private commands by using shell scripts or any other form of executable program.

UNIX resembles MS-DOS (or the other way around) in this respect, except that all of the standard shells in UNIX are extremely powerful interpreted languages in their own right. Thus, only in context does a UNIX shell script resemble a BAT file in MS-DOS.

Similarities between UNIX and MS-DOS

Other similarities between MS-DOS and UNIX abound. For example, both UNIX and MS-DOS enable the user to create subdirectories with the MKDIR command. In UNIX, directories are expressed in the form /usr/joe/subdir; in MS-DOS, directories take the form C:\joe\subdir. In UNIX, all disks on the system are connected, so they appear to be one large file system, starting from the root directory (symbolized by /). In MS-DOS, of course, each physical disk or partition is designated by a letter, as in C:, and each disk has its own root directory.

With respect to the individual user, the UNIX shell script /etc/profile serves the same purpose as the AUTOEXEC.BAT file does in MS-DOS: to set environment variables such as PATH. Like MS-DOS, the UNIX shell uses the value of the PATH environment variable as a guide to search for executable programs. Unlike MS-DOS, however, file-name extensions such as BAT, COM, or EXE are not necessary in UNIX. Instead, programs are marked as executable in UNIX by using the chmod (change mode) command (discussed later).

In UNIX, once a file has been marked as executable and is in the search path defined by the PATH environment variable, the new command can be run as if it were the same as any other of the hundreds of UNIX commands. Indeed, this is how many of the UNIX commands were created and why each release of UNIX has added commands—someone recognized a repetitive function, created a command for it and it was then adopted as part of the standard set of UNIX commands.

The last similarity between MS-DOS and UNIX is that they both permit pipelined instructions. (A *pipelined* instruction automatically places the output of the first command into the input of the second command.) The command `sort file | more` is a pipelined instruction that works in both UNIX and MS-DOS. In this case, the *file* is sorted and `more` displays the sorted output one screen at a time.

MS-DOS is a *single-tasking* operating system, which means that only one program can run at a time. For the previous pipelined instruction, the output of the `sort` command is placed in a temporary file. When the sort is complete, the `more` program takes the temporary file and displays it.

UNIX is a *multitasking* operating system, so all the elements of a pipelined command are executed simultaneously. Unlike MS-DOS, which uses temporary files to store intermediate results, UNIX uses buffers in memory to pass the output of one command to the input of another. Thus, with the command `sort file | more`, output from the `more` command is displayed before the `sort` command is finished in UNIX, and not until after the `sort` command is through in MS-DOS. Because MS-DOS is a single-tasking operating system, pipelined commands are an interesting idiosyncracy that are rarely used. In UNIX, pipes are an integral part of the way commands are structured.

UNIX Multitasking Capabilities

Because UNIX is a multitasking operating system, it can offer more services to the user than a single task system like MS-DOS can. For example, UNIX enables the user to place a program in the *background*—the program can run concurrently with a program that is executing in the *foreground*. Both tasks may be connected to the terminal. That is, any output from either process is displayed on the terminal. As you learn in later chapters, output can be redirected to an alternate device or file.

There are three layers of background processing. The first level, the *near background*, enables you to run a shell at the same time that a task is running in the background. The background task is still connected to the terminal, unless you have redirected inputs and outputs, and it displays messages on your screen and takes input from your terminal. This is accomplished by placing an ampersand, `&`, after the command you want to run. If you log off, the near background task is killed before the system displays a new login prompt.

The next level of background processing is the *far background*. Far background programs start out as near background programs, but they will not be stopped when you log out. Far background tasks are launched with the `nohup` (no hangup) command, but they must still be placed in the near background by the use of an ampersand. The syntax of a far background program is `nohup command &`. Any output generated by a far background command is placed in a file named `nohup.out` in whatever directory you were in at the time you ran it. Near and far background tasks inherit the environment and all variables in existence at the time the tasks were run.

The third level of background tasks, *deep background* tasks, are controlled by the UNIX daemon called `cron`. In UNIX, *daemons* are programs that continually run in the background and provide a useful service. For example, the print spooler in UNIX is controlled by the printer daemon `lpsched` (line printer scheduler). The daemon `cron` offers a range of services, including scheduling repetitive tasks (like backing up the system at 4 a.m. every Saturday morning) or running a one-time job sometime in the future (this task is as close as standard UNIX comes to classic batch processing).

A fourth level of background processing that more closely approximates the style and level of control expected in a mainframe batch environment is introduced in a later chapter.

Contrasting UNIX and the Mainframe Environments

So far, this chapter has examined the differences between UNIX and MS-DOS. The following section examines the differences between UNIX and the classic mainframe environment.

The Mainframe Environment

The greatest difference between UNIX and a mainframe is the way in which their terminals work with their respective hosts. Unless the mainframe is running TSO or CMS, it remains essentially a batch-processing environment, with CICS transactions being a batch program with one data record.

The traditional terminal on a mainframe, the IBM 3270, is a *block mode terminal*, which means that a screen image is passed from the mainframe to the terminal, where the user fills in the blanks. When the user is finished filling in the blanks and presses the transmit key, the terminal waits for the mainframe to poll the terminal and retrieve the data. Thus, the mainframe is free to poll terminals when it is free—not when the user wants to send data.

This process has advantages and disadvantages. Many more terminals can be supported by a mainframe than can be supported by a system that is more responsive to users' demands. On the other hand, this creates an impediment to users, especially at peak periods.

If mainframes are optimized for the support of vast amounts of hardware, UNIX is optimized for the convenience of the individual user. As with all choices, this has advantages and disadvantages. The major disadvantage is that, given the same hardware, UNIX cannot support as many users. Fortunately, hardware is now generically priced and networks throw hardware at the problem.

Traditional mainframes operate as large batch-processing machines. Even CISC is a large-batch process that receives its input and distributes its outputs continuously from dozens, hundreds, or thousands of terminals. The only time a mainframe needs to suffer a context switch (multitask) is when a new batch program is run in the background. Basically, a mainframe is free from the kinds of interruptions that contribute to system overhead on a UNIX system.

The UNIX System Environment

UNIX systems, on the other hand, can be plagued with the overhead that is created by having to switch from one task to another. Although a mainframe might have a few dozen very large programs running concurrently, even a small PC running SCO UNIX might have hundreds of very small programs all vying for CPU time. In this case, hardware differences between a mainframe and the typical UNIX system minimize the differences in operating-system architecture. Even the smallest mainframe is a multiprocessor system.

In addition to the CPU itself, a mainframe has channel processors that remove disk I/O tasks from the main system and maintain a constant stream of data to and from the CPU. Mainframes also have terminal cluster controllers that remove the terminal I/O from main CPU consideration and, again, provide a constant stream of data to and from the mainframe.

UNIX systems, in contrast, often have simple CPUs that perform all the functions associated with computing: they manage all terminals associated with the system, perform disk I/O, and monitor the network for messages. In short, UNIX systems, in contrast with their mainframe counterparts, are riddled with hardware and software interrupts. Fortunately, each interrupt affords each UNIX system an opportunity to switch programs, multitask, and respond to a pending request from a user or a peripheral.

There has been a tendency to add processors in the UNIX environment: smart SCSI processors relieve the CPU of some of the disk I/O burden, terminal I/O processors relieve the system of monitoring terminals, and specialized smart networking hardware perform the task of network management. Even with all the added hardware, the architecture of UNIX dictates that the CPU remain responsive to users. In the case of word processors, the CPU must respond to every keystroke. Thus, a mainframe is essentially free from any external interrupts, but the nature of UNIX ensures that the UNIX operating system, called the *kernel*, must respond to every keystroke, which is the reason why a UNIX system, given the same hardware, cannot support as many users as a mainframe system.

Differences between UNIX and Mainframe Environments

A *mainframe* is an interrupt-free system optimized for maximum throughput and average performance over the day. UNIX, on the other hand, is an interrupt-driven system, optimized for peak performance and end-user responsiveness. By way of comparison, a UNIX system that is used as a graphic workstation (equipped with a mouse) can generate hundreds of interrupts-per-second tracking the movements of a mouse. Such a system is capable of supporting one user.

With an almost identical system used to support dumb terminal applications, dozens or even hundreds of users can be supported because even the fastest typist can only type 30 characters-per-second and only for short stretches. If a mouse generates 300 interrupts-per-second on average, and the average dat-entry clerk or typist generates 10 interrupts-per-second (one for every keystroke), the average technical workstation is perfectly capable of supporting at least 30 users.

In the mainframe environment, in which block mode terminals are used, there are no interrupts of the system. If the transmission of one full screen has the effect of causing the same amount of work on the part of the mainframe, however, and if the average data-entry clerk transmits a transaction every 10 seconds, the same hardware used as a technical workstation should be capable of supporting 3000 terminals. This scenario is possible only in a theoretical sense, of course, because the disk I/O side of the system was not considered.

Logging Out of the UNIX System

This ends our users' tour of UNIX. You now know what UNIX looks like to the average user and the differences between how UNIX works and how PCs and mainframes work. All that remains is for you to log out.

 Logging out is accomplished by sending the shell an end-of-file signal (Ctrl-D) or by explicitly informing the shell that you want to exit. On directly-connected terminals, the login: prompt reappears; on remotely-connected terminals, the modem hangs up the phone line.

Having seen UNIX from the end user's point of view, the next sections discuss the view of UNIX as it bootstraps itself from a cold start (a powered-down state).

Analyzing the UNIX Bootstrap Process

Every computer system has a hardware mechanism for *bootstrapping* itself into full operation from a power-off state. In most cases, the CPU itself has a reset mechanism that detects an initial power-on state and directs the CPU to begin executing instructions at some predetermined address.

The initial address from which a CPU begins operation is usually the start of a program stored in permanent, read-only memory (ROM). The ROM program actually performs the bootstrap process by performing a system-integrity check, followed by loading the boot track from a disk.

In the case of an IBM PC, the system ROM program attempts to load the boot track from the first floppy disk (the A: drive in MS-DOS). If the ROM program detects an error (if there is no floppy disk inserted in the drive or if the drive door is left open), the ROM program attempts to load the boot track from the first hardware-defined hard disk (the C: drive in MS-DOS).

On most systems, the *boot* track is defined as track 0, sector 0. It contains information about the disk (such as partition information and other useful data), as well as a second small program defining what next to load into memory.

The third program loaded from disk in UNIX is another bootstrap program that prompts the console for the name of the UNIX kernel. The default name of this bootstrap program is `unix`, which is an ordinary executable file in the root directory. This program, in addition to loading the UNIX kernel into memory, also downloads any programs that are required by secondary processors such as intelligent disk and communications controllers.

The `init` Process

After subsidiary processors have been downloaded and the kernel is installed in memory, execution of the UNIX kernel can begin. Until now, very little could be configured by the user, and the process of bringing the system to full operation was automatic. Depending on the version of UNIX installed, the kernel creates a number of asynchronously-running tasks that perform such functions as managing virtual memory, servicing physical devices, and managing the system schedular.

The kernel also runs a program named `/etc/init`, which is the parent of all other tasks, both system and user tasks.

 In UNIX, any program that creates another running program is said to be the *parent* of the new task. Whenever a parent task dies, all of its children are automatically killed as well. This part of UNIX terminology sounds brutal. Parents can kill their children with abandon, but any child that kills its parents is committing suicide, and any child that dies but does not go away is said to be a *zombie*.

With the `init` (initialization) process, UNIX systems begin to differentiate themselves. Until `init` is run, all versions of UNIX are almost the same. The `init` process is the first of the UNIX subsystems that can be easily configured by the user or the superuser. The various UNIX subsystems work in roughly the same way.

Each subsystem has an initialization table that defines what the subsystem is supposed to do. The `init` process is no exception. As with most of the UNIX subsystems, these initialization tables can be reconfigured to make UNIX completely unrecognizable. This book helps you to identify those conventions that keep UNIX portable. Much of UNIX's portability comes from maintaining the integrity and conventions of the UNIX initialization tables.

Examining the `init` Process

From the user or system administrator's point of view, `init` is the only program that needs to be considered for controlling the behavior of UNIX as a whole. It brings the system up, takes the system back down, and enables the superuser to operate the system in single-user mode, as well as to place UNIX in multi-user mode within a network. Each of these different operating modes are called `init` states.

The meaning of these states is pure convention because what happens in each state is the result of entries made in the initialization table `/etc/inittab`. When `init` is run by the UNIX kernel, it scans `inittab` and executes those commands defined to be run at system boot, after which `init` places itself in whatever state is defined as `run`. This process is automatic—it is already defined in the `inittab` table. Once the system is in `run` mode, `init` becomes a command that can be used by the system administrator to change `init` states.

Once the system is running (usually `init` state 2 or 3) and `login:` prompts have appeared on all attached terminals, the system administrator can log in to the system console and issue further `init` commands to change the `init` state of the machine.

The syntax of the command for changing the `init` state is `init` *state*. The states are 0 through 6, S or s, Q or q, and a through c. The states 0 through 6 are true `init` states, that is, they change the way UNIX operates. The special state S or s stands for single user and is a usually a subset of state 1. States a through c are pseudo-states that can operate in any true state; the command `init q` tells `init` to rescan the `inittab` table for any modifications. What happens in any given state is the result of entries made in the `inittab` table, but the states are defined by convention (see table 2.1).

The `inittab` Table

A typical `inittab` table for a small UNIX System V Release 3 looks like the following (Release 4 `inittab` entries are similar, but the proliferation of `getty` commands are replaced by a single program, `ttymon`, that performs the same function):

Table 2.1

The init *States and their Meanings*

State	Meaning
0	System shutdown, ready for power to be turned off
1	Single user, no background tasks running
S	Single user, printers still running
2	Multi-user, login: displayed on all terminals, printers work
3	Network connected, superset of init state 2
4	User-defined state
5	User-defined state, sometimes used for warm reboot of the system or for panic system stops
6	System shutdown (for compatibility with XENIX)

```
init:2:initdefault:
bbrc::bootwait:/etc/brc < /dev/console > /dev/console 2>&1
run0:0:wait:/etc/rc0   < /dev/console > /dev/console 2>&1
run1:1:wait:/etc/shutdown -y -iS -g0   < /dev/console > /dev/console 2>&1
run2:23:wait:/etc/rc2   < /dev/console > /dev/console 2>&1
run3:3:wait:/etc/rc3   < /dev/console > /dev/console 2>&1
halt:5:wait:/etc/haltsys < /dev/console > /dev/console 2>&1
cons:23:respawn:env - TERM=wyse60 /etc/getty console 9600
tt01:23:respawn:env - /usr/lib/lpset serial tty01 > /dev/null 2>&1
tt02:23:respawn:env - TERM=vt100 /usr/lib/uucp/uugetty -t 60 -r tty02 MODEM2400
tt03:23:respawn:env - TERM=wyse30 /etc/getty tty03 9600
```

Each entry in an inittab table consists of four fields that are delimited by colons and terminated by a carriage return. The first field is a label used internally by init. The second field is a list of init states in which to run the command found in the fourth field. Thus, the line run0:0:wait:/etc/rc0 only runs when init enters state 0; the line run2:234:wait:/etc/rc2 runs when init enters states 2, 3, and 4.

The third field is termed the *action field,* and it defines the way init is to run the command found in the fourth field. The permissible values of this field are the following:

❖ initdefault. There can be only one entry marked initdefault in an inittab table. This value defines in which init state to place the system after booting. The desired init state is found in the second field of this record.

❖ bootwait. This value tells init to run the program in the fourth field and to wait for its completion when the system is first booted from a cold (power-off) state. The convention is to run a Bourne shell script named /etc/brc. The /etc/brc program is usually a shell script that determines if the system was shut down properly. If the system shuts down abnormally (due to a power failure, for instance), /etc/brc runs the fsck command to check and repair any damage to the file system. This shell script also synchronizes the software clock with the hardware clock, if necessary.

 All commands found in the fourth field in an inittab table must be able to run within the Bourne shell environment. That is, they can be Bourne shell scripts or executable programs, but they cannot be C shell scripts.

❖ sysinit. This value is similar to the bootwait instruction, except that sysinit is run before any attempt is made to read from or write to the console. For example, it can be used to download any code needed to a smart graphics controller card, but this value is not generally used very much.

❖ wait. This value is used to instruct init to run the command in the fourth field and to wait for its completion. The general convention is to run an rc shell script whenever init changes its state. For example, when init enters state 1, the convention is to run /etc/rc1 and wait for its completion. It is the shell script that actually performs any changes to the system. In this respect, changing init states has no real meaning beyond the conventions. (the rc scripts are discussed later in this section.)

❖ off. This value tells init to ignore the command if it has not been run. It also tells init to kill the command (after 20 seconds) if the command is still running—this only has real meaning if the init q command has been issued by the system administrator after changing the inittab table).

❖ once. This value tells init to run the command once—the first time init enters a particular state. If init re-enters the same state, it should not be run again.

❖ respawn. This value tells init to rerun the command if the command or its successors dies. This is commonly used to respawn the getty task in Release 3. The getty command is run, one for each physical or logical port, to determine what the communications character-istics are of a device that tries to communicate with the system (such as baud rate, parity, and so forth). When these characteristics have been determined, getty transforms itself, through a process called *execing*, into the login program that displays the login: prompt and verifies login attempts with the /etc/passwd file. Once a login has been completed, login execs into the shell defined for the user. When the user logs out, the shell dies. Throughout this entire process, getty, login and the user's shell have maintained the same process ID. When the shell finally dies when the user logs out, however, the *respawn* value in the action field of the inittab instructs init to rerun getty. The process then begins anew.

❖ `ondemand`. This value is used only with the pseudo-states associated with using the `init` states a, b, or c. It is the equivalent to `respawn`. The use of pseudo-states enables `init` to run commands without changing states. For example, if the system is in `init` state 2 and the system administrator gives the command **init a**, the command defined for `init` pseudo-state a is run. The `init` state remains 2, however.

Tip This command can be run in `init` state 1 or 3 and, although the command defined for pseudo-state a would run, it would have no effect on the `init` state.

❖ `powerfail`. This value is of interest only if your system has specialized hardware that can detect an imminent power failure. For instance, in the event of a power failure, an interruptible power supply may take over, enabling the system to shut itself down.

❖ `powerwait`. Like `powerfail`, this value requires specialized hardware to signal the kernel that a power failure has occurred. The only difference between the two values is that `powerwait` runs the command and waits for its completion. In most cases, the system should shut down immediately.

Whenever `init` changes states, any tasks not eligible to be run in that state are killed. For example, if `getty` is defined as "runable" in states 2, 3, and 4, whenever the system enters `init` state 1, all `getty` programs and their successors are terminated. This means that any users that are logged in will be logged off, and any offspring tasks will be killed. Many programs have `init` as their parent—for example, the print spooler and other UNIX daemons. None of these are affected by a change of state, so they must be killed independently. For example, any user task run with the `nohup` command is given `init` as its parent, so a normal change in state does not affect any of these tasks.

Running programs from `inittab` is, therefore, a mixed blessing. Any task that needs to be run in a given state can be run by `inittab`, as long as being killed arbitrarily does not affect future actions. For example, a transaction-processing monitor can be run from `inittab`, but the chances of damaging a critical file are very high.

Although UNIX provides other mechanisms for launching and controlling these kinds of programs, there are many instances in which running programs from `inittab` may be useful. For example, `init` state 4 is, by convention, user-defined. This state can be used to perform any automatic maintenance of the system, with a guarantee that no users would be allowed to be logged on. The following is a typical scenario.

Suppose that the system administrator writes a shell script designed to be run by the `cron` daemon, which is a background program that runs programs at predetermined times. In this case, the program is designed to run at 3 a.m., when few people are logged into the system. The shell script uses the `wall` command to announce to any remaining users that the system is going down.

After allowing ample time for logging out, the shell script runs the command `init 4`, which instructs `init` to change to `init` state 4. If all `getty` tasks (or `ttymon` tasks in Release 4), except for the console, are defined as runable in `init` state 2 and 3 (but not in state 4), any users are logged out and cannot log back in, except for the superuser at the console. The `init` program then runs any program defined for `init` state 4. An example of an entry needed for the `inittab` is the following:

```
int4:4:wait:/etc/rc4 </dev/console >/dev/console 2>&1
```

The shell script `/etc/rc4` contains the code required to clean up the UNIX environment, such as deleting temporary files from directories like `/tmp` and `/usr/tmp`, after which a backup of the system can be accomplished automatically. When the backup is complete, the shell script restores full service to the system by issuing the `init 3` command, which places the system back in `init` state 3 and allows users to log in again.

Most of the UNIX background programs, such as the `cron` daemon and the print spooler `lpsched`, are not run directly from `inittab` because, as soon as the `init` state changes, they are be killed without having the opportunity to shut down. Instead, these programs are run indirectly by the `rc` scripts that are run by `init`.

The /etc/rc **Startup Scripts**

The startup-script system has evolved from a single script named /etc/rc in the earlier releases (pre-System V), to a series of scripts in XENIX, to its full complexity in System V Release 3. With Release 4, the location of these scripts has also migrated, so there is no guarantee of their stability in this respect. Their structure has remained intact throughout System V.

For convenience, these scripts are described as they exist in System V Release 3. Check your manuals for further details.

The startup system consists of a single script, to be executed during system boot, called /etc/brc. There is also a script for each `init` state. For example, /etc/rc0 is the startup script for `init` state 0, /etc/rc is the script for `init` state 1, and so forth. These scripts are generic and virtually identical, and they only serve as vehicles for running programs found in a corresponding directory.

These directories have the same names as the `rc` file they belong to, but they have a .d appended to the name. For example the script /etc/rc1 runs programs in the /etc/rc1.d directory.

All or most of the programs run by the `rc` scripts are actually stored in a directory named /etc/init.d. Each script in the

/etc/init.d directory contains instructions to both start and stop a particular process. For example, there is a script called cron in the /etc/init.d directory. The cron program is a daemon that is supposed to be run in init states 2 and 3 and stopped in all other init states. This script contains instructions to both start and stop the cron daemon, depending on whether the script is run with start or stop as a parameter.

This script is then linked with the ln command to the proper /etc/rc.d directories with names that begin with S (for init states in which cron is supposed to be started and linked with a name that begins with a K), to directories in which cron is supposed to be killed. This enables UNIX to be far more flexible and makes the rc scripts far more portable. Thus, the file /etc/init.d/cron would be linked to /etc/rc1.d/Kcron, /etc/rc0.d/Kcron, and /etc/rc2.d/Scron. The cron daemon would be started in init state 2, stopped in init states 0 and 1, and remain untouched in all other states.

To see how this is accomplished, look at the cron script. Understanding how this script works requires a knowledge of the Bourne shell, which is beyond the scope of this book. For those just learning shell programming, however, the cron script provides a good example of shell scripts. The following is an edited /etc/init.d/cron shell script, as taken from a UNIX System V Release 3 system:

```
case $1 in
'start')
   set 'who -r'
   case $9 in
   [23])   exit ;;
   esac
   echo Starting cron
   rm -f /usr/lib/cron/FIFO
   /etc/cron
   ;;
'stop')
```

```
    pid='/bin/ps -e | grep cron | sed -e 's/^ *//' -e 's/ .*//''
    if [ ${pid} != ]
    then
        echo Stopping cron
        /bin/kill ${pid} > /dev/null 2>&1
        rm -f /usr/lib/cron/FIFO
    fi
    ;;
*)
    echo usage: /etc/init.d/cron {start|stop}
    ;;
esac
```

In the Bourne shell, positional parameters are represented by $1, $2, and so on. As the last line indicates, the command is started by using either start or stop as the only parameters. In the Bourne shell, the case statement is analogous to the switch statement in C, except that in shell scripts entire strings can be matched. In this example, once the script has determined that the command was called with start, it uses the set command to set positional parameters internally with the results of the who -r command. The who -r command places, in the ninth position, the last init state the system was in. This value is used in the next case statement to determine if the previous init state was 2 or 3. If so, exit the shell script—nothing needs to be done.

If the shell script passes this test, cron is run after first removing FIFO, a named pipe used by the at and crontab commands. If the shell script has passed stop as a parameter, the process ID (PID) of cron is determined and the cron daemon is killed. If neither start or stop is passed as a parameter, an error message is returned. This shell script should serve as a prototype for any new scripts that need to be run from an etc/rc script.

The importance of the crosslinks between /etc/init.d/cron, /etc/rc2/Scron, and /etc/rc1/Kcron, is illustrated by the rc script itself. Those programs that begin with K are run with the stop parameter and those that begin with S are run with the start parameter. Each of the rc scripts are almost identical—the only differences are from which of the rc.d directories the programs are executed.

The following is a prototype /etc/rc script. In this case, it is an edited rc2 script from a UNIX System V Release 3 machine:

```
set 'who -r'
if [ $7 = 2 -a $9 != S ]
then
    echo '\n\nChanging to run level 2.\n'
    if [ -d /etc/rc2.d ]
    then
        for f in /etc/rc2.d/K*
        do
            if [ -s ${f} ]
            then
                /bin/sh ${f} stop
            fi
        done
    fi
fi
if [ -d /etc/rc2.d ]
then
    for f in /etc/rc2.d/S*
    do
        if [  s ${f} ]
        then
            /bin/sh ${f} start
        fi
    done
fi
```

This prototype rc script begins by internally setting its positional parameters ($1,$2,...) with the output of the who -r command. In this case, the test makes sure that the current init state, $7, is 2 and that the previous init state, $9 is not S (single user).

Remember that the `init` state `S` means single user with all background tasks still running; there is no need to rerun them. If the test is passed, the `for` statement creates a list of file names that begin with K in the `/etc/rc2.d` directory. The list is in alphabetical order. This ordering enables you to arrange the names so that they execute in an order you select.

Next, a test is made to determine if the file exists and if it has a size greater than 0 bytes. If it does, the file is executed with `stop` as a parameter, as in `K123 stop`. After all the tasks that should be stopped upon entering this `init` state have been stopped, the process is repeated with any files that begin with S. These files are then run with `start` as a parameter.

 UNIX is completely configurable and the rules of UNIX are pure convention. You are free to change anything you like. By sticking to the rules and philosophy of UNIX, however, you are creating a portable and easily understood system.

There are other startup tables, such as `/etc/gettydefs` in Release 3, but they have no bearing on UNIX as an environment for a management-information system. There are, however, a number of subsystems in UNIX that have a direct bearing on developing an MIS environment. Several of these subsystems are controlled by UNIX daemons, which are started up by entries in the `rc` system. Some of the subsystems are passive—they are only active when needed (for example, the communications system `uucp`). Others, such as the file security system, are insidious (they are active all the time and are buried deep in the very fiber of UNIX).

Understanding UNIX Subsystems

These sections described a system that is capable of running programs and changing the way it behaves, depending on its `init` state. So far, however, UNIX does not do very much. Most of the services UNIX provides are found in the subsystems that make UNIX recognizable as UNIX. These systems enable users to access a printer, communicate with other systems, or run tasks in the background (or at predetermined times). They also provide security and enable the user (or system administrator) to tailor the system to individual needs. The way these systems work is an integral part of the philosophy of UNIX; an understanding of that philosophy is a prerequisite for reshaping and extending UNIX into a viable MIS environment.

UNIX Security

Much has been said about the lack of security in the UNIX system. Much more, however, should be said about the lack of enforcement of existing security arrangements by system administrators. Every user is assigned a unique login ID, a password, and membership in one or more groups. Conversely, every file and directory contains read, write, and execute permission for the owner, the owner's group and all others. Only users who have write permission to a file or directory can change its permissions. With proper policing of file and directory permissions and judicious assignments of users to groups, more than adequate security can be maintained, at least for most commercial purposes.

If tightened security is required, many versions of Release 3 and all versions of Release 4 offer mandatory security arrangements up to the U. S. Governments C2 standard. Of course, there is no substitute for a physically secure system, in which authorized personnel only are granted physical access to terminals and no connection to the outside world is possible.

A UNIX system can be made just about as secure as is required for any purpose. No security arrangement remains secure from prying eyes for long, however, if the system is not administered correctly. Thus, the onus for maintaining any secure arrangements must fall on management.

The UNIX Shell System

A shell is a user interface and UNIX comes equipped with at least two shells. In fact, almost any program that is capable of receiving data from a terminal and displaying results can be used as a shell. The creation of a user's shell is the last task in a process that began with the running of init by the kernel.

When init entered state 2 or 3, an entry or series of entries in the inittab table caused the creation of a getty (get tty) in System V Release 3 or the creation of ttymon (tty monitor) in Release 4, whose function was to detect activity on terminal ports. Once activity was detected (after getty or ttymon detected a flow of data) and recognizable characters were detected, the login process was initiated.

The /etc/passwd File

A typical /etc/passwd table from a Release 3 system follows (edited for brevity):

```
root:srm4UsF7CbG8A:0:2:The Super User,(617)484-4358:/:/bin/sh
adm:srm4UsF7CbG8A:4:4:The Systems Administrator:/usr/adm:/bin/sh
srg:ogCn2FNBYxxY.:203:1::/usr/srg:/bin/csh
jsr:yYgr2lOoaTlLk:239:1::/usr/lib/menu:/usr/bin/msh
```

The passwd table is an ASCII file that contains seven fields, delimited by colons, and readable by all users (but with write permission only for the superuser—user ID 0, usually known as *root*). The fields are defined as follows:

❖ The login ID text. What must be typed exactly in response to the login: prompt.

❖ The encrypted password. For the user on systems without the /etc/shadow table; otherwise, this field contains a place holder, *x*.

❖ The decimal user ID. The superuser is always ID 0, regardless of the login ID text.

- ❖ The default decimal group ID. In addition to the `passwd` table, there is also a `/etc/group` table that contains the text name of the group and a list of members. Thus, a user has a default group and all files created by the user inherit this group ID. The user can also belong to other groups and read, write, or execute files that have those permissions for any other group the user belongs to.

- ❖ Text information about the user. Although anything can be placed in this field, some programs (such as `finger`) expect this data to be in a strict format.

- ❖ The home directory of the user. Any directory can be given as long as the user has read, write and execute permission on that directory. Note also that the directory must be given as an absolute path name starting with the root directory, `/`.

- ❖ The absolute path name of the program to be used as a shell. In the example, three different shells have been used in the `passwd` table. The Bourne shell is actually an executable file named `/bin/sh`; the C shell is `/bin/csh`. There is also a shell named `/usr/bin/msh`.

- ❖ This is an example of the use of other programs as shells. The program `/usr/bin/msh` is a Bourne shell script used to run a menuing interface that precludes the user from ever running anything except what the system administrator defines. The `msh` command and its related programs are found in Section IV.

UNIX Shells

Shells, and indeed all UNIX programs, share many things in common, especially the use of the environment to personalize the way the system works. As with most things in UNIX, the way shells work is only convention.

For `login`, it only executes what it has been instructed to execute in the seventh field of the `passwd` table. The shell itself must seek its own configuration tables. For the standard shells `sh` and `csh`, it is done automatically. For any other custom shells, it should be done automatically by the shell when it first runs.

By way of example, the Bourne shell, when it is first run by `login`, looks for a shell script named `/etc/profile`. If it finds the script, it is executed. The `/etc/profile` script contains many shell commands that are designed to customize the system.

For example, `/etc/profile` is commonly used to define the `PATH` environment variable beyond the default `PATH=/bin:/usr/bin`. On many installations, locally created commands are kept in a seperate directory that must be included in the `PATH` variable. Once the Bourne shell has executed `/etc/profile`, it searches for another script, located in the user's home directory, named `.profile`. The use of the period before the name of the file hides the file from the most common form of the list command, `ls`, which is the equivalent of the DOS `DIR` command.

> The period does not hide the file very well because the command `ls -a` reveals any hidden files. Hiding files is useful, however, for keeping the home directory from getting cluttered. Most of the initialization scripts are thus named for the same reason. Almost every major program in UNIX has an initialization script, found in the user's home directory. Because you can end up with a dozen or more such scripts, it is useful to keep them hidden.

The C shell has its own set of initialization scripts. Like the Bourne shell, there is a system-wide script, written in C shell script, named `/etc/cshrc`. When this script has been executed, the C shell searches for, and executes first, a script named `.cshrc` in the user's home directory. It then executes `.login`, which is also located in the user's home directory. Any further C shell scripts run by the user also execute the `.cshrc` script.

When the user logs out from the C shell, another script, `.logout`, is searched for, and run from, the user's home directory.

Virtually any program can be turned into a shell by the following strategy: first, the program to be used must interact with the user in some meaningful way and have a way of terminating. For example, a data-entry screen can be used. Next, a small front-end Bourne shell script needs to be written that adequately customizes the environment and runs any startup scripts. The final step is to exec the program you want run. By execing you are replacing the current task with the execed task (for example, if you want to create a new shell called `/usr/bin/nsh`). The program `/usr/bin/nsh` is actually a Bourne shell script containing the following lines of code:

```
.  /etc/profile
.  $HOME/.profile
exec your_command
```

This script first runs the `/etc/profile`, followed by a `.profile` script in the user's home directory. Note the use of the dot (.) command in the shell script. Because no child process can modify the environment of its parent, the profiles have no effect on the shell when they are run as commands. The Bourne shell uses the dot command to run commands within the current shell—any modifications made to the environment by `/etc/profile` or the `$HOME/.profile` are retained when *your_command* is run.

 A program that is used as a shell must be either a native compiled program or a Bourne shell script. Executing native compiled programs is obvious; less obvious is the reason for executing scripts written in the Bourne shell. Like `init`, the `login` program executes its programs with the command `exec sh -c exec` *program*. Thus, any compiled program works, as does any Bourne shell script; shells written in C shell script, however, do not execute properly.

A slightly more involved shell script is used to launch the Menu shell, /usr/bin/msh. In the case of the Menu shell, the initial script detects the login ID of the user and the user's group. If the user has created a personal menu, that menu is run. Otherwise, if a menu is defined for the user's group, it is run. If neither of these menus is found, a default menu for the system is run. The Menu shell is one of many shells that exist or can be created to suit the needs of a particular system.

LP—The Printer Spooler

The print spool system has evolved considerably over the years, from a system that did little more than print documents on a first-come, first-served basis, to a sophisticated spooler that is equivalent to any found on a mainframe. In the original, pre-System V spooler, a print job was launched either by piping output onto the lpr command or launched directly by using the lpr *file* command.

The print command for each printer was labeled lpr, lpr1, lpr2, ..., which corresponded to the printers attached to ports linked to /dev/lp, /dev/lp1, /dev/lp2, ... The lpr command only copied the print request, or, in the case of piped input, copied the data to be printed into one of the printer directories within /usr/spool/lpd. The lpr command ran the printer daemon lpd in the background, which actually printed the file. The lpd daemon continued printing whichever files were destined for that printer until the queue was exhausted. The lpd daemon ran only when there was output to be printed (and only one daemon could run at a time). In other words, when the lpr program spawned an lpd daemon, the first task of the lpd daemon was to see if there was another daemon running, and if so, to die.

In the older system, all printing was done on a first-come, first-served basis (also known as first-in, first-out, or *FIFO*), and the only way to stop printing was to kill the daemon. Obviously, this arrangement cannot work in an MIS environment.

The newer system, called the *LP system*, was first introduced in UNIX System V and has been undergoing improvements ever since. Chief among the features of the LP system are the following:

❖ The capability to define multiple printers, of different makes and models, as a *class* of printers. In a large installation, you can define several printers to be members of a class and define that printer class as the default. Any output is then balanced between the members of the class.

❖ The capability to define a pre-printed form or type font for a printer. Any output requiring a special font or preprinted form is held until the system administrator confirms that the proper form or font has been mounted on the printer and aligned. Thus, you do not print checks on greenbar paper or perform word processing on preprinted checks.

❖ The capability to hold, cancel, reprint, or bump up the priority of any pending or currently printing job.

❖ The capability to define a remote printer, either over a network or via the `uucp` (UNIX-to-UNIX copy) wide area communications system.

❖ The capability to define a printer connected to the auxiliary port of a user's terminal.

❖ The capability to change the printer's interface program at will. The program that actually does the printing is usually a Bourne shell script, which means that not only is source code supplied, but changes are also easy to make and test.

The LP system is structured differently from the old pre-System V print spooler. Instead of spawning a temporary `lpd` daemon, the LP system uses a permanently running daemon, `lpsched`, which is launched by the `/etc/rc2` startup script. The `lpsched` daemon controls everything relating to printing a file.

The Print Spooling Process

The process of printing a file works like this: to print a file, the user either pipes input into the command `lp` or gives a file name as a parameter, as in `lp` `filename`. In the case of the former, the actual data to be printed is copied to a subdirectory within `/usr/spool/lp`; in the case of the latter, only the name of the file to be printed is recorded. When this process is complete `lp` notifies `lpsched` that there is a file to be printed. Everything is then handled by `lpsched`.

When a file is printed, it is given an ID that consists of the name of the printer that the job is assigned to and a serial number. This job ID serves as a handle with which the user (or the system administrator) may cancel the job, change the priority of the job, place the job on hold, release a job on hold, and change the printer for which the job is scheduled. Print jobs may also be scheduled with specific forms that are pre-defined—in this case, the job is printed only when the superuser has confirmed that the proper form is on the printer.

The system administrator can be notified whenever a change in form is required, either through the `mail` facility or, more directly, by having a message written to the administrator's terminal when a predetermined number of jobs, requiring a change in form, have been queued. In addition, any user can look at the full status of the print queue by using the `lpstat` command.

When a print job is ready for printing, the `lpsched` daemon finds and runs the interface program, which is usually a shell script. This interface program is the one that actually prints the job. In the LP system, each printer has a name rather than a number, and the interface program is a shell script named for the printer to which it interfaces.

Print Spool Directories

Although the structure of the files and tables governing the LP system are stable, their location is not. As of this writing, the location of the interface programs has been wandering through a number of subdirectories within `/usr/spool/lp`, but it is generally located in `/usr/spool/interface`, `/usr/spool/lp/adm/interface`, or another similar directory. Once you find the proper major directory, it will contain the following subdirectories:

❖ `/class`. This directory contains files named after the classes they represent. Inside each file are the names of the individual members of that class. For example, you can define a class named `laser` and include printers named `hplaser`, `okilaser`, or `tilaser`. Although you can edit this file directly, it is better to use the `lpadmin` program.

❖ `/filter`. This directory contains any filter programs needed to convert one kind of output to another. The LP system enables you to define different kinds of output-content types. This means that you can print Postscript output on an HP LaserJet if you have the right filter.

In addition to defining the type of form required for a particular print job, you can also define the content type of the file you want to print. You can define a filter to convert one content type to another. For example, suppose that you have defined three different content types: `dumb`, `postscript`, and `laserjet`. The default for all input is `dumb`, or normal ASCII files. You have also defined one printer as printing only `postscript` and another printer as only printing `laserjet`. You need at least two filters—one to convert `dumb` to `postscript`, and the other to convert `dumb` to `laserjet`.

If you print a normal file, the correct filter is automatically inserted in the data stream before being sent to the printer. If you have a word processor that is capable of either Postscript or HP Laserjet output, you can define, within the word processor program, the proper type of output. In this case, no filter is inserted because the LP system has been informed of the content type of the word processor. If you want to move a job from the laserjet printer to the postscript printer, you have to create and define a filter that converts postscript to laserjet (and vice-versa). Defining such filters (but not creating them) is the task of lpfilter.

❖ /forms. This directory contains the specifications tables for any forms you have defined by using the lpforms command.

❖ /interface. This directory contains the shell scripts that actually drive the printer.

❖ /member. This directory contains files named after the printer, and containing the name of the device to which the physical printer is connected. For example, this directory might contain a file named hplaser. The only entry in this file would be the name of the device, for example, /dev/tty011.

❖ /model. This directory contains templates for various printers. For example, it might contain files named okidata, epson, hplaser, and a few others. The content of this directory varies with the distributor of your UNIX software. In practice, when you are defining a new printer with lpadmin, you can define a new printer named okilaser and then use hplaser as the model. In this case, a copy of hplaser is created in the interface directory and named okilaser. You are then free to change the interface program to meet your needs.

There are other subdirectories, but they are subject to change as the LP system grows and matures. Obviously, there is a balance between the simplicity of the older versions of the UNIX print spooler and the complexity of the LP system. On smaller systems, the defaults will usually work. If no forms or content types are defined, the LP system closely resembles a simple print spooler. The `lp` command and the `lpr` command are significantly different in how they are run, however, which can lead to problems and confusion for users.

Print Spool Shell Scripts

In the old system, output was directed to each printer by the interface for each printer, `lpr`, `lpr1`. In the LP system, there is only the `lp` command, which must be told by a flag and parameter, to which printer the output is aimed. In the absence of an explicit destination, any output goes to the default printer, along with any default values associated with content type or form type.

The syntax for declaring a destination (other than the default) is `lp -d` *printer-name*. Any special handling, such as declaring proper form types and the like, must also appear on the command line. This can be confusing for ordinary users and programmers.

One solution is to create shell script programs that predefine various options. This option also enables the system administrator to create emulations of the older system. For example, the following shell script can be used to emulate the original `lpr` program:

```
#! /bin/sh
lp -s $*
```

Note that this Bourne shell script begins with `#! /bin/sh`. In the Bourne shell, beginning a line with a `#` means that the rest of the line is a comment. In the C shell, however, any executable shell script beginning with `#!` *command* means that *command* is the path name of the program to be used to interpret the script. In this case, a Bourne shell is run. If you intend to use the C shell instead of the Bourne shell, it is wise to begin all shell scripts with `#! /bin/sh`.

Note also the command `lp -s $*`, The `-s` flag tells `lp` not to report the job ID of the print process. This makes `lp` behave just like `lpr`. The `$*` at the end of the command is replaced with any other parameters given on the command line when the shell script is executed. If a file name is given, as in the command `lpr` *file*, *file* is the first parameter and the substitution generates the command `lp -s` *file*. If the command had been given as *command* | `lpr`, there would be nothing to substitute for `$*`, and the shell script would effectively become *command* | `lp -s`.

This process can be repeated for any number of special logical printers. For example, `lpr1` can be defined as the following:

```
#! /bin/sh
lp -s -d hplaser $*
```

As another example, `lpchecks` can be defined as the following:

```
#! /bin/sh
lp -s -f checks -H hold -d any $*
```

In this case, the command tells `lp` to use form type checks on any printer with checks mounted on it, and to hold the job until the system administrator releases it. As can be seen, a wide variety of special printers can be created with shell scripts.

The cron Daemon

The `cron` daemon is, except for the print spooler, the most useful daemon in the UNIX system. The `cron` daemon, launched by the `/etc/rc2` startup script, serves the purpose of running programs in the deep background at predetermined times or, in certain cases, when the load on the system permits. There are three ways that `cron` receives its instructions (and three ways it executes instructions).

The first method is *periodically*. Each user is permitted (or not permitted, at the system administrator's discretion) to use the `crontab` command to make entries in a personal `crontab` table. The `crontab` table defines which jobs should be repeatedly run and when. The options are minutes of the hour, hours of the day, days of the week, days of the month, and months of the year. Each table consists of records with seven fields in each record, delimited by a tab character. The fields are, in order:

Minute

Hour

Day of the month

Month of the year

Day of the week (Sunday is 0)

Program to be executed

For example, the following entries can be made to the system administrator's `crontab` file:

```
30 3    *   *   *   backup_program

0,10,20,30,40,50  7-18   *   *   1-5  communications_poling_program
```

In the first case, the backup program is run every night at 3:30 a.m. In the second case, the communications program runs every ten minutes between 7 a.m. and 1800 hours or 6 p.m., and it runs only on Monday through Friday.

The second method is *at any given time in the future*. Users are permitted (or denied) to run commands at any specific time in the future. For example, users can be reminded to file tax returns with the following command:

```
at 10 am apr 15 <<!
wall
TAX DAY
!
```

The syntax for entering the date is quite flexible and includes entries such as `now + 1 year`, and many others.

The third method is *whenever the load permits*. The final way to run commands in the deep background is with the `batch` command, which is logically equivalent to the command `at -now`.

The documentation for `batch` states that it will run programs whenever the load permits. This statement is not strictly accurate, however. The system administrator can determine how many programs can run in the deep background at any one time, but this does not reflect the load on the system created by on-line users or by tasks run with the `nohup` and `&` commands.

Tables Used by cron

From the system administration point of view, the entire `cron` system is controlled by a series of tables located in the `/usr/lib/cron` directory in Release 3 (and `/usr/sbin/cron.d` in Release 4). This directory contains tables such as `at.allow` and `at.deny`, which contain lists of login IDs that are explicitly allowed or denied access to the `at` command, with similar tables for `cron` and `batch`. The `queuedefs` table is the master control file for `cron`, with entries that control the behavior of the three queues. The queues are labeled `a`, `b`, and `c`, after the commands `at`, `batch`, and `crontab`. A typical `queuedefs` table might look like the following:

```
a.10j5n60w
b.10j15n60w
c.20j5n5w
```

The fields within `queuedefs` for the `at` queue may be read as follows:

❖ a. Defines the `at` queue. The `batch` queue is defined as b; `crontab` is defined as c.

❖ `10j`. Defines how many `at` jobs may be run simultaneously.

❖ `5n`. Defines the `nice` level at which to run the `at` job. The `nice` command, in theory, enables the user to be nice to other users by reducing the priority of a program. The levels at which a program can be niced vary from 0 to 39, with ordinary users running at nice level 20. Only the superuser can reduce the `nice` level (raise the priority level) on a task. If the user who runs a command with `at` is at `nice` level 20, the `at` command runs the command at `nice` level 25 with `5n` in `queuedefs`. This field applies to all queues.

❖ `60w`. If the number of tasks run from the `at` queue exceeds the value placed in the `j` field, the `w` field specifies how long `cron` should wait, in seconds, before attempting to run another. In this case, `cron` waits 60 seconds before attempting to run another `at` job if 10 jobs in the `at` queue are already running.

In a later chapter, you learn how to create a daemon that changes the number of jobs that are allowed to run in the deep background, based on the actual number of tasks running.

The uucp Communications System

Almost since its inception, UNIX has been an operating system that can communicate. (What can you expect, after all, from an operating system developed at Bell Laboratories?) The communications system is wrapped around the uucp (UNIX-to-UNIX Copy) program, but it also includes the transport system for remote electronic mail, a terminal login program called cu (call UNIX), and the capability to run programs remotely. These are all controlled by the system administrator.

Part of the UNIX philosophy is that programs should be split into as many functional units as is practical. This means, in the case of communications, that the code that controls the physical communications link should be separate from the code that handles the transfer of data, and also should be separated from the user interface. Thus, the user interface is independent of the transfer program and the transfer program is independent of the physical link. It also means that the speed of transfer is more dependent on the physical link than on the transfer program itself.

In the uucp system, the user interface consists of the programs uucp, cu, uuto, and uux. The data-transfer program is uucico, which in turn calls a program that handles the physical devices that are necessary to make the connection. The types of connections that can be made are direct connections between computers over a serial line, direct connections through any kind of network, and connections through a modem and telephone line. In the latter case, there is a database of modems that enables uucico to talk to virtually any modem on the market. In a network, any program that is accessible by a user that enables him to log in to a remote UNIX system can be used by uucico to make the connection.

Once the physical connection is made, the data-transfer program uucico is run on the remote system as a shell, and the two uucico programs transfer any pending files or instructions between them, with one program acting as master and the other as slave. When all permitted transfers have been made, uucico logs out, hangs up, or otherwise severs the connection.

The actual process of file transfer occurs in the background, independent of the user (or program) that initiated the transfer. For mail transfer, the uucico daemon may act as an agent picking up mail from one system and delivering it to another system without human intervention. On newer versions of the uucp system, file transfer and remote execution of programs over many hops is possible and, if the transfer medium is fast enough (as in a network), full network-wide programming is viable.

Structurally, the `uucp` system resembles the old `lpr` print spooler. When a user initiates a transfer with `uucp`, the file to be transferred is marked or copied into a directory in `/usr/spool/uucp`, after which the `uucico` daemon is run in the background if the window for communications is open. The system administrator may define when individual systems may be called by editing one of the `uucp` tables.

After `uucico` has made connections with another system, it continues to run until it has exhausted all legal file transfers both to and from the remote system. Again, the system administrator may define what constitutes a legal transfer, who may transfer files, which directories are accessible to what systems, and which commands may be run from what systems. The `uucico` daemon, spawned by a user, may continue running until well after the original user has logged out.

Summary

Although there are many other systems and subsystems in UNIX that have not been mentioned, this chapter has illustrated all of the major mechanisms used in UNIX.

As you learned, UNIX is driven by tables that are accessible to the user or superuser. These tables are ordinary ASCII files, located in specific directories and with a long history of conventional use. Some of the tables may be modified to render UNIX completely unrecognizable. The intent of this chapter was to instill respect for the UNIX conventions, so that as you modify the behavior of UNIX (in later chapters) to suit the demands of the MIS environment, the flavor, intent and brilliance of the UNIX design are not lost.

Chapter 3

Organization and Structure of the UNIX File System

W ithin the UNIX community, the structure of the UNIX file system has been the topic of much debate. *Structure*, in this case, does not mean internal file structure (that comes later in this chapter). Rather, structure represents the names, placement, and uses of different directories. Each faction of the UNIX community insists that its conventions are the right ones. What is "right" depends on your historical perspective and what you consider the "true" UNIX.

NOTE The earliest release of UNIX that gained stability and exposure was called "Version 7." Version 7 was not named after the release of the operating system; it got the name because the documentation achieved stability with version 7. (The seventh version of the documentation was the first version published to the external world.)

UNIX Version 7 formed the basis of both Microsoft's XENIX and the Berkeley version of UNIX. To many UNIX fans, Version 7 was the quintessential UNIX; the kernel was very small (less than 64K on one Intel 8086 version), and most of the usual UNIX utilities were already included.

The design of Version 7's file system was dictated by the fact that disks of that era were small (disks contained only 10M, fitting in an eight-inch housing that was similar to today's 5 1/4-inch housing). Because disks of the era were small and UNIX was big (all things are relative), the operating system and user's data were unlikely to fit on the same disk. As a result, the files and directories were divided in a rather curious way.

When the system first boots, everything needed to run UNIX must be found on the *root disk*, which is the equivalent to the logical C: disk in MS-DOS. The process of booting includes mounting other disks on empty directories, which is usually accomplished in the /etc/brc script. Because you must run shell scripts and because the mount command is part of the boot process, at least part of the UNIX utilities collection must be present on the root disk itself, including the contents of the \bin and \etc directories.

Understanding Directories and UNIX Conventions

The constraints imposed by small disks in the early days of UNIX determined the design of the UNIX directory structure through UNIX System V Release 3. With Release 4, it was recognized that the old constraints no longer existed, and a more rational design could be created. Because Release 4 promised to be backward-compatible with older releases, there was a confusing mix of the old and the new. The following sections discuss the old systems.

The UNIX Directory Structure Prior to System V Release 4

On the earliest systems, the root disk was no bigger than 5M, which barely fit the basic operating system. On these systems, the root disk contained the operating system; other disks contained user's data. The root disk was configured as follows:

❖ `/unix`. In most cases, the kernel was the only file in the `root (/)` directory. After the kernel was loaded into memory, it required tables and files located in `/etc`.

❖ `/etc/`. This directory contains any files, programs, and tables required for booting and halting the system, as well as the `passwd` table, which is used to record data on users. This directory is the exclusive province of the system administrator; no user data should ever be permitted in the `/etc` directory. Indeed, no files in this directory should have write permission for anyone but the system administrator.

❖ `/lib/`. This directory is a library of binary-code fragments used by the C compiler. It also contains the second- and third-pass programs called by the C compiler (`cc`). By extension, it is now commonly used for libraries for all other compilers.

❖ `/lost+found/`. The UNIX file system is very susceptible to accidental shutdowns because speed is the primary factor in its design. Unlike many other operating systems, when a program writes to a file, it does not write to the physical disk, but to a buffer. The operating system then flushes these buffers out to the physical disk.

In addition to the physical file on disk, UNIX maintains an intricate system of file pointers, called *inodes* (index nodes), which maintain the location of the physical file and the directory to which a file belongs. If the inode system becomes corrupted, UNIX cannot differentiate one file from another or where a file belongs in the file system. Because of the file system's fragility, there are many file-repair programs.

The first program was fsck (file system check). This program is run automatically by the /etc/brc start-up script—first on the root disk, then on any other disks that are to be mounted. If the file system is corrupted, fsck tries to repair the damage by reconnecting files that were "lost". If a file is found for which there is no entry in any directory (a common problem), the file is placed in the /lost+found directory and named for its inode number. The system administrator must then figure out what the file is and where it belongs.

 UNIX cannot "mount" a corrupted file system. Every disk or disk partition has its own /lost+found directory.

❖ /tmp/. This directory is used for temporary files, such as those created during a sort or a compile. It is the standard UNIX convention (as well as good programming practice) for any programs that use temporary files to clean up after themselves. Because not all of them do so, the system administrator must periodically delete any files left in any of the temporary directories. This process is usually done when going from init state 1 to init state 2 or when the system first becomes a multiuser system.

So far, all UNIX systems, past and present, have been described. In the following sections, the uses and functions of various directories begin to change as the focus moves to the Berkeley version of UNIX and finally to Release 4. There is an ordered migration from a system design that is dependent on available disk sizes to a system design that is more ordered and convenient for backup and duplication.

❖ `/bin/`. This (binary) directory holds most of the important original UNIX utility programs. Any program required during the boot process must be located here. When the system is fully operational, this directory is first in the search path (by default, `/bin` is listed first in the environmental `PATH` variable).

That this directory no longer contains just binary programs is more a matter of evolution than design—originally, there were few Bourne shell scripts in the UNIX system. Through Release 3, this directory contained the smallest (or the most frequently called) utility programs and few user programs were placed here. With Release 4, all this changed (later sections discuss the new release in detail).

❖ `/usr/`. On the original system that had the 5M root disk, there was little space left for user data (this data had to be placed on a second disk).

 When disks are mounted in UNIX, they appear to the user to be part of one contiguous file system, unlike MS-DOS, which maintains a conceptual distinction between disks and partitions by naming each logical disk A:, B:, C:, and so on.

Because files cannot cross the physical boundary imposed by different disks (unless the disks are *stripped*), the separation of disks must logically be incorporated into the UNIX conceptual scheme of a file system. This is accomplished by *mounting* the disk on an empty directory. (Files cannot cross a directory barrier, but must exist within a directory.) Thus, before the second disk in the primitive system is mounted, the `root` disk contains an empty directory named `/usr`. When a second disk is mounted on the `/usr` directory, it appears that the contents of `/usr` are just a continuation of the `root` file system. The only indication that a second physical disk is in the system is the appearance of `/usr/lost+found`.

As UNIX matured and the number of programs and utilities increased, they overflowed the boundary of the `root` disk and a mirror image of the `root` disk began to appear. Because there was a `/bin` directory on the `root` disk that contained programs, there also appeared a `/usr/bin` directory to handle the overflow. Because there was a `/lib` directory on the `root` disk, there also appeared a `/usr/lib` directory. Because the `root` disk was small, and `/tmp` could not hold a lot of temporary data, there was also a need for a `/usr/tmp` directory.

By the time Version 7 made its appearance, most of UNIX was codified. The root disk had remained stable and the contents of the `/usr` directory, as far as UNIX went, also became stable with the following directory conventions:

❖ `/usr/bin/`. The environment variable PATH is set by the kernel to search `/bin`, and then `/usr/bin`, for any commands that are issued to the shell by a user. By convention, `/bin` contains any commands needed to boot the system; it also contains any small, fast, and often-used commands. In contrast, `/usr/bin` contains everything else: all of the obscure UNIX commands, the (relatively) large and sluggish commands, and any front-ends to third-party programs, such as database managers and word processors.

Many users or system administrators place their own privately generated commands here as well, but this is not a good idea. Instead, most systems also contain a directory called /usr/lbin (or something similar) to hold locally created commands. This makes sense because, when migrating from one system to another, it is easier to pick out local commands if they are segregated into their own directory. The system administrator has to place the local bin directory in the search path (in /etc/profile or /etc/cshrc), but this is easy compared to picking local commands from the hundreds that are normally found in the /usr/bin directory.

❖ /usr/include/. The first pass of the C compiler enables you to include source-code fragments into your programs before they are compiled into binary-executable form. These C source-code fragments are kept in the /usr/include directory. Because they are source code, the system administrator is free to change or add to any of the files in this directory. Because the C language derives much of its portability from these include files, however, such editing is discouraged. A good policy is to place any locally derived include files in a subdirectory within /usr/include. For example, the system administrator can create a directory named /usr/include/local, and programmers can insert locally produced include files in their C programs by using the following instruction:

```
#include <local/file.h>
```

❖ /usr/lib/. Unlike the /lib directory, the /usr/lib directory contains no archived binary libraries. Instead, it contains tables and secondary programs used and called by programs in /bin and /usr/bin.

The use of `/usr/lib`, in pre-Release 4 systems, grew in a haphazard fashion. Some commands (in `/bin` and `/usr/bin`) call programs directly from `/usr/lib`; others—such as `uucp`, `cron`, and `mail`—maintain subdirectories of their own within `/usr/lib`. The use of subdirectories is a better practice when a program uses several tables or calls multiple programs.

There are no real conventions on the use of this directory. Many new programs, postdating Version 7, use their own directories within the `/usr` directory to keep `/usr/lib` in its original state. There are arguments on both sides of the debate. For example, the directory containing the system dictionary used by the UNIX `spell` command has "wandered" between `/usr/lib/dict` and `/usr/dict`. Although it is necessary to avoid potential naming conflicts, it is probably better practice to create subdirectories within the `/usr/lib` directory.

❖ `/usr/spool/`. With the introduction of print spooling and background communications, it would have been logical to use one of the temporary directories. Because of the practice of cleaning the temporary directories, however, either at system boot or periodically, any pending file transfers or print requests would be lost. To avoid that scenario, the `/usr/spool` directory was created.

Originally, only transient files were kept in this directory. In recent years, however, there has been a tendency to keep programs that end up in `/usr/lib` here as well. For example, with the old `lpr` print spooler, the `lpd` daemon was kept in `/usr/lib`. With the introduction of the LP system, however, both filter and interface programs are kept in `/usr/spool/lp`, and the LP daemon and some of its associated control programs are still found in `/usr/lib`.

The Remaining Directory Structure

In addition to these system directories, the /usr directory also contains directories owned by ordinary users. These directories are where login places the user and where users work and store data. Obviously, the /usr directory can get crowded; because user and system directories are freely mixed in, it is not easy to separate static system data from dynamic user data when performing backups.

Life for the system administrator improves when a third disk can be added to the system. Customarily, when a third disk is added to handle the overflowing user data, it is named /usr2 (subsequent disks are called /usr3, and so on).

 On systems configured this way, it is easy to move all "real" users to the new disk and reserve /usr for the system administrator. This approach was practical and almost necessary in the days of 5M hard disks and reel-to-reel tapes.

The use and conventions of UNIX reached a first level of maturity with the release of Version 7. As was previously stated, the design of the file system was primarily dictated by the physical constraints of disk size. In the following period, UNIX underwent a tremendous metamorphosis.

Examining UNIX's Evolutionary Changes

After the release of Version 7, UNIX was given away to colleges and universities (and purchased by a few farsighted companies). It was sold or given away without support or warranty of any kind and, although it was portable because of its C language, it only ran on the pdp-11.

At the University of California at Berkeley, UNIX was ported to the VAX computer and given virtues that were lacking in Version 7, such as demand-paging into virtual memory, a larger and more resilient file system, and a built-in network capability. Microsoft, on the other hand, offered support and porting advice for other manufacturers who wanted to use UNIX on computers using the newly available microchips. Because of their origins in academia and in business, the Berkeley version of UNIX became a favorite for engineers. Microsoft's XENIX also became a standard for small businesses. UNIX became a standard in these niches and in this era by default because there were no realistic alternatives on the market, especially for microchip-based systems.

The Evolution of UNIX into System V

Spurred on by the acceptance of Berkeley UNIX and XENIX, AT&T sought to regain control of UNIX by proposing UNIX System III as a new and universal standard. This quickly became UNIX System V, on which such standards as POSIX and X/OPEN are based. One of the tenets of UNIX is that all new versions should be backwardly compatible with older versions of the operating system running on the same hardware and that, above all, there should emerge only one standard version of UNIX.

To encourage or even tolerate multiple standards defeats the entire philosophy of UNIX. Because UNIX System V was different from both XENIX and the Berkeley variety, AT&T sought to merge the three competing standards into one standard. Merging UNIX System V and XENIX was easy, and it resulted in UNIX System V Release 3. Subsequent minor releases (Releases 3.1 and 3.2) refined the merged systems and brought "standard" UNIX up to the full capabilities of the Intel 80386 chip architecture.

To merge UNIX System V with the Berkeley variant (specifically, the Sun version of Berkeley UNIX) required not only the evolutionary changes that took place since the introduction of Version 7, but also necessitated a revolutionary rewrite of UNIX from the ground up. This rewrite was dictated as much by differences between SunOS and System V as the changes that had taken place in the technology.

Because designers were no longer limited by small disks or limited random-access memory, they had the freedom to design a more rational system. On the other hand, new constraints were placed on the designers by end users and hardware-system designers. UNIX was growing up. The new UNIX, if it was to remain stable for any length of time, had to be backwardly compatible with both XENIX and BSD, to be open to full network and multiprocessing implementations, and to have the security features of the systems it was designed to replace.

In many respects, UNIX System V Release 4 is as different from Release 3 as the old Version 7 was from the original System V. There are new file- and directory-usage conventions, built-in networking, and many new features that can create larger systems. Unlike Release 3, Release 4 is a mainframe operating system. The result is far more flexibility at the price of complexity.

UNIX as an Emerging Standard

To remain backwardly compatible with Release 3 and XENIX, the directories remain (at least in the form of symbolically linked files and directories) and serve the same function. One notable exception is the /usr directory. All users have been removed from /usr and placed in a new directory named /home.

It has long been a practice on larger systems to create a new directory named /u, /user, or whatever (there have never been any conventions), and then to place users there. The /home directory resolves the issue of a conventional name for a directory with real users.

Another distinction is made in Release 4 between programs and tables used to drive programs and other variables. Data, whether temporary or not, are now located in the /var directory. This makes a lot of sense, except that for compatibility reasons, much of what is found in the /var directory is also found in the /usr directory. For example, the new spool directory is /var/spool; there is also the classic /usr/spool directory, which exists only as a symbolically linked directory.

If you use the change directory command to move into /usr/spool (as in **cd /usr/spool**), and then enter the print working directory command (**pwd**), you see that you are not in /usr/spool at all—you have changed to the /var/spool directory instead.

Another example is /usr/lib/uucp, which is the home of the tables and secondary programs that surround the uucp system. Although all of the expected tables and programs are there, programs like the daemon uucico are real and the uucp control tables (such as Systems and Dialers) are not real. Instead, they are symbolically linked to their real files, which ar located in /var/uucp.

A final confusing example concerns the actual location of the standard set of UNIX commands. In addition to /bin and /usr/bin, there now exists a third directory named sbin, within which all the actual programs are located and linked to their respective locations in /bin and /usr/bin with symbolic links.

The UNIX System V Release 4 Directory Structure

If Release 4 appears confusing, it is the price to pay for a final merge between the three main branches of UNIX. When the dust settles and users become familiar with Release 4, the symbolic links that are necessary for familiarity with the past will eventually disappear and a far more simple conception of UNIX will emerge. The following are the directories in Release 4:

❖ /sbin/. This directory contains all normal UNIX commands.

❖ /lbin/. This directory contains all locally produced commands.

❖ /var/. This directory contains all system tables and transitory files, related to some spooled event such as printing or communications.

For example, the uucp command maintains three subdirectories in /var: /var/uucp (containing system-definition tables), /var/spool/uucppublic (having the same function as /usr/spool/uucppublic), and /var/spool/uucp (the same as /usr/spool/uucp). The secondary programs, typically found in /usr/lib/uucp, stay where they are or migrate to /usr/uucp.

❖ /tmp/. This directory retains its current function.

❖ /etc/. This directory retains its current function.

❖ /lib/. This directory retains its current function.

❖ /home/. This directory is the home of all normal users.

❖ `/usr/`. This directory becomes what `/usr/lib` was in previous releases, except that major subsystems get their own directories, as in `/usr/uucp`. There is still a `/usr/lib` directory for single programs not generally accessible by users; subsystems requiring directories are moved to `/usr`.

Of course, this discussion is conjecture because there are few "official" guides to the use and conventions of Release 4. The definitions of directory usage in Release 4 can be found in the *System Administrator's Reference Manual*.

Understanding UNIX Files and their Extensions: Networks

It is an axiom that data and data-processing requirements expand and eventually exceed any known system. Recently, the data-processing capacity of equivalently priced systems has doubled every four years and that system capacity has largely kept up with demand. Processing power that was considered to be a mainframe in 1970 can now be found next to the desks of many users. Because of the life span of most computers, however, it is easy for any installation to outgrow a single system before obsolescence. The solution to this problem (and the problem imposed by migrating very large systems to UNIX)is found in networking.

UNIX Networks

There are many types of networks available, and each one has attributes and shortcomings. The OSI model of the logical layers of a network is shown in figure 3.1.

The concept of a *network* ranges from the inexpensive but slow *sneakernet*, which moves files and data by magnetic tape or floppy disk, to the current ultimate in network speed, FDDI (fiber optics network).

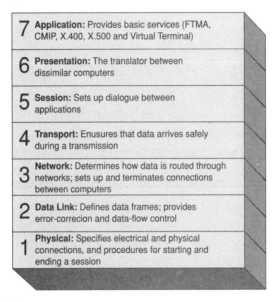

Figure 3.1:
The OSI model of a network.

The choice of networking hardware and software depend on three factors: the volume of data that must be shared between systems, the physical distance between systems, and the immediacy of the data-transfer need. On larger systems, a mix of technologies is often required, blending local area networks with wide-area packet switching or dial-up telephone lines.

The purpose of networking, of course, is to spread out the data-processing load across many distinct computers, while making the necessary data available to any systems that need it. The implication is that high-speed data links are required.

Nowhere are any of the popular network buzzwords, such as Ethernet, token-ring, X.25, or TCP/IP mentioned. There is a good reason for this. The efficiency of a network depends on delivering the right data when it is needed. To deliver it before it is needed does not improve the efficiency of the system.

For example, if the goal of an MIS system is to provide accurate financial statements four times a year, and the data required must be collected from widely dispersed sites, the postal service provides more than enough bandwidth and speed for the network. If less bandwidth is needed, but the information is more time-critical, the services of an ordinary telephone, modem, and the original networking program (uucp) may be all that is necessary.

 The design of a network and the choice of its file-sharing methods depends on the design of the MIS system. It is always the goal of a good system design to use the simplest method available to accomplish a task.

Electronic File Sharing

Most of the early electronic file-sharing systems, such as uucp, rely on copying the file from one system to another. This method is no different from using a magnetic tape because the data is duplicated on both systems.

The goal of a network-oriented file-sharing system is not to duplicate data, but to share the data resource over a reliable communication medium. On the surface, this sounds like a stretch of the art but, in reality, networks have always been an integral part of any computer system. Most computers have some sort of system bus that enables the CPU to communicate with memory, disks, terminals, and so forth.

The popular disk interface called SCSI is a small network that can address eight devices. This networking concept can be extended to local area networks or even to the telephone system. In each case, every device on the network has a unique address. (In the case of the telephone system, the address is the telephone number.)

What makes networking difficult is that different media have different bandwidths—they can carry different amounts of data. Thus, there is no guarantee that each node on the network will respond exactly the same way.

With wide-area networking, routing is an additional problem. On a single network such as the telephone system, routing is not a major problem. There are known paths between nodes (area codes, exchanges, and so forth), and the problem becomes establishing a semi-permanent path between client and server for the duration of the telephone call.

Unfortunately, establishing such semi-permanent links reduces the bandwidth of the telephone system. That is why modem links are generally restricted to speeds below 9600 baud. To increase the bandwidth of a given channel, it is necessary to multiplex the data (to recover the "dead air" inherent in voice communications) by digital packet-switching.

A *packet* is a predetermined block of data that contains the sender's and receiver's address. Each node in the network sends the packet on to the next node in the network closer to the destination, and each packet is handled independently. On a single network, it is relatively easy to establish a single packet-switching protocol, which is exactly what the X.25 wide-area networking is. If the packet must travel through a number of different networks, the Internet, a common internetwork protocol, is required. This is the function of TCP/IP and the OSI protocol suites.

Despite great promise, the OSI protocols have never gained much favor; the older TCP/IP system continues to gain acceptance within the data-processing community. Indeed, because of its wide acceptance in data processing and its origins in the Berkeley version of UNIX, TCP/IP is an integral part of UNIX System V Release 4.

The greatest advantage of the Internet Protocol, IP, is that it is independent of the carrier medium: it works over a 1200-baud modem line, as well as over a fiber optics cable. Of course, the rate at which a data packet can be transferred is dependent on the slowest link in the Internet, but a TCP/IP system connected to another system by any means can communicate.

A reliable communications mechanism is a necessary condition for establishing a shared file system. Because TCP/IP is a protocol designed to be run on almost any operating system, the basis exists for sharing files and other resources between any system on the Internet, regardless of make, model, or operating system.

Of the two file-sharing systems available on UNIX, Sun Microsystem's NFS (Network File System) and AT&T's RFS (Remote File Service), only NFS is based on the Internet Protocol. This has made NFS extremely portable and it has been ported to many non-UNIX operating systems, including DEC's VMS and IBM's VM.

There are pros and cons of both NFS and RFS. For example, NFS is portable and universal only as long as the underlying network is based on TCP/IP. RFS, on the other hand, is far less portable because it relies on being able to communicate with another UNIX system (this is not strictly true, but no other systems support RFS). RFS is not dependent on any one network protocol—the underlying network can be based on OSI, TCP/IP, SNA, X.25, or any other network protocol. With respect to the operating philosophy of UNIX, RFS may be more in tune with the concept of separation of function, but NFS—with its wider appeal and promise of interoperability—is almost a standard.

 One problem with NFS is its reliance on Sun Microsystem's defined Remote Procedure Calls. The TCP/IP protocol is only a communications system, so there must be programs at either end of the network to catch these data packets and decode them. In the case of NFS, a program at the remote site must catch the data packets and execute the instructions contained in them. These are called *Remote Procedure Calls (RPCs)*, and they must behave exactly the same on every system supporting NFS.

Part of the NFS package that must be ported to every system that shares files is a library of RPCs. If interoperable networking is to become a reality, there must be a standard library of RPCs. Unfortunately, the Open Software Foundation has adopted a different set of RPCs, based on pure technical merit for its OSF/1 version of UNIX. Should this decision stand, there will be two incompatible libraries of Remote Procedure Calls. Because RFS does not rely on any one protocol (it relies on an independent STREAMS interface to the network), it may turn out that RFS is more versatile after all.

So far, this discussion of networking has as much relevance to the way UNIX works as does a discussion of what disk interface to use: SCSI, IDE, or CMD. From the UNIX point of view, disk interfaces, and network types or network protocols are largely transparent after an appropriate device driver or other interface program is created. What is important is that both NFS and RFS create extensions to the standard UNIX file system that enable a remote resource to be mounted as if it were just another physical disk. Once mounted, a remote resource is used and accessed like any other UNIX file, program, or device.

For example, a system in New York can locally mount a remote printer device located on a system in Tokyo, and can spool print jobs to it with the LP print-spooler system. A more relevant example is when an IBM mainframe runs the VM operating system and NFS acts as a file server for hundreds or thousands of UNIX systems worldwide. The efficiency of such a system is governed only by the bandwidth of the network connecting the various systems.

Examining the Physical Organization of the UNIX File System

Designing an operating system is a thankless task because, inevitably, a system designed for one kind of application will be used for another application. For example, an IBM mainframe is designed to process massive amounts of data by using large files and large fixed-length records. A mainframe works fastest when programs request whole cylinders of data at a time from contiguous areas on a disk.

To define these files, a mainframe programmer may define disk tracks or cylinders, and block them according to the need of the program. Such large blocks improve the efficiency of classic data processing, but they make applications, such as those for word processing, inefficient by wasting disk space. On the other hand, an operating system that is "tuned" for word processing expects to manage many small files rather than a few large ones (the smaller the logical block size, the more efficiently a disk can be used).

 The smallest permissible block size determines the minimum disk space required to represent a file. An operating system "tuned" for word processing is inefficient for processing large files with large fixed-length records.

To understand the origins of the UNIX file system, you have to start at the beginning. When UNIX was created, disks had little capacity when compared to today's disks, so it was important to use this resource efficiently. It was also important, in the early days, to find users who wanted or needed UNIX. Without a user base, it would have been impossible to continue the development of UNIX. Within Bell Laboratories, such a user base was found in the need for technical documentation (word processing).

From its inception. the UNIX file system was designed to efficiently handle a large number of small files and the block size was originally set at 512 bytes. Later versions of UNIX increased the block size as disk capacity grew and applications became oriented toward larger files (specifically, the BSD block size is 2048 bytes). The basic UNIX file system still reflects its origins, however, with the basic file-system structure called the inode table.

The UNIX Inode

The *inode table* is to UNIX what the FAT (file allocation table) is to MS-DOS. It is a basic system of pointers to each item in a physical file system. Because UNIX places almost all manipulatable items (files, directories, devices, shared memory segments, semaphores, and named pipes) somewhere in the file system, each of these items is represented by an inode.

At the time a disk is formatted for use by UNIX, you are asked for the number of inodes to allocate. This number is the maximum number of files, directories, and devices you will need, including all temporary files and mount points for other disks. The formatter then creates a super block and the requested number of inodes for each physical disk volume or partition). The structure of an inode is discussed later.

Every physical disk or disk partition on a UNIX system is divided into four physical areas: the *boot block*, the *super block*, the *inode table*, and the *data blocks*. These areas are shown in figure 3.2.

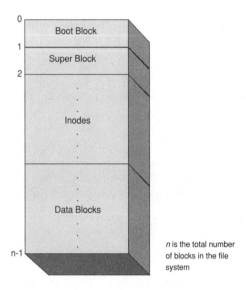

Figure 3.2:
The logical layout of a UNIX disk.

The *super block* contains the following information about the physical disk:

- ❖ The size of the file system in blocks
- ❖ The number of inodes
- ❖ The number of data blocks
- ❖ A list of unused inodes
- ❖ A list of unused data blocks

On a standard UNIX file system, this information is all that is required because the type of file system is assumed to be `unix` and the size of a block to be 512 bytes. UNIX System V Release 4 supports three different block sizes (512, 1024, and 2048 bytes) and an almost infinite variety of file types.

Several of these file types are pre-defined (for example, the Berkeley file system, XENIX, and MS-DOS). In this case, the super block contains more information, such as block size.

 The actual structure of the super block for a System V file system (s5), the Berkeley file system (bfs), and generic or Universal File System (ufs) can be found in the *System Administrators Reference Manual*.

Each s5 inode contains exactly 64 bytes of information, and all inodes are allocated before any data can be placed on the disk. Because inodes may be considered an array, the inode number is the address in the array (the tenth inode in the array has the inode number 10). The structure of each inode is as follows:

- ❖ Mode and type of file, an unsigned short integer (two bytes)
- ❖ Number of links to the file (a short integer)
- ❖ Owner's user ID (an unsigned short integer)
- ❖ Owner's group ID (an unsigned short integer)
- ❖ Number of bytes in the file (a long integer—four bytes)
- ❖ Forty bytes of disk-block addresses
- ❖ Time last accessed (a long integer)
- ❖ Time last modified (a long integer)
- ❖ Time status last changed (a long integer)

The structure of the inode imposes restrictions on the classic UNIX file structure. There can be no more than 65536 types of files, individual users, or groups on any UNIX system; the number of links to a file is restricted to 32767 links. The field representing the number of bytes in a file is a four-byte unsigned long integer, however, which means that in the classic UNIX file system there can be no file larger than four gigabytes. In most cases, this is not a problem, but in porting a large MIS system it can impose a constraint.

This constraint occurs only with the classic UNIX System V file system—there is also the Berkeley file system and the generalized Universal File System, in which blocks of any size can be defined. The maximum file size is represented by a *quad* (eight bytes) instead of by a long four-byte integer in a ufs file system.

A further problem with large files is imposed by the addressing scheme used to access the physical disk. The 40 bytes of disk addresses are organized as 13 addresses of three bytes each, with the last byte used as a *file-generation number*.

These three-byte addresses represent blocks in the file system. Because three bytes are just 24 bits, this represents a maximum address of 17 million possible disk addresses. With the standard UNIX block size of 512 bytes, the largest disk that can be addressed is eight gigabytes. At present, there are no physical disks of this size available, by using *disk stripping*, however, logical disks of this size can be created. (This occurs with the u5 file system and the minimum block size—there are fewer constraints in the ufs file system.)

The thirteen disk pointers contained in an inode are structured in a unique way. The first ten pointers point to the first ten blocks of data in a file system object (file, directory, or device). The first 5K bytes of a file (on a file system with 512 byte blocks) are directly accessible to a program from the files inode. This represents the contents of a two- or three-page letter, which is a typical word processing application. The eleventh address in an inode is called the *first indirect inode*, and it points to a block in the data space that contains 128 other disk addresses.

The 128 addresses contained in the first indirect block point to the next 64K bytes of a file. (The text of this chapter fits into that space, with a little room left over). Accessing larger files requires the use of double and triple indirect blocks. The twelfth address in the inode points to a data block, which contains the address of 128 additional data blocks (double indirect blocks), each of which contains 128 addresses of the next 16384 blocks (or 8M of the file). To reach still further requires the use of triple indirect blocks.

The thirteenth address in the inode points to a data block, which contains the addresses of 128 additional data blocks, each of which contain the address of 128 more data blocks (triple indirect blocks), each of which point to an additional 128 data blocks used in the file. In other words, to represent the largest possible file in the UNIX file system requires the use of an additional 16525 blocks (or over 8M) used for indirect addressing.

Figure 3.3 is a schematic representation of the inode-addressing scheme. UNIX is at its best with lots of small files.

So far, all system objects are represented by an inode number. A special file, called a *directory*, gives them a name. As far as the inode table is concerned, all objects on a disk have equal status, and a directory is just another object with its own inode. The fact that a particular object is a directory is signalled by a bit in the Mode and Status fields of the directory's inode.

This flag bit prevents users from writing to a directory file. The structure of a directory varies, depending on whether the file system is a normal UNIX, a u5, or a ufs. In a u5 file system, a directory contains any number of fixed-length records of 16 bytes each in the following formats:

> *node number*: two-byte unsigned integer
>
> *object name*: 14-byte string

The fact that the inode number is contained in an unsigned short integer implies that the maximum number of inodes on any one UNIX (u5) file system cannot exceed 65536. The remaining 14 bytes are dedicated to the name of the file.

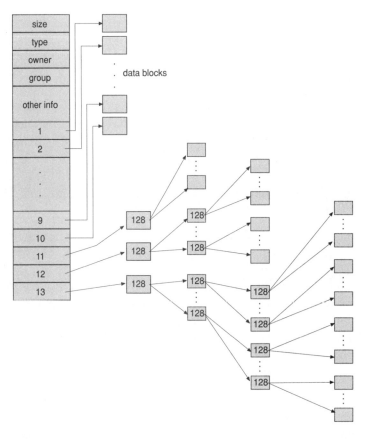

Figure 3.3:
The UNIX inode file-access system.

Each directory contains at least two entries: . and . . . The entry named . contains the inode of the directory itself; the entry named . . points to the inode of the directory directly above the current one. Thus, the directory named /bin points to the inode of the root directory, /. In the root directory itself, both . and . . point to the same inode. Although a directory file can contain any number of entries, only the first 320 (on a file system with 512 byte blocks) can be accessed without resorting to indirect address blocks.

You can access a file for reading or writing by finding the file's inode number from the directory block, and then looking up the inode and getting the logical block number required in the file system. If the file is a large one that requires indirect address blocks, reading and writing a file may consume many reads of the disk (it requires a maximum of five address block reads to reach the data block at the end of the largest file).

When a file is renamed or moved, only the appropriate entries in directory files are changed. If a file is moved from one directory to another, the entry in the original directory file is copied to the new directory file and erased from the original The file itself is not touched; it retains its inode number. If a file is removed, its entry in the directory file is deleted, the inode is freed, and any blocks used by the file are returned to the free block pool. The file itself is never touched.

In the classic UNIX System V Release 4 file system, only the root file system (composed of `/etc` and `/sbin`) need be of the type u5. The rest of the system may be composed of multiple ufs file systems.

The Universal File System is an outgrowth of the Virtual File System, which was created by Sun Microsystems to support NFS. To support differing file structures over a network, it was necessary to create a structure that could be mapped onto the UNIX file system.

Once a ufs file system has been created, either on a physical disk or across a network, it can then be mounted onto the standard u5 file system like any other device and accessed like any other UNIX file. A file-system design must be structured like UNIX (it can be made to look like the typical file within the directory tree structure of UNIX). Thus, files from diverse operating systems such as

MS-DOS, DEC's VMS, and IBM's VM can be used by UNIX, directly or over a network.

Almost all of the constraints imposed on file sizes, file-system sizes, and file names by the u5 file system are relaxed in a ufs system. They are more dependent on the nature of the file system the ufs is intended to mimic than on any real constraints. Many programs that are designed to run under UNIX implicitly assume UNIX's limitations and may not be able to take advantage of larger file sizes. An example of this self-imposed constraint may be found in many database-management systems, in which the maximum number of records in any one file is limited by a four-byte integer.

Summary

UNIX is mature and stable, as well as growing and evolving. The conventions of UNIX are really no more than time-honored traditions. As with all traditions, they are eventually broken by accident or intent.

This chapter covered the history of the UNIX file system, as well as its directory structure and file-sharing system. You learned about UNIX traditions and why many of these traditions evolved. Ultimately, the philosophy of UNIX can be summed up with the phrase, "if it ain't broke, don't fix it". Use the conventions, even if they do not make much technical sense any more, unless you have a dramatically improved way of doing things—then you should start a new tradition.

Topics covered in this chapter:

Categorizing UNIX Commands

Examining Program Tools

Understanding Shell Variables

Understanding Daemons

Examining the Data Workflow of an MIS System

Chapter 4

The UNIX Programmer's Toolkit

Some people consider UNIX difficult to use. At the same time, others consider it a "programmer's paradise." Although the first statement is arguably false, the latter is certainly true. UNIX is quite possibly the most complete operating system ever created because it incorporates more programming tools and utilities as part of its standard package than does any other operating system.

Categorizing UNIX Commands

The bulk of the UNIX commands and utilities fall into three categories: pattern recognition and manipulation, version control, and programming languages. UNIX provides the perfect environment to combine the basic commands and utilities into powerful shell scripts that can perform most of the functions of the typical management information system.

Pattern Recognition and Manipulation Commands

By far, the largest group of UNIX commands deals with pattern recognition and manipulation. This group includes the versatile `awk` interpreted language (named after its authors, Al *A*ho, Peter *W*einberger, and Brian *K*ernighan), the `sed` (*s*tream *ed*itor) and `grep` (*g*eneral *r*egular *e*xpression *p*arser) family filters, and the language generators `lex` (*lex*ical analyzer and `yacc`, (*y*et *a*nother compiler compiler) to name only a few. Within the group of pattern-manipulation commands are the database commands that manipulate whole tables, including the commands `sort` and `join`.

The UNIX pattern recognition commands search through designated files for text that matches some pattern passed to the command as an argument. For instance, the command `grep Glines authornames` searches the file *authornames* for all occurances of the text `Glines`. Any lines of text in *authornames* containing `Glines` is displayed on the screen. The lines containing `Glines` can be redirected to a second file with the redirection symbol: `grep Glines authornames > glinesfile`.

Version-Control Commands

The second major group of commands, unofficially called the *version control system*, are important when many programmers are working on a project or when a relatively small group of engineers are developing many programs. In either case, multiple versions of a program and its modules might be present on the system, which can create nightmares for programmers and program managers.

During the development process, the object file manager `make` compiles and relinks any modified program files and reconciles any *dependencies* by recompiling or relinking. A *dependent* file is a program module that requires another code module that was recently modified.

The UNIX *Source Code Control System* (sccs) is even more sophisticated. It enables the software project manager to control releases of software modules and to specify which version of program code is incorporated into the completed project.

UNIX Programming Languages

While the C language is the *lingua franca*, or "mother tongue," of UNIX, it is by no means the only language UNIX uses. For many applications, C is completely inappropriate. In fact, the Bourne shell, C shell and Korn shell constitute powerful languages in their own right. You can create programs in a few minutes using a *shell script* that might take hours or days using C. A shell script is a program written in one of the UNIX shell languages. Also, most shell scripts execute very quickly; implementing these same programs in C does not usually reduce execution time.

Using the C Language on a UNIX System

Aside from its raw execution speed, C's primary benefit is its capability to read and write binary files. Virtually all other commands and utilities found in UNIX are designed to read and write ASCII and EBCDIC files. EBCDIC is the character interchange scheme used on IBM-based mainframe computers.

UNIX's orientation to ASCII file manipulation has both advantages and disadvantages. ASCII files are generally bigger and require more disk storage than comparable binary files and, therefore, take longer (on large files) to access. On the other hand, ASCII files are a common medium on which all commands can operate.

The C Language in MIS Environments

The greatest drawback to using C for MIS purposes is that it was not intended for commercially produced application development. Although C is ideally suited for writing operating systems (which was its original purpose), it is a rather poor choice for transaction processing. It also has proved adept for creating word processors, spreadsheets, compilers, and even database managers. Because it is not well-suited to large-scale systems, however, C cannot completely replace other commercially oriented languages or database management systems (DBMSs).

Although C is of limited use to the MIS manager as a development language, it is the glue that binds UNIX applications together. Most, if not all, of the UNIX utility commands were written in C. Without access to the C libraries, few applications can take advantage of UNIX's resources and facilities. In addition, very few of the advanced facilities common in UNIX, such as named pipes and interprocess communications, are available in any other language.

From the MIS perspective, C is a useful tool-builder, but is not suitable as a primary language for most MIS tasks. For these tasks, you should use commercially oriented languages, DBMSs, and the rest of the UNIX toolkit. You might be surprised to learn how much you can accomplish with UNIX's remaining tools. You do, however, need to understand the uses of each tool in order to take full advantage of the toolkit.

Understanding UNIX Command-Line Parameters

The way UNIX tools are used depends upon how the shell interprets a command line. The *command line* consists of the command's name and the arguments passed to it. For instance, `grep james namefile` is a typical UNIX command line. The UNIX command is `grep`; while `james` and `namefile` are arguments passed to `grep`. If you want to create your own shell scripts, they should conform to expected UNIX conventions.

When a UNIX program or command executes, three parameters are made available to its main routine. The first parameter passed is an *integer*, the number of parameters passed (in the example, two parameters—`james` and `namefile`—were passed). The second parameter is the *starting address* of an array of characters passed to the command.

 Do not confuse *arguments* with *parameters* in this discussion. The command's *arguments* are text items entered as part of the command line (`james` and `namefile`). The *parameters* discussed in this section are made available to the `grep` command (in the example) by the UNIX system itself. The command can ignore the parameters if they are not important.

The first member of the array is a string that terminates with a binary zero or *null*. The string contains the program name, as it is called in the shell command line. In the example, `grep` was the name of the command, so it occupies the first position in the string array passed to the command.

 Remember that arrays in C are numbered 0,1,2,... instead of the conventional 1,2,3,... found in Fortran and COBOL.

 It may seem odd, but the command receives its own name as part of the parameters passed to it by UNIX. In the example `grep james filename`, `grep` is available to the `grep` command, if needed.

The first through *n*th elements of the parameter array are null-terminated strings that represent any command-line arguments as they are interpreted by the shell. Therefore, `james` is parameter 1 and `namefile` is parameter 2. Parameter 0 is always the name of the command itself (`grep`).

The final program parameter is the array's starting address, which contains all the program's environment elements in the form of null-terminated strings with the syntax `variable=value`.

Command-Line Parameters in a C Program

You can use any of the three parameters discussed in the preceding section; however, you always must pass them in strict order. To access the program's environment, the program must accept the *arg*ument *c*ount parameter (`argc`), the array of command-line parameters (`argv[]`), and the environment array (`arge[]`). In a C program, these paramaters usually are represented in the first few lines of the main program module, as shown in the following example:

```
main(argc,argv,arge)
int argc;
char *argv[],*arge[];
```

In this example, *argc* is 2 (there are two parameters—`james` and `namefile`—on the command line), and the `argv` array consists of `grep` (`argv[0]`), `james` (`argv[1]`), and `namefile` (`argv[2]`).

Command-Line Parameters in a Shell Script

A shell-script program passes the command-line parameters data in the same way as C; however, the data takes a different form. In the Bourne shell, the number of command-line parameters is placed in a variable named $#$ (equivalent to `argc`), and the name of the called shell script is located in the variable 0 (equivalent to `argv[0]`). The remaining command-line parameters are located in 1, 2, (equivalent to `argv[1]`, `argv[2]`) and so on, or can be used as a whole with the variable $*$.

A C program has access to the program's environment but defines and manipulates internal variables. A shell script, on the other hand, only manipulates environment variables.

UNIX Environment Variables

Those familiar with MS-DOS are acquainted with the concept of an operating system environment. On MS-DOS machines, the environment plays only a minor role in the operation of the system. In UNIX, however, the environment plays a far greater role. The UNIX shell is the prime manipulator and user of the operating system environment.

The *operating system environment* is the information the system uses for basic operations like finding commands (searching through directories specified by PATH). The environment also includes a set of variables that determine the shell-prompt display, certain information about the shell process itself, and where the user's home directory is located. Most of these environment variables have DOS equivalents.

Environment Inheritance by Child Processes

The growth of tasks in UNIX is like the growth of a single cell, through mitosis, into a large and self-sustaining organism. The germinal cell of UNIX is the init task, which clones itself into the processes specified in the /etc/inittab table.

This cloning process, called *forking*, is like the mitosis that results in new cells. The germ of the new cell, its "DNA," is the environment. Each new task is free to modify its own environment, but it cannot modify the environment of its parent. When a process forks to create a new process, it first clones its environment, then *execs*, or mutates, into the new process. The new process is usually referred to as a *child* process. The child process inherits the environment of its parent.

Although a binary program can manipulate its environment, it rarely does. Environment manipulation is largely a function of the shell and shell scripts. In this respect, you might recognize similarities to IBM's Job Control Language (JCL).

The shell, then, serves two purposes: environment manipulator and command interpreter. To interpret commands, the shell must first *parse* the command line into its constituents using the rules outlined in the following sections.

Parameter Substitution and Assignment

Values are assigned to variables in the environment with the simple string *variable=value* in the Bourne and Korn shells and with the command setenv *variable value* in the C shell.

For instance, in the Bourne or Korn shells, you might set the variable username to glines with the following command line:

```
username=glines
```

The equivalent C shell command line is as follows:

```
setenv username glines
```

Parameter Substitution

When working with environment variables on the shell command line, place a dollar sign (**$**) in front of the variable name. The shell replaces the variable name with the value of the variable. Thus, with a Bourne shell variable that is set as *username*=glines, use *$username* to use the value (glines) assigned to the *username* variable.

For example, to use the value of username as a command parameter, enter **grep $username myfile**. The shell replaces *username* with glines before it executes the command. When the command executes, the command line reads grep glines myfile. This process is known as *parameter substitution* because the parameter ($username) passed to the command is replaced with the value of the parameter (glines).

Command Substitution

Imagine a situation in which the parameters of a command depend on the outcome of another program. Better yet, assume the output of one program generates the parameters for a second program. This situation represents *command substitution*. The output of one command replaces the command name on the next command line before that line is executed.

The shell recognizes the *accent grave* (`—sometimes referred to as a *backwards quote*) as a signal that what follows is a command to be executed. For example, if you enter **grep `whoami` /etc/ passwd**, the shell runs the whoami command, replaces the string *"whoami"* with the results of running whoami, then runs the grep command. If you were logged onto the system as user mgroh, the whoami command returns mgroh, and the command line grep `whoami` /etc/passwd returns all of the lines in the /etc/passwd file with mgroh in them.

It is important to understand that the UNIX command enclosed in accent grave marks is run before the rest of the command line. The value returned by the command is substituted before the rest of the command line is processed.

Parameter Separation

Very few UNIX commands accept only one parameter. Instead, a command is more likely to have multiple parameters in the form *command param1 param2* and so on. For instance, the `cat` command (which displays files on the screen) can display multiple files: `cat /etc/passwd /etc/ttys`.

The shell separates items on the command line into fields by looking for one or more *field separators* between items. Field separators are defined by the environment variable *IFS*. The default values for the *IFS* variable are the Tab key, space bar, and carriage return. These values are sometimes referred to as *white space*. Fields on the command line can be separated by one or more of these characters.

The need for separators is obvious. We can recognize `echohello` as an attempt to have the system echo `hello` on the screen. Without field separation, the UNIX system itself, however, has no way to separate the command (`echo`) from the argument passed to it (`hello`).

For example, a command line might contain the command itself followed by three Tabs, a parameter string, a space, and a final parameter string. In this case, UNIX ignores multiple field separators (three Tabs) and parses the command line into a command and two parameters. The separators are necessary so that UNIX knows where the command leaves off and the arguments to the command begin.

By *escaping* a carriage return with a backslash (\), you also can use a return character as a field separator, as shown in the following example:

cat(tab,tab)*file1*(space,space)*file2*\(return)*file3*

Before it executes the line, UNIX translates this entry to the following syntax:

```
cat file1 file2 file3
```

In this example, *file1*, *file2*, and *file3* are displayed one at a time, in order, on the computer screen.

Rules of Quotation

Sometimes you need to pass strings with embedded spaces as a single parameter. For instance, you might want to pass the string `Hello world` to an application, as in `grep Hello world file1`. Normally, the shell separates `Hello` and `world` into two distinct parameters and discards the space between them. In this example, the `grep` command attempts to search for `Hello` in a file named `world` and ignores the `file1` parameter.

To ensure that the application receives only a single parameter, you must observe the *rules of quotation*. These rules state that any string enclosed in quotation marks (`"`) or surrounded by apostrophes (`'`) are treated as a single parameter. Therefore, the example above should be entered as **grep "Hello world" file1** or **grep 'Hello world' file1**.

However, the shell treats quotation marks and apostrophes differently. A string enclosed in apostrophes is passed exactly as written. A string enclosed in quotation marks is first subject to the rules of parameter and command substitution. Only the rules of parameter separation are suspended. Thus, using the example cited earlier in this chapter, the string *'$username'* (enclosed in apostrophes) produces the string $username (no substitution); *"$username"* (enclosed in quotation marks) is replaced with glines (*$username* is substituted with the value of *username*).

Wild Cards

By default, the shell expects all command parameters to be file names in the current directory. If the parameter contains *wild cards*, the shell attempts to resolve them into true file names before it passes them on to the command. Wild cards provide a short-cut means of referring to file names.

The *wild cards* include the asterisk (*), which represents any string of characters. For instance, the ls command, which lists the contents of the current directory, might be entered on the command line this way:

```
ls g*
```

This search returns the names of all files in the current directory that begin with the letter g.

The question mark (?) represents any single character in the file name, as in the following example:

```
ls for?
```

This syntax returns form, fort, fore, and ford, if all of these file names were found in the current directory.

A pair of square brackets in the form [...] matches any of the enclosed characters. If a pair of characters enclosed in square brackets is separated by a dash, as in [A-z], a match is made on any one character between or including the characters enclosed by the brackets:

```
ls b[a-o]rn
```

This line returns `barn`, `bern`, and `born` but not `burn`.

The square bracket syntax generates different results on ASCII and EBCDIC machines because the characters between any two are dependent on the sorting sequence of the machine. In ASCII, digits (0-9) are sorted first, then the uppercase alphabet (A-Z), followed by the lowercase letters (a-z).

The UNIX wild card rules represent a formal language, called *regular expressions*, that is used throughout UNIX to define and filter the content of strings. It is almost impossible to use the multitude of UNIX commands without resorting to regular expressions.

 The definitive explanation of regular expressions can be found in Chapter 1 of the UNIX reference manual.

Flags

In the UNIX toolkit, most commands have multiple but related uses. These uses are controlled by flags. Simple *flags* are represented by a dash, followed by one or more characters (`-abc`). A flag signals a UNIX command that an optional letter follows. MS-DOS also uses flags; however, the symbol is a slash, as in `DIR /P /E`.

 UNIX commands are not always consistent in the way that they use flags. Some commands require a flag for each parameter, as in `mv -f -i`; other commands enable you to concatenate flags together, as in `ps -aux`. Still other commands take the first parameter as a collection of flags and do not require the flag symbol itself (for example, `tar xvfb`).

The dash also has other uses and meanings that depend on the particular UNIX command. Experience with the UNIX operating system and a good reference manual help you to understand which flags are appropriate for which commands.

Some commands require a file name, and they generate an error if no file name is present. You can usually direct these programs to receive input from the standard input (your terminal) if the file name is replaced with a dash. Most commands, however, default to the standard input if a file-name parameter is missing.

Remember, the shell does not do anything special with flags. The flags are passed to the program as a command-line parameter. The program—rather, the programmer—must handle any flags that are passed. This fact might be why the conventions regarding flags are so loose.

Shell Escapes

Occasionally, a UNIX program provides an undocumented "door" or *shell escape* that enables the user to directly access the operating system command line. A shell escape is typically invoked through some unusual keystroke combination.

 Shell escapes can present a breach of security. Both the user and the system administrator should be aware that commands and application programs that contain hidden shell escapes enable the user to escape from the application and enter a subshell. These escapes can represent a serious security risk.

The most common escape enables the user to simply type an exclamation mark (!) to escape to a shell. The vi editor, for instance, provides this type of shell escape. For certain applications, you might find it useful to include a shell escape that enables the user to temporarily hop out to the operating system to perform an operation that is best performed at the command line (for instance, copying a file). Shell escapes are fine as long as the system administrator is aware of their presence and they do not pose a security risk.

Using Multitasking

While many operating systems are capable of *multitasking* (executing more than one task simultaneously), few use multitasking as a primary tool in programming. The IBM mainframe, for example, is capable of multitasking, but not many programming tools take advantage of it. For the most part, programming on a mainframe consists of multiple queues of batch processes; each process consists of a single task. For example, a classic mainframe batch job includes multiple job steps that are executed one step at a time as a single task, with intermediate results stored in temporary files.

The same job in UNIX runs quite differently. In UNIX, you can make a job behave like a mainframe batch job, processing one step at a time. Using a pipeline, however, is far more efficient. With UNIX, *pipeline processing* enables all the steps of a job to run concurrently.

The intermediate output of pipelined processes is passed directly from the output of one task into the input of the next. Instead of using temporary files to store the intermediate results, data passed from one task to another is stored in memory buffers. Thus, little extra I/O overhead is encountered. Data can come out of the end of the pipe before the first task has finished processing.

 Some tasks, like `sort`, require that all the data be processed before it can release any data to the next step in the pipeline.

The syntax of the UNIX pipeline was adopted by MS-DOS; however, because MS-DOS is a single-tasking operating system, no advantage is gained by using pipes. MS-DOS stores transient data in a temporary file at each stage of the pipe.

UNIX, on the other hand, automatically assigns each program a standard input, a standard output, and a standard error output.

Normally, the shell assigns the standard input to the keyboard of the terminal running a program and the standard output and error to the screen of the same terminal.

In a pipeline, only the standard input of the first task is automatically assigned to the terminal, while only the output of the last task appears on the screen. You can redirect input or output to a file, but the shell automatically redirects the standard output of one task into the standard input of the next.

The vertical bar (|) signals the shell that a command is a pipe.

If the vertical bar is unavailable on your keyboard, you can use circumflex (^) symbol.

The syntax for a pipeline, therefore, is stated as follows:

```
command|command|command|....
```

For example:

```
cat file1 | grep glines | wc -l
```

This example sends the contents of *file1* to the grep command, which then searches for occurances of the word glines. The search results are then sent to the word count (wc) command, where the number of lines are counted.

The equivalent command using the circumflex symbol follows:

```
cat file1^grep glines^wc -l
```

A pipeline in an MIS-oriented program might resemble the following:

```
data-entry|inventory|shipping|accounts-receivable
```

At each stage, data is extracted, modified and passed up to the next abstraction level in the MIS system.

The availability of pipeline processing has lead to more efficient programming. On systems that are essentially single-tasking, programs tend to grow and perform as many tasks as physical memory and programmer competence allows. The system overhead inherent in adding job steps, along with the required temporary storage, encourage a minimal number of steps in a job. Thus, the number of individual steps in a job grow. In an effort to minimize running time, programs grow until the overhead associated with debugging and maintaining the code puts a natural limit on their size and complexity.

True pipeline processing, as found in UNIX, encourages the opposite. Because very little penalty incurs for adding job steps in UNIX, the impulse is to create many minimal *filters* that accomplish just one part of the job. With luck and good design, you can reuse these filter programs in other pipeline programs, just as you can use a well-designed subroutine in an integrated COBOL program found on a mainframe. In fact, this impulse to create many small filters has given rise to the multitude of UNIX utilities in the programmer's toolkit.

The advantage to this approach is that, because each filter program is small, the individual programs are more easily maintained and debugged. If you change them, you do not have to exert a massive effort to recompile and relink the programs. This advantage is why so much effort has been made with each new release of the UNIX operating system to remain compatible with previous releases and why you are strongly encouraged to observe the UNIX conventions within your own applications.

It is also useful to note that, because of pipelined processing and the impulse to use small software tools instead of large programs, the importance of shell scripts as a primary programming language has grown immensely. The shell script that ties all the small tasks together is what blends a UNIX program into a coherent whole and enables the programmer to make full use of the tools in the UNIX toolkit.

Examining Program Tools

The scope of this book cannot cover all the software tools that are available in UNIX. Instead, a few of the major tools are discussed—enough for you to get a feel for the depth and breadth of the UNIX toolkit.

The system utilities that come with UNIX vary in their significance to the UNIX developer. Each tool's level of importance is measured by how well it accomplishes a particular job within a particular program. Of course, there are utilities that are used more often, but their signifcance diminishes if a more appropriate tool for a task is available.

In general, the most commonly used UNIX utilities include the following three programs: `grep`, `sed`, and `awk` (or `nawk`).

awk **or** nawk

There are two versions of this "mini-language" that are available on all UNIX System V releases, and one version that is available on all prior releases of UNIX. The `awk` programs are extremely fast interpreted languages and resemble, in syntax, a cross between BASIC and C. As with many commands in UNIX, the primary purpose of `awk` is to scan data in a pipe or from a file for text patterns. If the pattern is found, `awk` does something with the data. New *awk,* or `nawk`, is generally backward-compatible with `awk`, but has many new features. For example, the programmer can define new functions for `nawk`, and `nawk` can read command-line parameters.

The primary syntax for an `awk` program is as follows:

```
pattern { action }
```

The pattern portion of an `awk` instruction takes several forms. To execute commands before any data is received, `awk` recognizes the pattern `BEGIN`; `END` executes commands after the last record of data has been processed. In `awk`, a *record* is any variable-length ASCII line of text terminated with a new line character.

Between `BEGIN` and `END`, `awk` processes records based on a specific pattern. These patterns take three forms. The first pattern is as follows:

```
/regular-expression/ {action}
```

In this first case, if any portion of the record matches the regular expression, UNIX executes the actions delineated by the braces.

The following syntax shows a second form of the `awk` pattern syntax:

```
$1 ~ /regular-expression/ {action}
```

In `awk`, a record is separated into fields. These fields are determined, as in a shell, by using field separators. The default field separator is the contents of the IFS variable in the environment, but it can be changed by defining the FS variable inside the `awk` program. Fields are designated `$1`, `$2`, and so on, just as in shell scripts. In the pattern portion of an `awk` instruction, any of the standard logical relation operators (as used in C) may be used to test fields.

In the example above, the *matches* operator (~) was used. In this case, you are testing for a match between a field and a regular expression. Note the difference between the matches *operator* and the *test for equality operator* (==).

If you want to test for an exact match, you can be very explicit in the regular expression, or you can test for equality with the following pattern:

```
$1 == "string" {action}
```

Using the == operator implies that awk searches for an exact match to *string*, rather than matching a regular expression.

You also may concatenate patterns with the *logical and* or the *logical or* operators, as well as with inequalities. In general, the patterns used are identical to those used in the egrep command.

You can use several built-in functions and variables in a pattern as well. For example, length yields the number of characters in a record. NR, an internal variable, contains the number of records processed to date.

A special case of the search string is shown here:

```
{action}
```

When no pattern is given (a *null* pattern), the commands contained in the *action* portion of an awk instruction operate on all records. In this sense, a null pattern matches all patterns.

The action portion of an awk instruction, as mentioned earlier, resembles a cross between BASIC and C. Unlike C, variables in awk are defined at runtime and their *type* (integer, floating point, or string) is determined by their current usage.

For example, assume that $1 is always an integer and $2 is always a string. You could define x as an integer when you use the command x=$1+1, but x is transformed into a string when you subsequently issue the command x=x" "$2. As long as a string contains only numerals, you may use it as a string in one command and as an integer or floating point number in the next command. The *action* portion of an awk instruction can, in fact, contain many commands delineated by a carriage return or by a semicolon (;), as in C.

The logical control statements in awk more closely resemble some versions of BASIC than C. These statements include if, while, do, and for. Notably missing from awk is the case statement, which is similar to `case` in the Bourne shell or `switch` in C. You also find a host of built-in functions in `awk`. In addition, the `nawk` command enables you to create new functions. After the shell itself, `awk` and `nawk` are perhaps the most powerful and widely used utilities in the UNIX toolkit.

bc **and** dc

The commands `bc` (*binary calulator*) and `dc` (*desk calculator*) are miniature interpreted languages that were designed to create small special-purpose calculators. The syntax of `bc` resembles C; the syntax of `dc` more closely resembles an Assembly language. In fact, `bc` is actually a compiler for `dc`. When you use `bc` inside a shell script, you can easily create many of these calculators. For example, the following calculator prints the volume of a cylinder:

```
echo "Enter diameter\c"
read d
echo "Enter length\c"
read L
bc <<!
p=3.14159
r=$d*.500
r=r^2
p*r*$L
quit
!
```

cal

The `cal` (*cal*endar) command might not be as useful as an MIS-related utility, but it serves to illustrate the numerous small applications that are a standard part of UNIX. The `cal` command generates a calendar for any month or year in history after the year 1 AD. Leap-year rules are also incorporated into the program.

For example, according to the current leap-year rules, every year divisible by four is a leap year unless that year is evenly divisible by 100 or 1000. So, although the year 1900 was not a leap year, the year 2000 will be.

 Leap year rules changed in 1752, when the modern Gregorian calendar was adopted. In that year, 11 days are missing to make up for the incorrectly added leap years. Who in history was born on September 10, 1752? No one. Here is the result of the command `cal 9 1752`:

```
      September 1752
 Su Mo Tu We Th Fr Sa
        1  2 14 15 16
 17 18 19 20 21 22 23
 24 25 26 27 28 29 30
```

csplit

Context-sensitive *split*, `csplit`, is one of those highly selective commands that you might not use for years, then find it suddenly the perfect utility for a particular application. The `csplit` command divides files into components that are based on a series of regular expressions.

For example, if you are writing a program to translate a COBOL program into another programming language, one of the first things you might want to do is to place the four divisions (identification, environment, data, and procedure) of the COBOL program into separate files for independent processing. You could use an awk program, but using `csplit` is much easier.

The syntax for `csplit` is as follows:

```
csplit -flags file RE1 RE2 ...
```

In this case, *RE* stands for a regular expression. To split up a CO-BOL program, the command `csplit` *file* `/^ENVIRONMENT/` `/^DATA DIV/` `/^PROCEDURE` `/` takes the contents of *file* and places everything from the beginning of the file up to, but not including, a line that matches the regular expression `/^ENVIRON-MENT/` in a file named `xx00`. This includes everything in the Identification Division. The Environment Division is placed in a file named `xx01`, the Data Division in `xx02`, and everything else (the Procedure Division) in `xx03`. Other programs can manipulate the individual files (or COBOL divisions).

Later, you can put all four of the files back together in the proper order using the command `cat xx??`. The `cat` (con*cat*enate) command enables you to easily join files together in any order you wish.

 The `csplit` command requires a file on which to operate. If input is taken from the standard input from your keyboard or a pipe, the file name must be replaced with a dash (-).

As mentioned earlier, `csplit` is an obscure command, but, when properly used, it is a very useful one.

cut

The commands `cut`, `paste`, `join`, and `sort` properly belong to a subset of commands that can be called *relational database operators*. As with many UNIX utilities, you can write the cut operation as an `awk` program. Because "cutting" individual fields from a table is one of the most commonly used functions, however, it a separate command. Because `cut` is a *binary* or compiled program, it is faster than an equivalent `awk` program, and it is smaller in memory than `awk` itself.

The syntax for the `cut` command is simple. You can specify character positions to cut from a record or fields to cut. In the case of cutting fields, the default field delimiter is a tab. You can override the tab field delimiter by using the `-d` flag.

The `cut` command assumes that the input files are ASCII files consisting of rows and columns of data. Each row corresponds to a *record*; each column represents *fields* within the record.

For example, to display only the login name (field 1) and the numeric login ID (field 3) from the `/etc/passwd` file, display fields 1 and 3 using the following syntax:

```
cut -d: -f1,3 /etc/passwd
```

In the case of the `passwd` file, the field delimiter is a colon (`:`). The output resembles `name:221`.

egrep, fgrep, **and** grep

The members of the `grep` family are filters that search for occurrences of a regular expression in a file and print the record that matches. The primary differences between members of the `grep` family are as follows:

❖ `egrep` has the most features and enables the widest range of regular expressions, but it employs an algorithm that uses exponentially more memory with the complexity of the search. If you can use a more limited regular expression, use `grep` instead.

❖ On complex searches, `egrep` runs faster but uses more memory, while `grep` takes longer but is more memory-efficient.

❖ If the pattern to match is only a simple string with no ranges (such as `[A-z]`) or wildcards, `fgrep` is the most efficient.

❖ Each member of the grep family could be rewritten in awk or sed; however, if the function desired is a simple text filter, using one of the grep commands is more efficient.

Given the nature of UNIX, using grep as a pipeline filter before passing data on to an awk program is more efficient than simply using awk's pattern-matching capabilities. For example, the following two programs are equivalent:

```
grep '^hello' file|awk '{print}'
awk '/^hello/ {print}' file
```

The pipeline symbol (|) in the first example means to send the results of the grep command (that is, all lines in *file* containing the string "hello") to the awk command for printing. The second example uses awk to find all lines in *file*, then prints them. Although the second example uses only a second UNIX command (awk), the first example runs faster.

join

After two files have been sorted in ascending ASCII order, the sorted fields can be joined with the relational database operator join. The join command assumes that the input files are ASCII tables consisting of rows and columns of data. Each row corresponds to a record, while each column represents fields within the record.

The UNIX join command is useful for combining specific fields from the input tables. The command join -j1 2 -j2 3 *file1 file2* combines *file1* with *file2* with field 2 of *file1* joined with field 3 of *file2*. The output (which is displayed on the screen unless redirected into a file) contains everything in *file1* with all but the joined field of *file2* appended to the end of the matching record from *file1*.

You can cut specific fields from the output using the -o flag, which expects a list of fields in the form `file.field`. For example, -o `1.2 1.3 2.4` yields fields 1 and 3 from *file1* and field 4 from *file2*.

Even in large files, `join` is faster than similar statements in most database managers. The key to its speed is that both files must be already in sorted order in the key fields before `join` goes to work. All database managers expect the data stored in their tables to be in more or less random order. The ordering is imposed on the database tables by indexes. Searching and sorting multiple indexes takes much longer than searching a preordered file the way `join` does.

ksh

The Korn shell (`ksh`) is destined to replace the C shell, `csh`, as the shell of choice for interactive use by programmers, and to replace the Bourne shell, `sh`, as the main shell-scripting language. However, the Korn shell is only an option on some pre-Release 4 systems, and is unavailable or only available in unsupported C source code on other systems. The Korn shell has an advantage over the C shell and the Bourne shell because it embodies the best features of both and adds a few new features of its own.

For the programmer, `ksh` keeps a history of the previously issued commands (up to several hundred) and enables you to easily edit and rerun any command stored in this history file. The Korn shell also provides a more sophisticated job control system than does the C shell. This system enables a programmer full control over *jobs*.

As a shell-scripting language, `ksh` is a superset of the Bourne shell. Almost all Bourne shell scripts can run as Korn shell scripts, but not the other way around. The Korn shell makes an ideal scripting language for programs that execute in the foreground. Unfortunately, the standard Bourne shell, `sh`, is still the system default for many background tasks. For example, any program run in the background by `cron`, `at`, or `batch`, or from the `/etc/inittab` table, must be Bourne shell scripts. This step is only a minor impediment if the programmer remembers to add the following line of code at the head of any job destined to be run by `cron`, `at`, `batch` or from the `inittab` table:

```
exec ksh <<!
ksh text
```

The `exec` command "transforms" the Bourne shell into a Korn shell. The input redirection symbol (`<<!`) tells the resulting shell to read all text that follows into the standard input until it reaches the end of the file or encounters an `!`.

NOTE You can find details of the structure and control functions of the Korn and Bourne shells under `sh`.

paste

Any system that has a `cut` command must have a `paste` command. The `paste` command creates output like `join`, but does not syntactically pair fields. Instead, `paste` matches one record in one file with its ordinal match in another.

The output record of the `paste` command consists of the first record of one file pasted to the end of the first record of another file, and the second record of one file to the second record of another, and so on. You also can instruct `paste` to merge subsequent lines in a file and produce multicolumn output from a single stream of data. For example, the command `ls|paste - - - -` transforms the simple output of `ls` into four-column output, similar to the results of the `ls -c` command.

Together, `cut` and `paste` provide the UNIX developer with powerful table-manipulation capabilities.

pr

There are several text formatters in the UNIX toolkit. The fmt (*format*) command is a very primitive and basic text formatter. A more powerful formatter, which is ideal for most types of documentation, is pr.

Using pr, a user can specify the number of columns, double or single spaces between lines, tab positions, column width, white space between columns, page length, space between columns, and so on.

The default print format prints 66 lines-per-page with a five-line header and five-line trailer on each page. The default header consists of the file name, the current date and the page number. An optional pause stops output at the end of a page and waits for a carriage return. This feature is ideal for displaying formatted data on a screen and negates the need to pipe the output of pr through more or pg.

rsh

With the advent of Release 4 and its assumption of a networking environment, the art of shell scripting is raised to a new height. Using rsh (*remote shell*), scripts are no longer restricted to running on a single system. The rsh command enables you to run a command or program from another machine on your network.

You could run a program remotely using the older uux (*UNIX-to-UNIX*) command; however, such a remotely running program is queued for transmission to the remote system by uucp, (*UNIX-to-UNIX copy*), then executed.

The reply is queued for transmission back to the local user. This cycle can take seconds, minutes, or days to complete; therefore, you cannot use uux and its reply in a pipeline or for other time-critical uses.

Using `rsh`, however, you can run a program on a remote system in *real time*, that is, as though it were in a shell on the local system. Thus, you can imbed tasks run by `rsh` within a local pipe with any portion of the pipe running anywhere on the Internet.

Suppose, for example, a widely dispersed network of UNIX systems is connected by a TCP/IP network. Orders taken in Boston must be relayed to a distribution point in Omaha, then forwarded to the home office in New York City. The syntax is `rsh` *hostname command*. A single pipeline process might look something like this:

```
order_entry|rsh omaha ship|rsh nyc accnts_receiv
```

 Using `rsh` on a widely dispersed and interconnected network can pose security nightmares for a system administrator. Malicious users can trigger disasterous events (such as file or directory deletion) on remote workstations if they are not restricted by permissions, login passwords, and other security measures.

Also note that `rsh` does not work as advertised on early versions of UNIX. In these earlier versions (except Berkeley), `rsh` stood for a restricted Bourne shell, which prohibited a user from changing directories.

sed

Every user and programmer is familiar with the use of *text editors*. UNIX provides two editors for general text editing tasks: `ed` (*editor*) and `vi` (*visual editor*). These editors are commonly used for writing shell scripts, changing start-up files, and other text-editing tasks.

Many users are familiar with word processors, which are really editors "tuned" for use with text instead of programs. UNIX provides an editor tuned to work in a pipeline: sed (stream *edi*tor). The syntax of sed is very similar to that of ed, but with branching and limited testing capabilities.

You can insert sed in a pipelined command line to extract or change textual data as it flows from command to command, making it one of the most powerful of the UNIX utilities. By all measures, the sed syntax is perhaps one of the hardest to master in UNIX. It combines the power of full regular expressions with an arcane but powerful editing construct.

Although you can duplicate almost all the utility of sed in awk, it requires many more lines of code to accomplish. Sometimes, it is simply easier to code in either awk or sed, but the penalty for using awk over sed is clear: on an Intel-based system, sed requires about 26K bytes of disk storage; nawk needs over 100K. The sed command is simply smaller and faster. When working on large files, it is worth the trouble.

For instance, take the trivial example of printing the login name and the numeric login ID from the /etc/passwd file. In sed, the code to perform this feat is:

```
echo "ex:PewoqhxthOYRg:255:1::/usr/exx:/bin/sh"|
sed 's/:[:,A-z,\/]*:/:/g
s/:[A-z,\/]*$/:/
s/:[0-9]*:$//
s/:/ /'
```

Identical results are printed with the following awk command. Again, echo is used to print a passwd entry into a pipe, which is read by nawk:

```
echo "ex:PewoqhxthOYRg:255:1::/usr/exx:/bin/sh"|
nawk 'BEGIN{FS=":"}
{print $1,$3}'
```

Although the `sed` script is somewhat longer than the equivalent `awk` script, it executes faster and requires less memory and disk space to operate.

If you are familiar with the MS-DOS EDLIN editor or others like it, you probably recognize the `sed` syntax. The major difference is in that `sed` uses the full set of regular expressions to match fields.

Selecting a Shell

One of the underlying principles governing the UNIX system is that there are several *shells* (also referred to as *command-line processors*) that you can install and use on any UNIX system. Many vendors supply more than one command-line shell with the particular version of UNIX they sell. The system administrator must decide which shell to use.

Although very similar in most ways, the scripting language and many commands vary somewhat between shells. These differences can become quite important when considering which shell to use.

Although the Korn shell is likely to eventually overtake the Bourne shell in popularity, at the moment the Bourne shell is the default shell for UNIX. Because the Bourne shell is loaded by UNIX at startup, any shell script run from the `/etc/inittab` table must be a Bourne shell script. The shell scripts run from any of the `/etc/rc` programs also must be written in the Bourne shell. This fact is true of any scripts or commands run by `cron`, `at`, or `batch` as well.

Users of the Korn shell should be aware that not all Bourne shell scripts work in `ksh`, which has no built-in mechanism for detecting which kind of shell script is running. The same is true for `sh` (the Bourne shell). However, advocates of the C shell (`csh`) are quick to point out that `csh` first attempts to run a file containing text as a `csh` script, then executes as a simple interpreter the first line of text in the form: #! *command*. Failing that, the C shell attempts to run the ordinary Bourne shell. In this respect, the C shell is the "smartest" of the three commonly available shells and generally remains the shell of choice for programmers.

Exploring the Bourne Shell as a Programming Language

The Bourne shell is not a programming language in the same sense as COBOL, Fortran, BASIC, C, or even awk. Instead, this shell's main function is to manipulate variables in the environment, to manipulate files and directories in the file system, to parse command strings, and to run commands. In this regard, the Bourne shell is very similar to the DOS command-line interpreter. A UNIX shell script is analogous to a DOS batch file, although a UNIX shell script is normally much more complex than the typical DOS batch file.

If you think of a programming language as primarily a manipulator of numbers, the Bourne shell is not a language. It can do simple arithmetic, but only by resorting to the binary program expr (*expr*ession evaluator), which performs the arithmetic and returns a value on the standard output. To perform simple arithmetic, sh must use command substitution.

The sh syntax for such manipulation resembles the following:

```
x=`expr $a + 2`.
```

This simple command line assigns the value of the expression $a + 2 to the variable x (remember that the accent grave [`] is a signal to UNIX to return the result of the command contained within the grave symbols). The variable x and its value are then maintained as part of the shell environment.

With the introduction of the `let` command, stolen from BASIC, the Korn shell is more of a true language. Using `ksh`, the same arithmetic problem is resolved within the shell, rather than by using command substitution.

The Korn shell syntax looks like this:

```
let x = $a + 2
```

In both cases, the results are placed in variables maintained by UNIX in the shell environment. Because no shell really has internal variables in the sense of a compiled program, the environment represents the entire data space of a shell.

Understanding Shell Variables

Now that you know what the shell is not—it is not a good vehicle for crunching numbers—you might well ask what it is good for. You can get a glimpse of its use from the following fragment:

```
FILE="/usr/lbin/progx"
if [ -x $FILE && ! -d $FILE ]
then
$FILE
else
echo "File not found:"$FILE
fi
```

When you assign the name of a prospective command to the shell variable `FILE`, UNIX tests to determine if the file exists and is executable (`-x $FILE`), and checks to see that it is not a directory (`! -d $FILE`). If the test is passed, the command executes; if the test fails, a warning is displayed.

In `sh`, the test is made with an external program named `test`, which is linked to a program named `[`. In `ksh`, however, the test is an internal function signaled by `[[` and terminated with `]]`. The previous example works in `ksh`, but uses the command `test` rather than the internal function. This syntax change also applies to the `while` and `until` statements.

Controlling Processes with Shell Scripts

The shell's purpose is to manipulate files and run programs. Consider the situation in which only a single copy of a particular UNIX command can run at any one time (remember, in a multitasking environment like UNIX, there is normally no prohibition on starting the same command or program multiple times). Other users might try to run the same command at unpredictable times. Assume that the command always runs in the background and that no user intervention is necessary. You also want the command to abort if it finds another instance of the command already running. This is the situation managed by the UNIX print spooler `lpr`. After you start it, there is no need to start another instance of the print spooler—the print spooler currently running in the background is sufficient to manage all printing jobs.

In order to prevent multiple instances of `lpr` from starting, an environment variable named `LOCKFILE` is set to the path of a file that is located somewhere in the file system. The shell script preventing multiple `lpr` instances resembles the following fragment:

```
if [ -s "$LOCKFILE" ]; then exit;
else
echo $$ > $LOCKFILE
lpr
rm $LOCKFILE
fi
```

In this example, a test determines if $LOCKFILE exists and if its size is greater than zero (-s "$LOCKFILE"). If the result is true, the program simply exits because the lpr is already running. If the result is false (that is, LOCKFILE does not exist), the shell script creates the file named LOCKFILE and places the process ID ($$) of the current process in it (echo $$ > $LOCKFILE), then runs the desired command. After the command runs, the program removes the $LOCKFILE so that the next invocation of the program can run.

The following shell script represents a perfectly usable version of the lpd (*line printer daemon*) print spool daemon:

```
# A simple print spooler
# S. Glines - 1992
set `ls`
while true
do
for i
do
cat i >/dev/lpr
echo $FORM_FEED>/dev/lpr
rm $i
done
x="`ls`"
if [ -z "$x" ]
then
set $x
else
exit
fi
done
```

In this example, the set `ls` command places the results of ls, through command substitution, into the parameter variables *$1*, *$2*, *$3*, and so on. The while loop executes continuously unless interrupted by the exit command. The for loop places successive elements of the parameters into the environment variable `i` until the list is exhausted. In other words, the first loop places *$1* into `i`, the second loop places *$2* into `i`, and so on, until all positional parameters have been processed.

When that step is complete, the environment variable *x* receives a new list of files in the current directory (`x="`ls`"`) and a test is made to see if `$x` is a string longer than zero bytes (`-z  "$x"`). If it is longer than zero bytes, there are more files to process and their names are placed in `$1`, `$2`, and so on using the `set` command, and the loop continues. If the directory is empty, `$x` is zero length and the script ends. The entire command is terminated with the `exit` command. While the loop runs, each file in the directory is concatenated to the printer device by using the `cat` command. A form feed echoes after each print job, and the file is deleted after printing.

This print spooler shell script is primitive by the standards of the `lpd` print spooler system, but it illustrates how a simple a print spooler can be written in Bourne shell script. It also illustrates the utility of shell scripting in general.

sleep

One of the simplest and most useful commands in the UNIX toolkit is the `sleep` command. This command puts the shell "to sleep" for a predetermined time. During the sleep period, virtually no system overhead is required. The `sleep` command is often employed when a shell script needs to wait until some task is completed or to pause a while before starting another session of some task (like printing).

The following example illustrates one use of `sleep`, as well as another feature of the Bourne shell. Bourne shell scripts can "trap" some interrupt signals, then execute a program when the signal is received. If a task needs to wait for a signal, it must continue running:

```
trap "command" 15
while true
do
sleep 60
done
```

This script loops forever, waiting to receive signal 15. When it does, it executes *command*, then continues to loop as long as it does not encounter an exit. Without the sleep command inserted in the loop, considerable overhead would be generated by the do-while loop. If you use the sleep command, almost no overhead is required because the loop is completed only once per minute.

Other Tools in the Toolkit

Several hundred commands and utility programs are available in the UNIX toolkit—this chapter touches on only a few. Most of the remaining tools, like csplit or sleep, have specific functions. Other tools are designed to perform specific tasks, like maintaining compiled programs (make, for example), but can be used as a more general-purpose dependency checker and program sequencer.

Beyond the specific commands in the UNIX toolkit and perhaps of greater importance are the collection of concepts—some new, some time-honored—that are embodied in UNIX. These concepts are part and parcel of the UNIX philosophy and, in themselves, constitute part of the UNIX toolkit.

Examining Conceptual Tools

Individual programs are no better than the support they receive from the operating system in which they run. For example, the `grep` program would be of little consequence if UNIX did not support pipes and redirection (redirection is discussed later in this chapter). On a mainframe, the function of `grep` would be buried in a library of string-handling subroutines and would never emerge as a major stand-alone component of the operating system itself. In other words, the design of the operating system determines the way programs are written and used.

The design of the UNIX operating system supports small, special-purpose utility programs and encourages programmers to create new programs in a style that allows them to become part of the next generation of UNIX. UNIX is extendible only if new programs conform to the conventions of the old ones.

In this section, you explore many of the conceptual tools available in the UNIX toolkit. *Conceptual tools* are not UNIX commands or programs; instead, they are part of the UNIX architecture that enhances UNIX as a general-purpose operating system that you can apply to such diverse environments as science and engineering and to the transaction-processing world of most MIS shops.

Each UNIX concept stands on its own, but contributes to the generality of the UNIX system as a whole. Some of the concepts are based on the way the UNIX shells work, some are extensions of services already discussed, and some are services only available to the C programmer.

Examining I/O Pipelining and Redirection

Much has been stated already about the concept of pipes and the contribution they have made to the UNIX programming style. If utility programs such as `grep` are reusable because of pipeline processing, much more must be said about the generalization of pipes—especially the redirection of inputs and outputs.

The concept of pipes exist because every UNIX program can automatically assign a standard input, a standard output and a standard error output. In a shell script, these *I/O definitions* are assumed. In a C program, they are assumed when the `stdio.h` header is added to `/usr/include`, which is generally included as a matter of course by most C programmers.

When a shell runs a program, the three standard I/O *ports* are attached by default to the terminal from which the program was run. The *standard input* is the keyboard on the terminal. *Standard output* and *standard error* are the computer screen. Unless otherwise instructed, the program accepts input from the keyboard and displays results and error messages on the computer screen.

When the shell encounters the pipe symbol (|), however, the standard output is assigned not to the terminal, but to the standard input of the next command in the pipeline. For instance, the command line `grep glines /etc/passwd | wc -l` takes the output of the `grep` command and pipes it into the input of the `wc` (word count) command. This process takes place automatically and seamlessly without creating temporary intermediate files. The result of this sample command line is the number of lines in the `/etc/passwd file` that contain the string `glines`, which is displayed on the computer screen.

The pipelining process continues until the shell encounters the end of the pipe. To the user, a pipeline appears as a single process, with the front end taking input from the terminal and the back end returning data to the terminal. Generic I/O redirection using pipes enables the user or programmer to reassign the standard inputs and outputs of a pipeline anywhere.

You also can *redirect* the output of a command into a file rather than being displayed on the screen. This feature is useful if you want to preserve the intermediate result of some series of commands.

For instance, the command line `grep glines /etc/passwd >` `myfile` takes all of the lines appearing in `/etc/passwd` that contain the string `glines` and puts them into a newly-created file named `myfile`.

The syntax of the shell requires that the command or pipeline be listed first, followed by any I/O redirection instructions. The following illustrates the structure of redirection:

```
pipeline < input > output
```

In this case, you can use `pipeline` as a single command or a stream of commands. When I/O is redirected, it is assumed that the object of that redirection is a file or device somewhere in the file system. Put another way, processes only exist within a pipeline, while files exist outside the pipe and are the object of redirection. Directing the output of one program to another creates a pipe (*command | command*); directing output from a command to a file uses standard redirection (`command>file`).

Simple redirection can have three minor variations. Output can be appended to the end of an existing file by using `>>` rather than `>`. The single right pointing arrow (`>`) creates a new file, overwriting any existing file with the same name. Using the previous example, `grep glines /etc/passwd > myfile` creates a new file named `myfile` (destroying any existing file of the same name); `grep glines /etc/passwd >> myfile` appends the results of the `grep` command to the file named `myfile` (a new file named `myfile` is created if none exists).

A second variation of redirection enables input in shell scripts to be taken from the end of the script rather than from a file or the user's keyboard. To use this variation, include the `<<` operator in the sytax:

```
echo <<!
Hello,
brave
new
world
!
```

In this example, the exclamation mark (`!`) in the first line signals the shell to continue taking input from the script itself (`Hello`, `brave`, `new`, and `world`) until the exclamation mark at the end of the script is encountered.

The final variation on redirection enables you to reassign any of the standard ports in a program. Normally, when a program opens, UNIX assigns each port a numeric *file ID*. In the case of the standard I/O ports, 0 is the standard input (normally, the keyboard), 1 is the standard output (the computer screen), and 2 is the standard error (also the computer screen). The standard redirection symbols assume the standard input for `<` and the standard output for `>`. Redirecting the standard error, however, requires the syntax `2>`.

 Remember that the standard error is automatically assigned the file ID `2`.

You can clone file IDs using the syntax `2>&1`, which assigns the standard error (`2`) to wherever the standard output (`1`) is assigned.

This example illustrates that, in UNIX, the assignment of input and output is "bound" at the time of execution. Most operating systems support this in one form or another, but only with UNIX's introduction of pipes has this concept been generalized.

Understanding Daemons

The concept of the UNIX *daemon* (pronounced like "demon") was introduced in Chapter 2. It is difficult to talk about UNIX without referring to one or more of the standard daemons. Print requests are serviced by the daemon of the LP system (`lpd`, the *l*ine *p*rinter *d*aemon). Communications requests are serviced by one or more daemons; system maintenance is routinely accomplished by the services of yet another daemon.

As you recall, a UNIX daemon is any program that runs continuously in the background or as a result of a command issued in the foreground. Daemons can also be started as part of the boot procedure. A daemon normally operates without benefit of user intervention. The user (or system administrator) can control the daemon, but the daemon automatically performs its function deep in the background.

The relevance of the daemon concept in the MIS world should not be overlooked. Daemons can perform many useful services, and there is little magic in their design or creation.

 Many DBMSs, like Oracle, use a daemon to manage the database files and reserve the foreground for data entry and reporting programs.

The *foreground/background* approach represents a compromise between the virtually monolithic method of a transaction processing monitor, such as CICS, and the approach of PC-oriented languages such as dBase.

In traditional PC-based languages, the data entry and file management portions of an application are integrated as a single task. Each user must run a copy of the task. UNIX daemons, like pipes, offers a way to cleanly separate functions into discrete programs.

There are many tasks best left to daemons. Examples range from the management of Automatic Teller Machines (ATMs) to the automatic manipulation of data received over the Internet from widely dispersed remote systems. In the latter case, a daemon runs continuously, looking for files received by uucp or some other mechanism. When a file is received (when its presence is detected), the daemon runs a program to handle the data.

Another example of a useful daemon is a nightly inventory monitor that receives data from widely dispersed sites and automatically triggers restocking reports to be printed in the morning. No human intervention is required to determine whether stocking orders were received or to print the reports.

As with many other UNIX tools, there are several types of daemons, and several ways to launch them. Although there are no specific conventions regarding the use of daemons in UNIX, chaos would result if there were no guidelines. Daemons are characterized by how deeply they run in the background, their running time, duration, and frequency. The following sections begin with the shortest and shallowest-running daemons and progress from there.

On-Demand Daemons

The purpose of an *on-demand daemon* is to complete a long-running task in the background that began in the foreground. One of the best examples of this type of daemon is the uucp daemon uucico (*UNIX-to-UNIX copy in, copy out*) which starts when you run uucp, uux (*UNIX-to-UNIX exchange*), uuto (*UNIX-to-UNIX-to-user*), or mail if the recipient is on a distant system accessible only by uucp. The pre-System V print spooler also employed this kind of daemon.

On-demand daemons are also excellent for post-processing data, such as printing job orders after data entry. For instance, if a user is expected to run a task only intermittently, and normal post-processing would delay the user, an on-demand daemon provides an ideal solution. The user can launch the on-demand daemon when he exits the task to finish the job in the background. You can launch an on-demand daemon using a script that resembles the following:

```
foreground-task
nohup background-task &
```

The nohup (*no h*ang *up*) command disconnects the task from the user's terminal, while the & places the task in the background. This permits the daemon to continue running in the background even if the user logs off the system. The standard output from any commands run with nohup is appended to a file named nohup.out in the user's current directory if no I/O redirection exists. When the user logs back onto the system, the nohup.out file is available as an audit of the process.

Login Daemons

A *login daemon* runs only when the user is logged in, and is *killed* when the user logs out. You can use login daemons for the same purposes as on-demand daemons; however, login daemons have additional advantages. For example, if your terminal can display a status line, you can use a login daemon to announce the arrival of incoming mail, even if you are in an application that does not allow interaction with the shell.

One way to launch a login daemon is to place the command *background-task*& (for instance, mail&) in the user's .profile file (if the default shell is the Bourne or Korn shell) or in the .login file (if in the C shell). The .profile and .login files are normally found in the user's home directory.

Notice that the `nohup` command was not used this time. The login daemon must remain attached to the terminal so that, as a child process, it automatically ends when the user logs out. In this case, the standard I/O must be redirected because a daemon of this sort remains connections to the terminal—unless, of course, it is your intent to allow the daemon to continue running after the user logs out.

Background Processes as Daemons

Little distinction exists between running a task in the background and running a daemon in the background. Background and foreground processes are managed by UNIX in equivalent manners.

In fact, the distinction between foreground and background processes exists only in the definition of a daemon. If the task performs some service to a user, such as looking for events to occur and processing them, then the task is a daemon. If, on the other hand, the background task merely performs some function unrelated to servicing a user, it is not a daemon. The distinction is a fine one and of little real consequence.

There are four ways to run background tasks, whether they are daemons or not. The most shallow of background tasks is initiated simply by placing an ampersand after a command (*command &*) and is subject to termination when the user logs off. To place a task further in the background, use the `nohup` command to detach the task from your terminal and use the ampersand to place it in the background, as in `nohup` *command* `&`.

The final two methods, `batch` and `at`, are virtually identical, except that one runs the task almost immediately, the other at some predetermined time and date in the future. Both commands have a unique place in the library of UNIX commands because they require UNIX to read the program to be run from the standard input, not from the command line.

For example, if you want `batch` to run a shell script file named `program`, you can use any of the three following syntax lines:

```
cat program|batch
batch<<!
program
!
echo "program"|batch
```

The last two examples assume that `program` is in the search path as defined by the `PATH` variable; the first example assumes that `program` is a Bourne shell script located in the current directory. In the case of `at` and `batch`, the program to be run must be a shell script written in the Bourne shell.

The `at` command syntax is identical to that of `batch`, except that a time and date must be specified on the command line to indicate the time you want the command to run. Because `at` (as well as `batch`) is actually controlled by the `cron` daemon (which is discussed later in this chapter), the *granularity* of `at` is one minute. In other words, you can specify the time a command must be run down to the minute, but no finer.

The date format accepted by the `at` command is very flexible. For example, UNIX understands the command `at today + 1 week`. The `batch` command is the logical equivalent of `at now`, except that, in the logic of the `at` command, `now` has always past.

System Daemons

The bulk of the background services provided by UNIX, from printing to managing the network, are provided by *system daemons*. System V Release 4 includes four main daemons: `cron`, which provides time-dependent task processing; `lpsched` (*line printer scheduler*), which is the daemon for the LP print spooler system; `ttymon`, (*teletype monitor*) which replaced a multitude of `getty` (*get teletype*) tasks in Release 4; and `listen`, which is the network-servicing daemon.

 Early versions of UNIX ran mostly on teletype hard-copy terminals. Throughout discussions of UNIX, you encounter references to tty. Almost without exception, *tty* refers to the user's terminal.

Of these four system daemons, `cron` is the oldest. In fact, `cron` was the only system daemon used in XENIX, an early version of UNIX. Release 3 introduced `lpsched`; `listen` is part of the UNIX Networking System.

These four daemons are required to provide the minimum standard UNIX services. You can create other daemons, and, in the case of many DBMSs, some are part of standard application packages.

A *system daemon* is an executable binary program or a shell script. You can launch a system daemon at system startup in one of two ways: from the `/etc/inittab` table (directly by `init`) or from the appropriate `/etc/rc` file or directory. Convention suggests that only the higher-level system daemons be run from `inittab`, but, in truth, the function of launching system daemons is evenly split between `inittab` and `/etc/rc` files.

 The `inittab` and `/etc/rc` scripts are run by UNIX as the system boots.

In practice, daemons that are well-behaved binary programs, such as `listen` and `ttymon`, are run from `inittab`. Other daemons have potential side effects, such as removing lock files or clearing FIFO buffers. Those daemons that must be shut down gracefully are run by `/etc/rc` files. In the latter category are `cron` and `lpsched`, which are driven by FIFO special files.

NOTE FIFO buffers are discussed later in the chapter.

If the system crashes, you must remove these special files and clean up the file-system environment (for instance, by removing lock files) before these daemons can operate again. This is more easily accomplished in a shell script than embedded in a binary program. Therefore, they are usually run from the appropriate / etc/rc script. These same considerations should be applied to user-created daemons.

TIP If you cannot determine why a daemon fails to restart, you might have to manually search for a lock file left behind by the daemon when it failed. Well-behaved UNIX daemons remove lock files before they exit. However, in the event of an unscheduled system crash, lock files might have been left behind, preventing the daemon from restarting.

Periodic Daemons

Periodic daemons can be private or system-wide. These daemons are regulated by the cron daemon. Chapter 2 discussed the workings of the cron daemon and the way jobs are controlled and run. This section examines situations in which the use of cron is preferable over other forms of daemons.

By nature, every job takes its toll on the system. Each job requires some system resources, and, more importantly, every running job gets its turn in the run queue. Even if a job is sleeping, when its turn to run comes up, the currently running job is paged out of active memory and the next job is paged into the system's environment. At the very least, all the processors' registers are written to memory. The registers of the new task are read in, and any memory references are checked in the system's memory.

If the memory addresses of the current and next instructions are not in cache memory, they are fetched from regular memory. If they are not in regular memory, a *page fault* occurs. UNIX then swaps the least-used page of memory with the required memory page from the "swap space" on a disk and reads it into cache. Only then is the processor ready to determine if the task actually can run. In the case of a long-dormant task, like one that is currently sleeping, this system overhead, called a *context switch*, can be a waste of time and memory.

The `cron` daemon, which runs as a permanent fixture of UNIX, already requires a certain amount of overhead. Because it can control a virtually unlimited number of scheduled tasks, there is little point in running an independent daemon if that daemon is expected to sleep for more than 60 seconds at a time. Instead, you can put the daemon's task into the `crontab` file and periodically execute it by using `cron`.

Put another way, if a daemon can expect to operate only once every minute or so, run it as a `cron` task to create less system overhead than running it as an independent daemon.

Understanding the UNIX Binary Resources

Not every programming task in UNIX is accomplished with shell scripts and `awk` programs. Eventually someone has to write "real" code. Although everything you can accomplish in shell scripts you also can do in C (never with the same brevity, however), some things can only be accomplished by using C.

You do not need to learn C to create a well-tuned MIS, however. On the contrary, you can use many excellent DBMSs and high-level languages instead. If you are building a system from scratch or creating your own MIS environment, you should be aware of the resources in the UNIX binary toolkit.

There are hundreds of functions in the standard UNIX C libraries. Most are duplicated in any ANSI-C compiler on most operating systems, and are very well documented elsewhere. There are, however, several functions (in the broader sense) that, while occasionally duplicated in other environments, are transportable only among UNIX systems. Broadly speaking, these functions fall into two categories: I/O to terminals and interprocess (or internetwork) communications.

curses

The `curses` library contains device-independent functions that control or "paint" an ordinary character-based terminal. Because UNIX must be able to control the literally hundreds of different *dumb terminals* on the market, a generic screen-handling system is essential.

In pre-System V versions of UNIX, terminals were defined in an ASCII database named `/etc/termcap` (*termcap* is an abbreviation of *term*inal *cap*abilities). In all releases since then, terminal definitions are kept in a compressed form in the `/usr/lib/terminfo` directory. (*terminfo* is a contraction of *term*inal *info*rmation.) In fact, most System V versions of UNIX maintain both databases.

A conversion program called `captoinfo` converts `termcap` definitions to `terminfo` definitions. The `curses` library can read definitions from either database for backward compatibility with C programs written for XENIX and BSD.

Virtually every database and screen-design package available on UNIX, as well as standard UNIX programs like `vi`, use the `curses` library. The driving force behind proper screen operation is the definition of the environment variable TERM. The TERM environment variable is normally set as the user logs into the system. Erratic terminal behavior usually result from the misassignment of the TERM variable or a bad definition of the terminal in either the terminfo or termcap databases.

Any of the terminal control sequences are available from the shell with the tset and tput commands. For example, the clear command clears the screen based on the TERM variable. The clear-screen control sequence is defined in the termcap or terminfo database. The clear command is equivalent to tput clear.

Using the UNIX terminal control sequences in shell scripts, although effective, is very slow. For instance, it is much faster to use the UNIX clear command to clear the screen than it is to use the equivalent tput clear.

Understanding Interprocess Communications

The power of UNIX is based on two factors: the ability to multitask and the ability of different tasks to communicate with each other. In its most primitive form, the UNIX pipe is an example of this *interprocess communication*. Each task in a pipe is a free-running program with its own time slice, environment, and I/O ports. As a task, its only connection to the rest of the pipeline is the fact that each task in the pipe is the recipient of the output of the task that is immediately upstream from it.

No task included in a pipeline is aware that it is part of a pipe. The task of setting up the interprocess data stream (a pipe) belongs to the shell.

Another capability of UNIX is to send *signals*, which is a form of software interrupt that can be received (using the `trap` command) and processed by a shell script or by a binary program. For example, almost any program can be terminated from the shell with the `kill` command, which takes the form `kill process-ID signal`. The `signal` is an integer from 1 to 18, possibly higher, depending on the system. Signal number 9, for example, is nonmaskable (it cannot be trapped or ignored by the receiving process). Signal 9 results in the immediate termination of the target process.

Signals and unnamed pipes are the only forms of interprocess communications you can easily access from the shell. Other forms require the use of the binary libraries.

The interprocess communications facilities and their uses are as outlined in the following sections.

Signals

Signals are software interrupts that are sent by one process to another in which some data can be trapped and processed. Most signals are related to operating-system conditions such as memory violations or illegal instructions. The following signals are relevant to the user:

❖ **1 - hangup.** This signal is sent to all processes when the user logs out. Any tasks run with the `nohup` command are rendered immune from this signal, but all others are automatically terminated unless the signal is trapped and processed.

❖ **2 - interrupt.** This signal also kills a task unless trapped. The interrupt signal is sent to a foreground task when the interrupt key is pressed.

❖ **3 - quit.** Similar in effect to `interrupt`, but used as a software-generated signal by shells and pipes.

❖ **9 - kill.** This signal cannot be caught or ignored. Unless the target process is a *zombie*, (a task that is already "dead" but not yet purged from the run list) the `kill -9` command almost surely removes it from memory.

❖ **14 - alarm clock.** This signal is returned to a process by the kernel when an alarm, set by `alarm()`, expires.

❖ **15 - software termination.** This signal is never sent by any kernel process—it is reserved for users. By convention, it signals a process to terminate.

❖ **16,17 - user-defined.** User-defined signals.

❖ **18 - death of a child.** All versions of the UNIX System V documentation contain the warning that this signal might not be supported in its present form in future releases of UNIX. So far, however, this signal is still supported. Signal 18 is sent by UNIX to the parent of a child process that has stopped running. This signal is useful if the parent process needs to clean up intermediate files created by the child process or perform other housekeeping tasks.

❖ **19 - powerfail.** This signal also carries the warning that it might not be supported in future releases. Signal 19 is sent to all processes started at boot time to inform them that the system is rebooting as the result of a power failure. This permits these processes to perform any housekeeping duties (like removing lock files) that might be left on the system as a result of the power failure.

For a complete discussion of other UNIX System V Release 4 signals, see the *Programmers Reference Manual* that is part of the standard UNIX documentation.

Pipes

All examples of pipelining described so far in this chapter have used *unnamed pipes*. An unnamed pipe is indicated by including the vertical bar character (|) on the UNIX command line between two commands and indicates the flow of information from the command to the left of the pipe symbol into the command on the right of the symbol.

There is nothing special about any of the pipes included in the examples presented so far in this chapter. Unnamed pipes can thread their way through an almost unlimited number of tasks and in and out of systems on a network by virtue of the remote shell. Only one process can read or write to an unnamed pipe at a time, however. This is a natural consequence of the pipe syntax `command|command|....`

Since the introduction of System V, UNIX has had the facility for *named pipes*. Named pipes are not created or used the way unnamed pipes are. Instead of appearing on the command line as the vertical bar character, named pipes are managed as part of the UNIX file system and appear as ordinary files. They are distinguished, however, when listed with the `ls -l` command, by a p in the leftmost column of the permission field.

For instance, in the output of the `ls -l` command shown below, `lppipe` is a named pipe:

```
$ ls -l
total 20
drwxr-xr-x  2 mikeg nrp    96  Sep 13  10:04  chap01
drwxr-xr-x  2 mikeg nrp    96  Sep 17  09:37  chap02
drwxr-xr-x  2 mikeg nrp    96  Aug 01  19:15  chap04
drwxr-xr-x  2 mikeg nrp    48  Aug 23  07:21  chap05
prwxr-xr-x  2 mikeg nrp     0  Aug 01  12:01  lppipe
```

Because pipes enable data to flow in only one direction, a named pipe is essentially *a first-in, first-out (FIFO)* buffer. Data that is put into the pipe first is the first data removed from the pipe by a receiving process. The input side of the named pipe is available for any process to pour data into; any process can take data from the output side.

Both cron and the LP system use named pipes as the interprocess-communication system for their user front ends. The command lp uses a named pipe to signal lpsched about new print jobs. Like at and batch, the user command crontab uses a named pipe to signal the cron daemon of new tasks to run. In both cases, the pipe is named FIFO after its function. After a named pipe is created, any process—binary or shell-script—can write to it as long as normal write permission for the pipe (or special file) allows it.

In general, named pipes are best used as a low-volume conduit to a single daemon when the input is from many users (or processes) and unpredictable in nature. Any unread data remains in the queue until processed by its recipient.

Using Shared Memory as Interprocess Control

Like most other things in the UNIX environment, a *shared memory* segment is represented in the UNIX file system, complete with ownership and file permissions that are honored. The "file," however, is really an address in the logical memory space of the processor. When the file is opened, a memory address is returned instead of a file descriptor.

As with normal files, multiple processes can simultaneously access the shared memory. The shared memory area may be used to transfer data between processes, or may store variables and other data required by the processes at runtime. Using shared memory reduces the overall memory requirements for multiple processes because you only need to establish a single copy of the data in the memory space of the computer. Alternatively, you can let each process allocate memory for data storage, replicating what the other processes have allocated.

Programs that use shared memory must have a structure that defines what the address is pointing to. Because a shared memory segment becomes part of the address space of the process using it, the processes using the memory must arbitrate which process is permitted to read and write to the shared memory.

Normal file permissions apply to whom can read and write to the shared memory, but no file-locking mechanism, mandatory or otherwise, is provided. You must use semaphores (see next section) or some other mechanism to assert a write demand and to synchronize access between the processes.

Shared memory is the fastest of the interprocess-communications methods available in UNIX. Like shared memory on any system, however, it suffers from being resource-hungry, and it is limited by the scope of the common data. All the processes sharing memory must agree, in the form of a data structure, to the contents of the shared memory segment.

Semaphores

The UNIX semaphore also is represented in the file system. A *semaphore* is a small piece of memory, just large enough to contain its value and identification, that is managed by UNIX. Multiple processes access a semaphore.

You can use a semaphore to pass information (but not *data*) between processes. For instance, a process might set a semaphore to a particular value to indicate that it successfully opened a file or to indicate a file open error. Another process can examine the semaphore, then determine whether the file had been opened. This is not the same as dynamically exchanging data (such as database fields and records).

After it is defined by a process, a semaphore contains a semaphore number and a semaphore ID. Each semaphore ID is unique and can contain any number of individual semaphore numbers. Each semaphore number is a short, unsigned integer that can be set anywhere within a positive range of 0 to 65536.

System calls enable an individual semaphore to be cleared (set to 0), altered (set to almost any value relative to its previous value) and tested (higher, lower or equal to a specified value). The process can wait until a specific condition is met.

On a well-tuned set of synchronized processes, semaphores are extremely useful. If any of the processes fail, however, the entire set might "lock up" if processes are waiting for a semaphore value to change or reach a certain value. The semaphore value, of course, can not change if the process responsible for changing the semaphore has failed.

If large numbers of processes are using a single semaphore, you might have trouble keeping the system running. In cases like these, other methods of interprocess communication might be more forgiving. Otherwise, you might have to introduce a semaphore daemon into the system that is smart enough to police a semaphore and signal possible errors.

One excellent use for semaphores is to synchronize shared memory usage. An unlimited number of processes can read the shared memory, but only one task can write to it at any one time. You can define a semaphore monitoring shared memory use as follows: a value of 0 means that no process is reading or writing the shared memory. When a process wants to read from the shared memory, it increments the value of the semaphore by 1 only if the value of the semaphore is less than 32767; otherwise, the process waits. When it has finished reading the shared memory, it then decrements the semaphore by one.

In this scheme, if a process wants to write to a shared memory segment, it waits until the semaphore's value is zero, then increments it by a large number—35000, for example. When the process has finished writing, it clears the semaphore for other processes. Obviously, if any task dies without resetting the semaphore, any process wanting to write to the shared memory is forever frozen, and a deadlock can eventually occur. Because they are nothing more than memory locations, semaphores are extremely fast.

Message Queues

Message queues have been described as a cross between a bi-directional pipe and a semaphore. They serve as a buffer in memory, with a predefined number of bytes allocated for buffering, and are controlled by the UNIX kernel. If messages aren't read, they sit in the queue. Eventually, the queue fills up.

Each message has a *type* followed by an ASCII string. Like a named pipe, a message in the message queue can be of any length as long as it fits in the preallocated buffer.

A message queue works much like a semaphore. A sending process can be instructed to wait until the buffer is free to receive the message of the desired length, and a receiving process can be instructed to wait until a message of the desired type is placed in the queue.

The message *type* is defined as a long, unsigned integer. A receiving process might request any one of the following: the first message of a specific type (with a specific valid number), the first message of any type, or the first message less than or equal to a specific type.

Another way to look at message queues is as a peer-to-peer message channel within memory. This analogy suggests the type of program topology common between systems on a network. Instead of using a semaphore to synchronize operations, for example, you might use a message queue. The processes included in the message network exchange messages that enable them to stay synchronized.

To stretch the network metaphor a little further, picture the use of a semaphore like that of Ethernet. On an Ethernet network, any system can broadcast a message; that message is received by all nodes on the network. If a collision occurs, all nodes back off and wait. Ethernet requires a clear channel for communications to occur. When you use semaphores to control access to shared memory, anyone can read shared memory but only one process can write to it at a time. Another process wishing to write to the shared memory must wait until the semaphore is clear before it asserts the right to write to the shared memory segment.

If you picture a message queue like a token ring network, each process in the chain has a chance to communicate before it passes the token on to the next. If the synchronization process uses message queues, one of several methods can be employed. The process at the head of the chain places a message on the queue directed at the next process on the list. When the second process receives the token, it also receives exclusive access to the resource—in this case, the shared memory segment containing the message. When the process is finished, it places a new token in the queue directed to the next process on the list, and the messaging procedure continues. Each process gets a chance to use the resource.

The message queue procedure works well if all the participating processes cooperate and continue to function, and if the processes are entirely dependent on access to the resource (if the process is fast and predictable). Otherwise, a process might well hog the message queue resource by delaying the tken's passage.

You also can use a *message arbitration* daemon to place the tokens on the queue. The daemon can detect if the token has been received, by what process, and when. If the intended recipient dies without picking up the token, the daemon can reclaim it and pass it on to the next in line. Conversely, the message arbitration daemon, knowing when the recipient picked up the token, can determine how long the recipient has had it, and if the daemon determines that the recipient has had it too long, the daemon can signal the errant process and force it to give up the resource. The recipient process can pass the token back to the daemon or simply wait to be signaled.

Message queues also can play a limited role in a client-server system. In this kind of system, any number of client processes send requests to one or more server processes. The most common approach is to use the uniqueness of the process ID of each task as a *handle* for the message type.

Because the process ID is an unsigned, short integer, the maximum process ID is 65536; however, the *message type* is a long or four-byte unsigned integer. A *client* task can make its request using its process ID as a message type. The server(s) then requests the first message in the queue with a message type less than or equal to 65536. The *return channel* is the incoming message type shifted by 16 bits, or multiplied by 65536. Because each process knows its process ID, it also knows the returning message type.

Using this type of architecture is more resilient than the semaphore/shared memory system; however, because of the extra overhead required to sort through so many messages, it is not as fast.

So ends the list of interprocess-communications facilities available through UNIX System V Release 3. Each has its uses and short-comings. Singularly or in combination, each can accomplish almost anything the programmer might want, however awkwardly.

Sockets

The concept of sockets originated in the Berkeley version of UNIX. With the Release 4 merge, sockets are now a part of UNIX System V. The essential idea behind sockets is to extend the file system to interprocess and interprocessor communications. The following discussion avoids using socket terminology any more than is necessary.

A *socket* is a gateway to a resource. The process in possession of the resource advertises its availability by creating a socket. A process wishing to use the resource attaches to the socket, and, if successful, receives a *file descriptor* as if the process had just opened a disk file.

The process with the resource must accept the request from the client. In doing so, it also receives a file descriptor. Both processes now have what appear to them as open files ready to read and write.

One unique aspect of sockets is that the socket can be local (and represented in the local UNIX file system), or it can be an *internet process* (IP) address anywhere on the Internet. Thus, the socket can connect to a non-UNIX system as long as a program at the other end is ready to service the socket.

Obviously, the architecture of sockets resembles client-server architecture, but the actual communications is peer-to-peer because both processes are equally predisposed to read and write to the open file descriptor.

Using the network analogy one more time, a socket resembles a hub-and-spokes or star orientation; message queues resemble token rings and semaphores resemble Ethernet. All in all, sockets are the most flexible means of interprocess communication, and they are as fast as message queues for local connections. They do not suffer from the same strict memory limitation of message queues and semaphores. Sockets, however, are limited to BSD and System V Release 4 only.

Examining The Data Workflow of an MIS System

Imagine the design of an MIS system within the context of available UNIX tools. From the outside, raw data is obtained from dozens of sources, including automated test equipment, bar-code scanners, electronically-placed orders, and data-entry clerks. From there, the data progresses up the ladder of abstraction, generating reports (like shipping, receiving, and purchase orders) as it goes.

Each level of abstraction implies some management action, which can come from equally varied sources: a foreman releases a job order, an MRP system generates pick lists and inventory requirement reports that might lead to purchase orders. At a higher level of abstraction, senior management might be required to plan staffing levels and equipment inventory or to allocate financial resources. As the data moves up the chain, decisions and directions move down in a (theoretically) well-ordered fashion.

The Traditional Design of an MIS System

In designing an MIS system (or any system, for that matter), it is difficult to separate the hardware architecture from the software design. Each dictates the other. The efficiency of a mainframe MIS system depends on its capability to move massive amounts of data at a time. Programming methods followed that permitted the greatest throughput with the least system overhead.

At the time mainframes were introduced, networking was in its infancy. It was unreliable and was expensive in terms of equipment and overhead. The cheapest approach from a hardware perspective was make the same centralized hardware work harder, so bigger and faster mainframes were built.

Today, of course, network hardware is much cheaper. It is easier now to put computing power where it is needed rather than make users conform to the requirements of the centralized system in the "back room." This mindset has lead to the opposite extreme—networking PCs with virtually unlimited power at the fingertips of the end user.

Networked PCs as an MIS System

Networked PC arrangements are just as inefficient as a mainframe in respect to an MIS system because every MIS system is a blend of foreground activity (primarily interacting with users) and background activity, such as posting orders to inventory or to a general ledger. With networked PCs, too much horsepower is at the front end and too little horsepower is left over for the back room. This is particularly true of PCs running DOS, because a DOS-based PC cannot multitask or run processes in the background.

The Ideal MIS Design

Picture the ideal data-processing environment as a sphere of uniform density, with *density* representing the balance between the demand and the supply of computing power. The surface of the sphere—the shell—represents the user interface, and the depths of the sphere represent the demands of background processing. At the center is the kernel that represents the requirements of the entire system: the operating system.

In this metaphor, a network of personal computers is an empty shell, which, although fast and responsive to users' input, has little available power for background tasks.

A mainframe, on the other hand, resembles an overripe peach with a soft, unresponsive exterior and a large, extremely dense pit at the center. The connections from the pit to the surface are a network of soft, easily disrupted fibrous tissue. A mainframe is strong on background batch processing and very unresponsive to the demands of the user.

The balance between the mainframe and the PC network is generally called a *client-server system* or, in our metaphor, perhaps a watermelon with dense, evenly dispersed little seeds (kernels). Although you can never truly achieve the ideal of uniform processing power, you can achieve greater uniformity by placing relatively small processors wherever you need more power. Thus, the backbone of the system becomes the network itself rather than a single large processor. On small systems, of course, a single processor can suffice.

The point is that an MIS network based on distributed UNIX machines is almost infinitely scalable.

Planning System Resources

As a point of reference, start with a very small system—a single personal computer or a small network of personal computers. The questions to ponder are these:

❖ How will the system grow?

❖ Is it operating efficiently now?

❖ Does everyone need a personal computer?

Not everyone needs a personal computer. Examine the applications used in an office environment. There are, of course, word processing applications, spreadsheets, an accounting system, and so on. As the system grows larger and larger, however, fewer people are required to "do it all."

Jobs become specialized—some use word processing all day, others perform data entry, still others might perform some kind of analysis using spreadsheets, while others might be involved in graphically intensive engineering or other tasks. As the work becomes more specialized, many—indeed most—of the tasks become unsuited to the capabilities of a personal computer.

For example, many word processing programs offer sophisticated graphics capabilities. In common office practice, however, how often are they used? How many people developing spreadsheet models need to see sophisticated graphics before they print it? How often, in an office environment, does a user need to be in two or more applications at once? What accounting application needs capabilities beyond those offered by a simple dumb terminal? The answer to most of these questions can be summed up with the words "never" and "none".

A different complication arises for accounting applications on a network. Accounting systems, by nature, are interrelated and use overlapping files. Thus, file sharing is mandatory. But this brings other problems, such as file and record contention. PC network operating systems like Novell go a long way towards solving these problems, but the fundamental problem of where the processing takes place persists. On networked PCs, tasks that belong in the background are performed in the foreground while the operator waits.

Building a UNIX-Based MIS System

Growing a UNIX-based MIS system from a network of PCs is both easy and managerially more difficult. Fast, expensive and super-fluous personal computers are often underutilized. Specialized tasks like word processing and accounting need specialized tools—for instance, dumb terminals connected to a local UNIX System. You can still use UNIX systems as file servers even if you need networked PCs, but the efficiency of the MIS system improves if you use dumb terminals.

The architecture of a growing MIS system begins with a single UNIX system. The classic functions of data entry are performed on dumb terminals. Using a daemon started by `cron` or initiated by a user, collected data is collated, sorted, posted, and so on.

As the MIS system grows and functions become even more specialized, so too do the hardware and software systems supporting it. Dedicated hardware systems could support customer order entry, a second could support accounts receivable, a third could support inventory control, and yet another could run the MRP (Material Resource Planning) system. Common files could be shared using NFS, and pipeline programs could drop data off on one system while picking other data up in another.

Designing an MIS system from scratch or migrating from a main-frame to a distributed UNIX network is not much different than building a system from a network of personal computers. Functions are isolated from one another in the smallest practical unit. With pipes or networks or file-sharing technology, they are joined together.

The key to success is to isolate functions, reduce them to the smallest practical tasks, place them on the smallest practical hardware platform, and carefully design the flow of data as it works its way up the ladder of abstracted information. A well-designed system can grow almost without bounds.

Summary

UNIX has come a long way from the early versions and portable games. As an environment for business applications, UNIX reached an early maturity with XENIX, which, in the 1980s, helped hundreds of thousands of small businesses to grow.

In the 1990s, UNIX has evolved into a mature operating system with the tools and capabilities to support an MIS environment of virtually any size. There are still limitations and considerations to be made in the use of UNIX, however. In the next chapter, you take a close look at what does not work, but in later chapters, you learn how to overcome some of the problems.

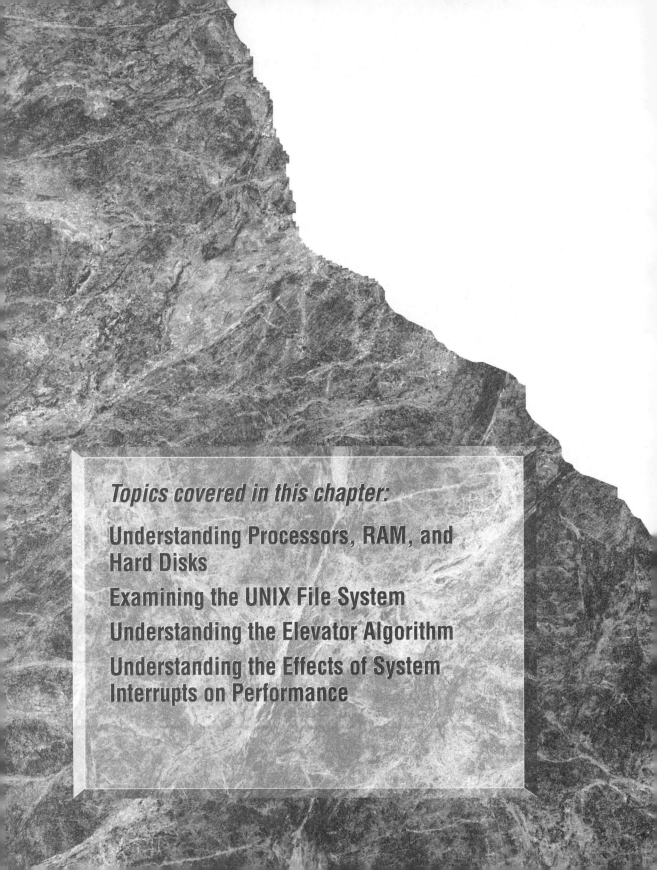

Topics covered in this chapter:

Understanding Processors, RAM, and Hard Disks

Examining the UNIX File System

Understanding the Elevator Algorithm

Understanding the Effects of System Interrupts on Performance

Chapter 5

Limitations of
UNIX Resources

L ike all things in life, designing an operating system is
an exercise in compromise. Every portion of the OS
(operating system) is fraught with decisions to be made
between imperfect alternatives. One of the most difficult balancing
acts in OS design is the pursuit of performance versus the cost of
the product. Typically, designers err on the side of price as measured by hardware requirements, building into the software the
inefficiencies of the hardware they are using to run their prototype.

This chapter discusses the inefficiencies that are inherent in the
design of UNIX and explains how designers improved these perfor-
mance-degrading features, seeking to enhance the overall performance of UNIX, while not increasing hardware requirements. The
chapter is divided into subjects dealing with each type of ineffi-
ciency:

❖ Processor, RAM, and hard-disk relationships

❖ File-system design

❖ File-compatibility issues

❖ Reliability issues

Understanding Processors, RAM, and Hard Disks

The performance of any system is affected by the design decisions made to overcome two major data-transfer inefficiencies: how to overcome the differential between the very fast speed of the processor(s) and the comparatively slower speed of RAM; as well as how to overcome the differential between the relatively faster speed of this RAM versus the comparatively slower speed of storage media.

 In the early 1970s, the average time it took to access a cylinder on a disk was 90 milliseconds because of fixed-head drums with access times of only 20 milliseconds. Today, the fastest disks access data in fewer than five milliseconds. This is less than one order of magnitude improvement in speed, yet RAM access times increased from milliseconds to nanoseconds over this same time period.

The capacities of both disks and RAM have improved one order of magnitude every four years. Thus, the relative storage speed of disks versus RAM speeds is getting slower, and 15 to 30 milliseconds is an eternity when compared with the speed of RAM.

Computer-processing cycles are also getting faster and the time required to access data in RAM is not keeping pace with the requirements of these faster processors.

There are two kinds of memory chips used in computers: Static RAM (SRAM) and Dynamic RAM (DRAM) chips. *Static RAM* chips are fast and hold their data when the power goes down but they cannot hold as much data as *Dynamic RAM* chips can (they are less dense).

At this time, the densest SRAMs in commercial use contain only 256 kilobits. Dynamic RAMs, on the other hand, are cheap and more dense, but they are relatively slow. This is because between every read or write cycle, DRAMs must be refreshed. Currently, four-megabit DRAMs are commercially available (eight-megabit DRAMs are on the way). Unfortunately, the access speed of DRAMs has not kept pace with the speed of the current crop of processors.

For example, in an ideal world, a processor should be able to fetch data from RAM in one clock cycle. A *clock cycle* is the time a computer takes to complete one operation. The Intel 486 chip is now available in 25-, 33-, and 50-megahertz clock speeds. Table 5.1 shows the hypothetical speed required of RAM for a *memory fetch* to occur in one clock cycle. This ideal performance is then compared to the actual clock speeds of processors.

Table 5.1
Hypothetical and Real RAM Access Speeds

Clock Speed in Megahertz	RAM Access Time in Nanoseconds
1 megahertz (MHz)	1000 nanoseconds
8	120
10	100
12	80
16	60
25	40
33	30
50	20

With the fastest DRAMs hovering around 60ns, only a processor with a clock speed no faster than 16MHz can fetch data without having to wait. To get around this problem, the designers of faster hardware employ cache memory that is composed of the swifter (more expensive) SRAM and pipeline or prefetch instructions from DRAM, and then place it in the SRAM. To run at full speed, these fast processors can only run programs, or program fragments, located in cache or in the cache pipeline. When an address is referenced that is not in cache, the processor must wait for that page of data or program to be brought in.

On multitasking operating systems, this represents an opportunity to run some other program that is still in cache while the required page of the paused program is brought in. This represents an opportunity, however, only if the operating system is aware of the cache. On some systems, the memory-management system is written in firmware or ROM beneath the cognizance of the operating system.

 There are no perfect solutions, and problems are compounded with the trend toward RISC (Reduced Instruction Set Computing) architectures, which increase the demand for memory even more by minimizing the effects of any single instruction. Thus, they require more instructions to be available in memory at one time. Even so, pipeline processing and fast cache dramatically increase the speed of processing.

There is a large litany of complaints about hardware design constraints, as voiced by system software designers. As a result of these constraints, any operating system, especially a multitasking system, ends up being a *most reasonable* compromise because of the designers' decisions based on the limitations of the hardware.

An example of this compromise is the design of a *real-time operating system* (versus a *multiuser operating system*). A multiuser operating system can rely on supporting many non-demanding tasks to provide enough free cycles to serve each of its users. It is therefore designed for maximum throughput.

The drawback of this design decision is that to be efficient for all tasks means that the response time of the system to any one task is more or less indeterminate. Real-time systems do not have this luxury; the response of the system to any given condition must be very precisely determined. This is accomplished at the expense of overall efficiency.

What follows are problems that, although associated with any multitasking operating system, are more acute in UNIX as a result of its "most reasonable" compromises.

Thrashing: Uncontrolled Growth in UNIX Processes

Most modern operating systems, including UNIX, are called demand-paged, multitasking operating systems. *Demand paging* means that if the total RAM required by all the programs that the system is attempting to run exceeds the actual amount of RAM in the system, the operating system *pages* portions of RAM into the *swap space* on a disk.

The page size on most UNIX systems is 4K bytes. Thus, all programs currently running on a UNIX system are, theoretically, divided into pages of 4,096 bytes each. If the system runs out of RAM, the least-used page is swapped out to the disk and replaced with a needed page. The operating system keeps track of which page is where, and if a program requires a page that is currently on disk, the system generates a *page fault*, which suspends the currently running program until the required page is brought into RAM. On fast systems, page faults can be generated if the required page is not in the cache.

Whenever a page fault (or some other fault, such as a request for I/O services) occurs to block the continued execution of a task, the operating system must perform a context switch. A *context switch* saves the state of the currently running process and prepares the next task in the memory queue to run. This switch involves a lot of overhead (time spent in performing housekeeping tasks). UNIX is notorious for being burdened with context-switch overhead.

This overhead is largely the result of a design decision that enables UNIX to be almost a *virtual machine* environment, in which each user thinks he has the machine to himself. If most processes are blocked, the operating system spends its time performing endless context switches—this is called thrashing.

Thrashing occurs when the computer performs endless I/O activities that do not lead to the completion of any task. When a multitasking system thrashes, it uses up the idle time that enables it to service multiple users. Thus, no one is serviced. Thrashing has been described as that point when a system's disk is doing so much input-output that the disk head activator moves like a Maytag washing machine's tub during its spin cycle.

 Many things can cause thrashing. For example, thrashing can occur with disk-intensive applications, such as those caused by a DBMS or a few very large unstructured programs.

Of most concern to UNIX users is the fact that the more tasks a system has to service, the greater is the chance that the proper pages are not where they are required to be. UNIX, by its nature, encourages a multitude of processes. The user shell is a process, every command the shell runs is another process, every command in a pipe is yet another process, and all daemons are processes, as well.

 One or two large processes on a mainframe can easily become dozens of small processes on a UNIX system (the result of the programming techniques encouraged in UNIX.)

Every system reaches its thrash point eventually, but it is impossible to determine in advance what that point will be because it depends on the mix of programs being run. On UNIX systems, there are a predefined, maximum number of tasks that the system allows to be created; when it reaches that limit, the message `cannot fork another process` appears on the system console.

 This process-acceptance limit can be changed by relinking the kernel to increase or decrease the maximum allowable processes. The allowance only represents a "best guess" of the upper limit in the number of processes that any one system can support without thrashing. If system defaults in versions of commercial UNIX systems (such as SCO UNIX and XENIX) are a valid indication of the thrashing threshold, it is easy to determine the number of users a given system can support.

For example, some versions of XENIX that were designed to be run on Intel 286-based systems have a default maximum allowed job acceptance limit of 80 processes. Subtracting 10 for system process slots and daemons, 70 processes remain to service users. If each user is allowed seven processes (a shell and six other commands) in a pipe, for example, an Intel 286 running XENIX should be able to support at least 10 users without thrashing.

Early versions of UNIX System V, designed to run on slow (16MHz) Intel 386 machines, came with a default maximum number of processes set at 180. Using the same logic yields a maximum number of users of 24.

More recent versions of SCO UNIX, designed to run on Intel-486 processors with ESIA buses, arrive configured with over 460 maximum processes (yielding a support level of 64 users). These numbers are so dependent on individual system characteristics that they are of little use to anyone and may bear no relationship to the actual thrashing point on any of these systems.

To illustrate the problem of thrashing, the following example from *Operating Systems* by Madnick and Donovan (1974) calculates the thrashing region for an IBM 360 mainframe, which was the pre-eminent computer of the 1960s and early 1970s. This theoretical system had the following characteristics:

❖ The system had 256K bytes of core memory, 0.5 MHz clock speed, 20ms average access fixed-head drum for paging, and a 4K-byte page size.

❖ Each program required 160K bytes of memory, ran for 1,000,000 instructions (two seconds of run time), and had 60 I/O requests-per-program at 50ms-per-request: 20ms to request the data, 20ms to get the data, and 10ms to be safe, for a total of three seconds of I/O).

❖ Each program then required a total of five seconds to run, of which three seconds were devoted to I/O processing. Thus, in a monoprogramming (single-tasking) environment, the efficiency of the CPU can be calculated by dividing the two seconds of run time by the five seconds of total time, yielding a CPU efficiency of 40%. In a multiprogramming (multitasking) environment, the system is in the thrashing region if the CPU utilization drops below this same 40%. Figure 5.1 shows what the results were for an IBM 360 multitasking environment.

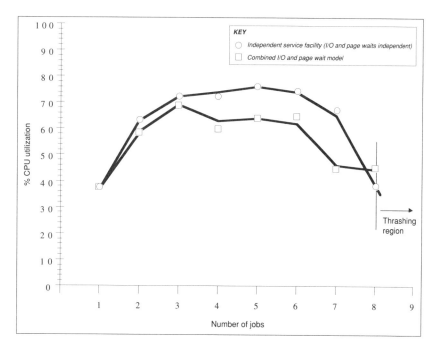

Figure 5.1:

Sample program analysis: CPU utilization percentage.
Courtesy of McGraw Hill.

The results for an IBM 360 show why mainframe programming evolved the way it did. If a mainframe was most efficient running just four or five tasks, it is understandable why a monolithic transaction processor, such as CICS, was developed. A typical mainframe, in the mid-1970s, had two CICS programs and four or five batch spools running at any one time.

Although the primary cause of thrashing is the lack of fast RAM, vis-a-vis the RAM required by all the currently running programs, this is only half of the story. Thrashing can also occur if there are too many processes for the system to handle.

The problem of too many processes is similar to the activities that occur during paging. Whenever an operating system must perform a context switch, it unloads the registers of the currently running program, loads the registers with the previously stored registers of the next program in the run queue, and moves a lot of pointers in memory. These pointers point to I/O buffers, IPC (interprocess communications) buffers, and the data space of the now running program. Each time a context switch occurs, the operating system must determine if the process is ready to run.

 This determination (that the process is ready to run) may take some time. For example, the operating system must determine why the process was previously blocked and if the condition causing the blockage has been rectified. If the process was blocked for a pending I/O operation, has that operation been completed? If the process was blocked because of an alarm timer, has the timer run out? If the process was blocked because of a page fault (either to disk or to cache), has the page been restored? If the operation is still blocked, the operating system must perform yet another context switch. All of this activity occurs, not matter how much RAM is installed or how fast it is.

If the operating system can perform a context switch on all processes in its run queue in less time than it takes the average process to become unblocked, the overhead associated with multitasking has no effect on the efficiency of the system. Because the context-switch overhead rises linearly with the number of processes in the queue and the time it takes the average process to become unblocked remains constant, eventually the operating system will not keep up with demand.

This form of thrashing is encountered most often in modern UNIX systems because of the unlimited number of processes that can be generated at any one time. Only faster processors, faster RAM, more efficient kernel programming, and a conscious design of application programs (to avoid paging) can alleviate this type of thrashing.

The programmer or system administrator can do little about the speed of the processor or RAM, and can do nothing at all about the kernel or the application design. There is a lot that can be done, however, to impose limits on the number of processes that can be spawned by users.

Thrashing occurs when permissions are provided for the user to create pipes with many processes and to run them with the nohup command in the background. The problem with nohup is that there are no checks on the use of programs run with this command, other than the system-imposed maximum number of processes. There are, however, controls on the number of processes that can be run simultaneously by cron, which means there are also limits imposed on batch and at. Chapter 12 introduces a system that imposes even tighter controls on background processes.

One last mechanism for avoiding thrashing is useful only to C programmers and is not yet widely available (it will be available with the next edition of SUID Release 4 and in some UNIX clones). This mechanism is called threads. A thread is a semi-process—a task that is so closely associated with a normal process that a full context switch is not necessary. Threads are helpful only if the number of processes in a system can be reduced or if they enable a context switch to actually perform some useful work.

Examining the UNIX File System

Any system design is the result of imperfect choices, based on a field of inadequate alternatives. The UNIX file system design is an example of this kind of choice. On a mainframe (and on many other systems), the user or programmer has a choice of what the file will look like.

 For example, a programmer can define block size, based on a disk's cylinder size, and then define the number of records in a block. He can also preallocate contiguous cylinders for fast response times. This entails a lot of work of work to design, and any program that accesses this data also knows the details of the file structure it will use. The structure that is defined in this manner is not very convenient for the system because it is so hardware-dependent. Because such file structures are not portable (a criterion for a UNIX file system), they cannot be used.

The organization of a file system also depends on the ways it is accessed. If a file is only to be read sequentially, the data may be scattered all over a disk—the only organizational requirement is that each record or block should contain a pointer to the next record or block in the chain. Conversely, if the data is to be read at random, either the data must reside in contiguous blocks (so that the operating system or user program can calculate the offset of any one record from the starting address), or some form of indexing must be used.

Loose-file organizations, such as those just described, are flexible—but only at the expense of extra programming and file-maintenance work to ensure that the pointers and offset tables remain reliable. If the underlying structure of the file system is intended to be transparent to the user or application programs (as it must be in

UNIX), the design must favor the speed of the operating system at the expense of some speed in applications. Such a requirement dictates fixed blocks and an indexed access method—hence, the fixed block and Information Node (inode) tables of the UNIX file system.

The inode tables are only one type of many indexing schemes that can be applied. This scheme is a compromise, favoring fast access of many small files over the slower access of a few very large files.

 With Release 4, you can define the block size of the file system; with the `ufs` file system, almost any kind of file system can be created. Even a `ufs` system, however, requires some indexing scheme that can be superimposed on top of the inodes.

Every choice that a system designer makes has implications that reach far beyond the original design concepts. (In the case of UNIX, these original concepts were to produce a good system for writing documentation and for playing Space War) The following sections discuss some of these additional design implications.

 UNIX Space War, a video game from the mid-1970s, consisted of two spaceships orbiting the sun in two dimensions. The spaceships could alter their orbits and fire projectiles at each other, but the projectiles were also in orbit.

Practical File Limitations

On the first UNIX systems, the block size was set at 512 bytes, which yields a theoretical maximum file size of eight gigabytes. The Berkeley file system used a block size of two kilobytes, which allowed a theoretical maximum file size of 32 gigabytes.

Unfortunately, the true file-size limit turned out to be only four gigabytes because each inode contained an unsigned four-byte integer that recorded the file size.

In addition, accessing four gigabytes requires *tipple indirection* in the inode tables. This means that the disk must be accessed four times to retrieve a single block.

 In real terms, if a modern database management system (DBMS) is superimposed on top of this raw file, accessing a single record can require a dozen accesses.

With `ufs`, all constraints are off. The maximum file size is 2^{64} bytes long or a 20-digit (base 10) number (in other words, well beyond the limits of foreseeable technology). In addition, the block size can be almost anything short of the number of bytes in a cylinder or physical block on the disk.

It is difficult to find fault with the `ufs` design because it is fast, efficient, and it supports Sun/OS Network File System (NFS) and non-UNIX file. Its only disadvantage is the added overhead associated with data access on `ufs`, in contrast to the standard UNIX file system. This lack of size constraints would have impacted any operating system by making the kernel larger.

UNIX's fundamental reliance on inodes to support `ufs` can be criticized for its dependence on multiple indirect access. Although any indexing design adds complexity and overhead into systems, some kind of indexing methodology is needed for flexibility.

The only drawback to the introducing `ufs` is that each physical file type requires its own disk or partition on a disk and that the root disk must be a standard UNIX `u5` file system. Thus, to escape the limitations of the `u5` file system requires either a partitioned disk or a separate disk.

On very large systems, in which multiple disk drives are used, this obviously is no hindrance. In fact, on the largest systems, there can be multiple `ufs`'s, each configured with a different block size, optimized for different types of applications. In complexity, this is no more of a problem than preallocating contiguous space for files in other operating systems. What it removes from UNIX in the form of simplicity and uniformity it more than gives back in flexibility because you can now design the file structure to meet the performance requirements of your software, instead of constraining the applications to fit the hardware.

File-System Speed Considerations

The access speed of a file system depends on how easily the data can be found. The ease of access is directly related to how well the data is indexed. Thus, file-system speed is directly related to indexing methodologies.

Many books have been written about file-indexing methods, and the truth is that every method is flawed in one way or another. The problem is not that the algorithms do not work; rather, it is that each algorithm favors one kind of file size and organization over another and, thus, multiple disk accesses (such as indirect address blocks) are required to find data.

Small files require less time to access than large files. In fact, any byte in an open UNIX file can be found with a maximum of four-disk accesses. This is surprisingly efficient, but data, especially in an MIS environment, is rarely accessed by record number. Instead, data is searched for by a key such as part numbers or customer codes, which usually requires a separate index. Several indexing schemes that are suitable for this kind of searching (most often a B-Tree search). In other words, this kind of database more often than not requires a DBMS.

Virtually all DBMSs use a B-Tree algorithm to search for pointers to data records; the number of searches that are required to find a randomly located record increases logarithmically with the number of records. In addition, these DBMS fall into two categories:

those that use the UNIX file system and those that do not. The DBMS that do not use the file system rely on their own disk-accessing system that parallels that of UNIX. The problem is to access the disk blocks that contain the index. Then, once the right key has been located, finding and delivering the data. On UNIX systems, these DBMS access raw devices that are minimally known to UNIX in the device directory.

The DBMSs that use the UNIX file system must also use the inode system to locate keys in an index and then locate and deliver the data containing the key to the DBMS. The DBMSs that use the UNIX file system fall into three categories that have varied efficiency. Some DBMSs store both data and indexes in one large file, others store data in one file and all the indexes in another, still others store data and each separate index in separate files.

DBMS Single-File Systems

The worst-case scenario for degrading file-access speeds are nearly full databases (those nearing the four-gigabyte limit) that keep both data and indexes in one file. There are several databases that do this—and at least one stores both data-entry screens and reports in the single file. To make matters worse, suppose that the algorithm they have chosen uses only the most primitive B-Tree methods. Assume that the index consists of 20 characters in the key and 12 bytes of pointers, and that the database itself consists of 128 byte records, which translates to roughly 16,000,000 records and an equal number of index pointers.

 Because the bulk of the data is stored in blocks that require tipple indirection to access, assume that it requires four-disk accesses to retrieve anything. Also, assume that half of the branches in the index require a new block and that the block size is only 512 bytes. This is truly a worst-case scenario because an *inode* points to a block, and if the blcok size is small, then it requires lots of reads to find the index pointer (many of which can fit into a single block).

If the algorithm used for searching requires the natural log of the number of keys to find a match, 16 comparisons are required to locate the key and the data (this translates to eight disk accesses to find the key).

Because each block requires tipple indirection to find the data that matches an index search, the real access of the disk consists of eight index searches times four inode searches, or 32 accesses of the disk. Multiply this by 20 milliseconds' access time, and you get more than one-half second per record found.

DBMSs with Separate Files

Because UNIX is most efficient when accessing many small files, the most favorable file-system performance situation occurs when each table and each index in a database resides in a separate file. Suppose the same situation exists as in the previous example. With the same data and index, you now have two files: one containing the data, the other containing the index.

The data file is now 3.5G in size. The index, having been put into a separate file, contains 500M (16 million times 32 bytes). If the block size expands to 2048 bytes from the original 512 bytes, the index will require more than 250,000 data blocks in the UNIX file system. This still requires tipple indirection, but now 64 keys in the index fit inside one data block, thus reducing by four the number of accesses required in the same B-Tree algorithm.

 Using one of the better B-Tree algorithms yields about five comparisons, or 20 accesses of the disk (given tipple indirection), plus four to retrieve the data. This still yields nearly 480ms of disk thrashing to find the data you are looking for.

Further Performance Enhancements with ufs

When a ufs file system with 8K blocks is applied to the DBMS with separate files for index and data, the B-Tree overhead is reduced to three accesses and the number of blocks required for the index is reduced to about 65,000 (within the limits of double indirection). The total number of disk accesses is now six accesses to find the right record and another four to get the data, for a total of 10 disk accesses, or 200ms.

How I/O Affects File-System Performance

In a single-tasking environment, the best performance rate for a DBMS is to complete five transactions-per-second. Because UNIX is a multitasking environment, performance can be further enhanced, beyond simply tuning the file structure. The I/O provides plenty of opportunities to service other processes. By incorporating an *elevator algorithm* in the kernel, more transactions can be serviced than would be indicated by the raw I/O time alone.

Understanding the Elevator Algorithm

Normally, disks are rated by their average access time—the time it takes for random reads and writes of the disk. This means that the read/write heads of the disk are thrashing all over, and they require time to settle into the groove of a track before any I/O can take place. Many operating systems, including pre-System V UNIX and MS-DOS, service I/O requests on a first-come, first-served basis.

In addition, commands from many processes or widely fragmented files effectively randomize the locations of data addresses on a disk. Thus, on "first-come, first-served" systems the read/write head performs a wildly gyrating dance, accompanied by the familiar "tic, tic, tic" of the head moving, stopping, and settling into a track. UNIX has always buffered its disk I/O, which means that the act of performing the actual I/O is divorced from the process that actually requests it.

The elevator algorithm might be explained this way: as I/O requests are collected in a buffer, they are sorted into ascending or descending order, depending on the current position of the read/write head. As a result, multiple reads and writes to an individual cylinder are accomplished without moving the heads.

As the head moves on to the next required track in the buffered list, it is more likely to be adjacent or nearly adjacent to the previous track. This is because UNIX files are laid on the disk sequentially, and it is likely the head will not have to move much to access the next set of records. Response times are typically measured from track-to-track in buffered I/O. This measurement basis is more accurate than the calculation of an average access time. In track-to-track algorithms, the head does not have to move as far. Because the track has a lower velocity, the time it takes to settle is less (in most instances, track-to-track access time is about half that of average access time).

In other words, the heads move back and forth or up and down in a smooth motion, like an elevator picking up and discharging passengers. The result is a significant improvement in throughput, and the average time it takes to deliver a passenger or the total number of disk accesses divided by the total elapsed time also improves. Thus, whereas it can take as much as 200ms to access an individual record in the previous example of the DBMS with a single file structure, UNIX can deliver several dozen other records to or from different processes in that same period. This is the way a DBMS can legitimately claim to perform dozens, or even hundreds, of transactions-per-second.

Non-UNIX File Systems

Access to raw disks has always been possible, but on pre-`ufs` systems any data located on a raw device could not be made visible to UNIX. Such data was the exclusive property of proprietary programs.

The `ufs` file system is a generalization of the standard UNIX file system. As a result, in `ufs` nearly anything resembling a UNIX file can be made to behave like a standard UNIX file by the system, complete with access by all the standard UNIX utilities. These programs include those that deliver data in the form of UNIX files, such as remote NFS.

UNIX has only one compatibility requirement for a new file system—that it should be capable of being manipulated to look and behave like a UNIX file. Can it be manipulated to appear to have a directory structure, does it have file names shorter than the 128-byte maximum, and can it can "speak" ASCII?

These capabilities are not very hard to accomplish. In fact, many versions of UNIX (both Release 3 and 4) permit the creation of MS-DOS partitions and, once mounted, to access MS-DOS files like any other UNIX files. This makes running MS-DOS under UNIX a lot easier and begins the merging of distinctions between the two operating systems.

The concept of the `ufs` enables the creation of a file system and access method that is better suited for large-scale use by databases and their file-server programs, bypassing the multiple indirection of the inode system. Unfortunately, no standards bodies have convened to discuss this—you and your DBMS vendor are on your own.

Discussing Reliability Issues

UNIX is very fragile. For example, you cannot turn the system off, as you can when using MS-DOS or a Macintosh. A bad disk crash or the threat of one can give system administrators nightmares. The effect of accidentally pulling the plug on a UNIX system is almost as catastrophic as pushing the panic button on a mainframe for potential file system damage.

 UNIX has a number of utility programs that are designed expressly for checking and repairing ruptured file systems. The utility `fsck` checks the file system for inconsistencies and repairs most of them, and `fsdb` (file system debugger) enables you to fix almost everything else.

The source of all this anxiety is also the source of the strength of UNIX—the fact that all I/O is buffered. *Buffering* enables the operating system to separate physical I/O and inter-process communications from the processes that use the resources. For example, all traffic to and from disks, terminals, and networks (and anything else represented in the file system) must pass through the buffer of a device driver.

Device drivers are part of the kernel, and they represent the only kernel component that is visible to the file system. In fact, the transparent window of the device driver provides communication to the shell. It is the device driver that buffers data.

When a request to write to a disk (or any other device) is passed to the kernel, the data is actually stored in a buffer defined within the device driver for later disposal.

The sync **Command**

Once the system is up and running, much of the data required to maintain the file system is maintained in memory and only periodically flushed back to the disk. The superblock of each disk, for example, is stored and updated in memory and not on disk. UNIX provides the sync command to flush superblock data back to disk, but only periodically.

The sync command forces the updating of the superblock on the physical disk. If the system crashes after a new block has been allocated but before the superblock has been flushed, inconsistencies occur in the file system. There will be file blocks allocated in the inode table that have not been allocated in the superblock. The fsck command detects these inconsistencies and corrects them. In addition, any data still in buffers that have not been physically written to disk when the system crashes are lost.

Although buffering improves the speed of UNIX, there are repercussions. A user should be cognizant of the dangers and appreciative of the advantages of the UNIX design. Eventually, there is a failure in one or more components of every system. The problem can be mitigated if there have been frequent backups of the system and if efforts have been made to minimize the most frequent causes of system failure.

These system-failure causes, in order of frequency, are the following:

❖ Power failure

❖ Disk failure

❖ RAM corruption

❖ RAM failure

❖ CPU failure

Software rarely if ever "breaks." If it does break or if there are bugs in the software, it breaks in the same place every time. Hardware failures often begin with intermittent "soft" failures.

 There are other types of hardware failures that can be called "soft" hardware failures. These are environmental conditions that play havoc with system components, such as static, radio broadcasting, and even cosmic rays. As system components become smaller, denser and faster they also become more sensitive to these environmental hazards. Only uninterruptable power supplies (UPS), frequent backups, and disk mirroring can begin to alleviate these problems.

Understanding the Effects of System Interrupts on Performance

Almost nothing happens in UNIX without intercession by the kernel. Most function calls in C (or any other language) are actually requests for the kernel to do something. Any input or output by a program must pass through the transparent veil of a device driver. In fact, whenever there is a need to perform a context switch; a call to a kernel; or a hardware interrupt from a disk, network, or terminal; the kernel must take control from the shell. In this respect, the kernel performs a lot more work than is readily apparent, and the demands imposed on the kernel can be a source of extra system overhead. Fortunately, a lot of this overhead can be alleviated by extra hardware.

On a mainframe, all terminal I/O is performed by terminal controllers. The mainframe polls the controllers to see if they have any data to deliver, and the controllers in turn poll the terminals. The only thing the transmit key on a block mode terminal does is to signal the terminal that it may transmit data the next time it is polled. In this respect, mainframes create a situation in which there are no system interrupts as a result of human action.

In contrast, on UNIX systems using dumb ASCII terminals, each keystroke is transmitted, whether the system is ready or not, and each keystroke must be serviced. On generic UNIX-based systems, such as a PC running SCO UNIX, there are no special processors that trap keystrokes. Thus, the kernel accepts full responsibility for the interrupts caused by activity on the port. These interrupts can, of course, be masked and ignored until the processor has the time to service them, but each keystroke by each user must be processed, one at a time, by the device driver.

Fortunately, the average typist types only ten characters-per-second, and he types only in short bursts. If the system performs 100 context switches per second, that is one hundred times per second that the kernel has an opportunity to service I/O from terminals, disks, and so forth.

Workstations, or systems supporting X-Window terminals create a third type of interrupt situation. Because workstations use both a pointer system, such as a mouse, and keystrokes to input data, the kernel must work with even more inputs and output.

The buffering device must not only support dozens of dumb terminals, it must also be able to service, at a high priority, all interrupts generated by a mouse (these can range into the hundreds-per-second).

This is why workstations or systems supporting X-Window terminals must be fast (if they are not fast, they would have no time to perform any useful work, other than to position the cursor on the screen). Graphical user interfaces, such as X Windows, require file servers to buffer the I/O, thus reducing the overhead to the kernel.

In recent years, even small UNIX systems have taken on more of a mainframe look with subsidiary processors that manage the actual I/O. On these systems, terminals, disks, and even networks are managed by local intelligent processors that trap and service interrupts from devices in the outside world, which reduces the demands on the kernel and enables the system to perform more useful work.

Summary

UNIX designers compensated for the inherent performance inefficiencies of their hardware platforms (the comparative differences in data-access speeds of processor(s), RAM, and storage media) that lead to system thrashing by introducing hardware- and software-based cache memory schemes that act as buffers.

As was mentioned at the beginning of this chapter, an operating system is a compromise based on a set of design goals. In the case of UNIX, the goal is to support as many interactive users as the hardware permits and to offer a file system that is transparent and identical to all applications. These design goals lead directly to the concept of the shell and the simple file structure of the inode system.

Originally, UNIX was intended to support a multitude of small files, but with the introduction of the `ufs`, files and database structures of almost any size and design can now be supported within the context of the UNIX file system.

UNIX is not perfect, but with skillful system administration, the traditional problems of overloaded systems can be avoided.

Part Two: The Design of a Management Information System

Work and Data Flow in an MIS

Resource Management

Migration Strategies

Topics covered in this chapter:

Describing a Management Information System

Collecting and Verifying Data

Using the Data

Describing the Typical MIS System

Chapter 6

Work and Data Flow in an MIS

T he most significant difference between a management information system (MIS) and the use of computers in engineering is the tremendous amount of data collection required by the MIS versus the emphasis of engineering applications on data manipulation. A CAD or CAE application generates far more data as output than it takes in as input. Every hour of data entry in an engineering application may yield megabytes of data in the form of engineering drawings. In contrast, the bulk of the data generated in a management information system is generated by human data-entry clerks or their automated surrogates, and the amount of additional data generated by post-processing is small compared to engineering applications.

Management information systems are data-intensive and engineering applications are usually CPU-intensive. This is why engineering applications are written in efficient and fast languages such as FORTRAN or C, and why interpreted or tokenized languages like COBOL, business-oriented BASIC, and fourth-generation DBMS languages are used in commercial applications. The CPU cycles required to service a business application generally pale in comparison to the overhead associated with that application's disk I/O.

 There is a further difference between engineering and business applications: an engineering application, once written and debugged, requires very little maintenance. How often, for example, does the accepted algorithm for the surface area of a cylinder change? (Not very often.)

Business applications, on the other hand, are driven by the tax code; by accepted practices in accounting; by new products and manufacturing techniques; and by managerial whims. The very essence of business-oriented applications is maintenance, which means that cryptic languages such as FORTRAN and C cannot readily be used—more descriptive languages such as COBOL are required.

Many useful business applications were written in the 1960s in COBOL. Even with hundreds of changes in the tax code and in accounting practices, many of these applications are still maintained today.

 Because COBOL is a descriptive language, programs written in COBOL can be easily passed from generation to generation of programmers without great disruption. In contrast, imagine having to maintain a program written in C for 30 years, given the propensity of many C programmers who, for efficiency, write cryptic code with very few comments.

The term *management information system* has a ring to it that elicits nods of approval and understanding from most high-level managers. When asked "What is an MIS?", however, they will give different and sometimes conflicting answers. This chapter establishes the general characteristics and minimum requirements of a management information system.

Describing a Management Information System

An MIS invokes the image of the fully-automated corporation, in which most managers sit in their offices making decisions with the push of a button (or the click of a mouse), based on data that is only seconds old. The details of how this works are always vague, but this "grand vision" is in the back of every executive's mind.

 A management consultant tells the story of a consultant who was called into the CEO's office of a Fortune 500 company in the mid-1970s. The CEO asked the consultant to build him an MIS. The consultant asked the CEO if his accounting and inventory control systems had been automated yet. "That was done years ago," replied the Chief. "What I want is a management information system." "What information do you need that you aren't getting now?" asked the consultant. The CEO could not tell him.

Needless to say, the consultant did not get the job, and the CEO retired after spending millions of dollars on a system he did not need and could not use. An MIS system is no more than a tool used by management—a tool like the screwdriver used by a production worker. If the tool is too big or too small (or the wrong kind) it does not get the job done and might, in fact, damage the product.

The goal of any MIS is to gather relevant information and to disperse exactly what is needed when it is needed, so that managers can make intelligent and informed decisions. Too much or too little information that is badly timed performs no service.

Too much information leaves the manager with the problem of trying to glean useful data from reams of printouts or cluttered screens. Too little information forces the manager to rely on "gut instincts" and other risky methods. Badly-timed information has equally disastrous results.

Consider the predicament of an executive in a company that manufactures products with long sales cycles and equally long production cycles, so that it takes a long time between the first contact and the sale (and an equally long time between the sale and final delivery).

If the cycle, from first contact to delivery, takes two years to complete, for example, do monthly sales and production statistics make sense? Would quarterly averaging be helpful? Academic research suggests that five-year running averages are the most informative and least disruptive from a managerial point of view. With these lead times, imagine the chaos that would occur if managers based hiring and firing decisions on instantaneous information.

 Sometimes the speed of computers are a disadvantage because instant information is sometimes wrong information.

What then is the ideal management information system? First, consider its origins.

The Accounting System

Fundamental to every business is some form of an accounting system. It is not enough to collect and distribute invoices and cash. Accounts have balances, vendors and customers owe or are owed the sum of their outstanding invoices, and the net inflow or out-flow of cash determines the health of the business. These net flows and balances are the components of which an accounting system and an MIS are made.

Although accounting is primarily concerned with the ebbs and flows of income, an MIS is concerned with a lot more than that—it is the feedback mechanism that closes the loop between good ideas and reality.

A Classic Feedback Loop

Feedback is when an MIS is designed. In this context, it is part of, and separate from, an accounting system. A pure accounting system must comply with the tax code and accepted accounting practices, and these practices can sometimes distort the operations of a company. The purpose of a classic accounting system is to mini-mize taxes and maximize the apparent wealth—wealth as deter-mined by the tax code and accounting practices—of the entity.

Although minimizing taxes and maximizing apparent wealth is certainly one of the goals of management, it is not the only goal. Others include the overall health and prospects of the company which, in the long run, translate to profit for the owners.

The MIS of a Pushcart Vendor

Imagine the management information system of a pushcart ven-dor. It is a cash business: items for the pushcart are paid for in cash, and the only accounting system consists of cash receipts for the day, paper receipts for items purchased, and an itemized ac-counting of items that were lost, stolen, or given away. This system may be sufficient for taxes or for profit/loss knowledge, but it is insufficient for what the pushcart vendor needs to know to create a successful business.

Suppose that this vendor's goal is to be the proprietor of a small, profitable, stable enterprise. The goal of the MIS is to provide him with knowledge about the most profitable locations and items.

Information collected for accounting purposes only provide part of the data. Also important are data on the weather, location, vendor integrity, competition, and items sold. When a sufficient impression is made on the vendor (when he has enough feedback), he makes changes to his practice to improve his overall business. It is the process of data collection, hypothesis, and action that forms the feedback system of this vendor's management information system.

Outgrowing the "Seat of the Pants" MIS System

Larger organizations cannot rely on personal impressions for their management information systems because they are simply too big, and data that is collected in the normal course of business is too useful to be ignored. Because an MIS is a feedback system, the data collected and the data-processing methodologies used are constantly changing. As a result, a typical computerized management information system is distinguished by two factors: data collection and verification, and constant changes in the way that data is collected, processed, and analyzed.

Collecting and Verifying Data

The single most important task of an MIS is the collection of accurate data. The importance of the data-collection function is often minimized because what the executive sees (and what most of the programming effort goes into) are the reports and summary screens that close the feedback loop. Unfortunately, the axiom "garbage in, garbage out" is especially pertinent in the data-intensive, data-sensitive MIS. In this respect, data verification is as important as its original collection.

Data verification—the data you have is the data you want—poses a problem. Because any MIS is an open-ended design, you often do not know what you want or need. In this case, data verification can sometimes consist only of checking the spelling of customer names or verifying that a part number actually exists. After data has been captured, however, there are ways of ensuring its integrity throughout the system.

Data-Entry Screens

The source of data for an MIS is usually human data entry, which is relatively slow and can be error-prone. The speed of human data entry, which approaches 10 characters-per-second in short bursts, offers an excellent opportunity for software verification of the data.

Typically, data can be verified in one of two ways. Stand-alone screen-painting programs are fast and relatively compact, but they offer only *field verification*. This means, for example, that a telephone number field can be checked for numerics, but the programmer must supply the code to verify that a telephone number entered in the field belongs to the customer or that the area code and exchange are indeed located in the right town.

What is true for stand-alone screen programs holds true for data-entry screen generators that are supplied with stand-alone languages such as RM-COBOL. Data entered in this fashion can only be checked or verified off-line in a background program run at a later time. This approach's necessary delay, however, may guarantee that some data is never corrected (or may get lost).

 Because data entry is a low-overhead operation (the rate of keystrokes-per-task is low), many data-entry programs and terminals can be supported, even in a paging environment. This puts the extra overhead that is associated with modern database management systems in its best light, and it negates any advantages that stand-alone screen generators have in terms of raw speed.

The screen generators that are associated with modern DBMSs enable quick prototyping and maintenance of data-entry screens, and they have the advantage of built-in support for data verification, both in field editing and automatic data lookup in the database tables.

 An additional advantage that most (but not all) DBMSs possess over stand-alone or conventional language screens is the automatic maintenance of the integrity of each transaction. Should the system fail before all the relevant data has been entered and posted to the disk, partial transactions can be "rolled back," leaving only fully-verified data.

The penalty for the extra convenience and service of a DBMS is not very severe. Typically, a DBMS divides its activities between a data-entry process and a file-server process. Depending on the nature of the screen process, it contains the curses library, some interprocess-communications code, and field-parsing routines. In other words, the screen-presentation portion of many DBMSs is not much bigger than a stand-alone screen program.

Competing Philosophies of Commercial DBMSs

Depending on the DBMS, the file-server process can be a single large task, as with Oracle and Sybase, or a series of individual processes—one per screen—as with Informix and Progress.

From the point of view of system thrashing, a single monolithic file server is a better system, but only if no paging takes place. A monolithic file server can be locked in memory, but only at the price of reduced flexibility because these file servers are very large (typically requiring a dozen megabytes of memory). Thus, the availability of RAM for other processes is reduced.

The "one file server-per-task" philosophy has the advantage of only using system resources when needed. The disadvantage of this concept, however, is that you use more resources on a heavily loaded system.

If many users spend most of their day in the DBMS environment, a single-file server process should be the choice. If, on the other hand, users change applications frequently, and only a limited number are expected in the DBMS environment at any one time, the "one file server-per-task" system should be selected.

The decision is determined by the number of users that access the DBMS at any one time and how often the average user enters and exits a DBMS environment.

In determining which DBMS to use, you also should consider the way reports are to be generated. If all (or most) of the post-processing is to be done in the DBMS' native 4GL, the single file server is most advantageous. Often, greater advantages are to be found in using a database only as a source of raw data, with post-processing performed by using a conventional language or the UNIX tools. In these cases, no advantage is gained by a single file server.

The collection, verification, and integrity of data collected manually for an MIS is so important that the added overhead of a DBMS is a small price to pay for this service.

On networked systems, the use of remote files and database servers can impose such a strain on the network as to make their use impractical. The system designer should remember this fact when planning the placement of database tables and file servers. On networks, keeping traffic low is essential.

After verified data enters the system, it is safe from human error, except for a system crash or from errors in programming.

Automatic Data Collection

Human data entry is not the only source of information needed and used by an MIS. In a manufacturing environment, for example, an obvious source of reliable data is intelligent production machinery. The reliability of this data has more to do with programming and extra sensory equipment than with human mistakes. As a result, this data can be considered already validated, for MIS purposes, and the burden imposed by immediate processing by a DBMS is unnecessary.

The previous sections discussed the safety of data that is captured, but this safety applies to data stored internally (on disks, tape, and so forth). There also are ways to track external events and items with the same relative safety of disk storage.

Consider, for example, a company selling products from a warehouse. Orders are placed by telephone and entered by a data-entry clerk. This data entry is, of course, subject to validation. Once the data has been entered and validated, it is transmitted to the warehouse, where a *pick list* is generated. Clerks then pick the items from the shelves, pack them, and ship them.

Ordinarily, items on the pick list are checked off as they are packed. The pick list then has to be re-entered manually before an invoice can be generated. With three manual steps, the chances of error are multiplied. If the validation of the pick list could be automated, however, errors would be reduced. The solution is magnetic and bar coding.

Data Integrity—the Magnetic Strip

Magnetic coding, except on credit cards, has not been popular because it is volatile—it can be erased accidentally, for example, and you cannot visually determine if the magnetic strip is readable. There are still applications for magnetic strips—after all, it cannot be photocopied. When rigid security precautions are not necessary, however, visual bar codes are preferred; they are inexpensive and non-volatile because they are made of ink and paper.

Data Integrity—the Bar Code

One unique aspect of today's bar codes is that there is enough redundancy in the code to guarantee that, if the bar code can be read at all, it can be read correctly. Thus, a bar code that is read once is considered to have been verified, and an extra verification process is unnecessary.

There are three standard bar-code formats in use today: the familiar Universal Product Code (UPC) that is found on retail packages, and two related codes: Code 39 and Code 93. Most modern industrial bar-code readers can read all three codes, which make these codes useful in many distribution applications.

 The UPC code is assigned to every product by a standards body, which makes the UPC useful for retail-product distribution, but it is worthless for most other applications. Code 39, the de facto standard for American industry, represents the uppercase letters of the alphabet with the numbers and punctuation. Code 93 is an extension of Code 39 that is designed to encompass the entire ASCII-character set.

In the example of the product distribution company, imagine a pick list that consists of a bar-coded customer order number and bar-coded items. All the clerk has to do is to "wand" the pick list with a bar-code reader to establish which customer order is being picked, and "wand" each item as it is packed. The bar code axiom "if it can be read, it can be read correctly" ensures that whatever data is captured can be captured without error.

Similarly, serialized inventory tracking or work in progress tracking can be bar-coded with the certainty that if the item has been "wanded," the data will be recorded correctly. Bar coding can be used to replace error-prone data entry in an unlimited number of applications, and the number and diversity of bar-code reading and printing equipment is immense.

Printers include thermal-label printers, high-speed pin printers, laser printers, and even Postscript fonts for typeset-quality output. On the input side, hand-held and fixed industrial lasers are capable of reading a bar code at some distance, as well as pen and badge readers. Interactive bar-code readers resemble small ASCII terminals that have one or more lines of display, and a wand and/or keyboard for input.

 From the system integrator's point of view, bar-code readers are simple ASCII devices that are easily interfaced and defined (with easily defined `stty` parameters and—for readers with screens—as `terminfo` or `termcap` definitions).

Using the Data

Collecting data is important, but if no rational use for the data is found, its collection is a wasted exercise. Like the "chicken and the egg" syndrome, creating an MIS is difficult if what is needed or what is available is unknown.

The reality is that the most expensive study by a consultant can sometimes yield a first approximation of what is really needed. What appears to be needed often is not necessary; what is thought to be available often is not. Thus, an MIS can sometimes be considered a maintenance task as well as a design task.

An Electronic Paper Trail

A less-rigorous approach, but one that often yields better and quicker results, is to mimic an existing paper trail. This process yields efficiencies over the existing system, and it usually exposes flaws in the methods by which executive decisions are made. (These flaws are not those of the actual executive decision process; rather, they are in the validity of the data upon which those decisions are made.)

After such a system is in place, the executive will know what data is actually available and how best to use this data. Only then can the true process of designing and implementing an MIS begin.

The goal of any MIS is to give the executive what is needed to make decisions; without this knowledge, it is impossible to collect the right data in the first place. Still, a good place to start an MIS is by automating what is already available and being used, even if it is inefficient.

A good example of this design process is the automation of a very small bank. Account balances are kept on paper ledger cards using mechanical accounting machines. The first attempt at automation is to use a PC and Lotus 1-2-3 spreadsheets to create reports for regulatory purposes and account balances. At the end of each period, these are manually copied from the ledger cards into Lotus. (Lotus is used because the bank needed to calculate the balance and interest on its loans to customers and on the loans or lines of credit it had with other banks.)

After the decision to automate the entire process, the Lotus spreadsheets are discovered to be hopelessly out of sync with the ledger cards. Thus, the management has been basing decisions on false data. In this case, there is no choice except to enter and validate every entry from the ledger cards for every open account. Only then can they get the data they thought they been getting all along, and only then can they see the flaws in their accounting methodology.

The bank officers also are lucky to discover the flaw because they had been cheating themselves out of earned interest. The bank has only one kind of user account—an interest-bearing N.O.W. account, and interest on deposits were calculated and credited at the end of the accounting period. The bank also offers its customers conventional loans and leases.

The difference between a *lease* and a *loan* is simple, although the results are nearly the same. When a bank loans a customer money, the interest on the outstanding debt is charged at the end of the accounting period. (This is called calculating interest in arrears.)

A lease, on the other hand, is technically a rental in which the bank buys some equipment, holds title to it, and rents it out to the customer or lessee. Because a rental is paid for in advance, the bank calculates the lease payments, based on repayments of a loan with the interest calculated in advance.

Banks generally "sell" the lease agreement (or, more precisely, borrow against it) to a bigger bank for the amount of money equal to an equivalent loan paid for by the lease payments. The bank makes its money by keeping the first payment and any residual gained from the sale of the equipment at the end of the lease.

In this example, the bank has mistakenly calculated lease payments the same way they calculate loan payments, which raises the lease payments by about one percent. Because the bank has its own loan from a bigger bank (with interest calculated in arrears), the smaller bank overpaid the larger bank on its lease payments.

Who Needs What and When

It is essential, when designing an MIS, to determine who needs what information and to determine when they need it. As a general rule, the higher one goes in an organization's management structure, the more abstract the information becomes and the less its delivery is time-critical.

 Imagine the structure of an MIS as a great pyramid with data collected at the bottom and flowing upward. Between each level in the pyramid, the data is abstracted, summarized, or otherwise condensed with some necessary passing of time. (It is, after all, impossible to summarize data without collecting some of it first, which takes time). Abstracted data is a function of the data collected. Thus, even when you want data instantaneously, you cannot have it without some distortion of reality.

The Planning and Control Cycle

As has been said, a management information system provides feedback to management. Like all feedback mechanisms, an MIS can exert either positive or negative feedback. (It can either stabilize a company or destabilize it.)

 The difference between a stable system and a wildly unstable system is often very subtle, and the stability is completely dependent on the duration of the planning and control cycle.

The Planning Cycle for a Manufacturer of Widgets

Suppose, for example, a company manufactures widgets. It requires time to hire and train workers and more time to build inventory. Management has decided that it needs two months of inventory in its warehouse. At the beginning of the cycle, because they are manufacturing a brand-new widget, the warehouse is empty. Management hires a few extra workers to manufacture the extra inventory. If sales are static, management lays off some of the workers so that production rates equal sales rates. Sales are rarely static, however—they are subject to random fluctuations (noise in the system) and the influence of the economy as a whole, both largely unpredictable factors.

Maintaining two months' inventory is designed to absorb these fluctuations, and management has determined that two months is sufficient for changing production rates enough to meet any change in demand.

Because rises and falls in sales can temporarily raise or lower inventory levels and because maintaining inventory costs money, management is quick to lay off workers if inventory levels rise much and is slow to hire them back in the face of apparent rising demand.

Due to the time required for hiring and training workers, however, it is easier to lower production rates than it is to raise them. Thus, when sales rates return to normal, production rates are lower than needed, and management is reluctant to hire back workers. When inventory falls precipitously low, management hires back more workers—enough workers to meet demand levels and even more to raise inventory to its desired level.

The result is that the system, like all physical systems, finds its natural harmonic frequency. In this case, it oscillates between too few workers—too little inventory and too many workers—too much inventory. Management experts believe that this is the basis of the "business cycle" in the economy.

These oscillations are the result of trying to shorten the control cycle and are familiar to any engineer engaged in real-time process control.

This example was discussed to make the designer of management information systems aware of the consequences of the type of feedback provided and to suggest possible remedies.

Describing the Typical MIS System

No typical MIS system exists (except in the mythical widget manufacturing industry). Most industries have the same problems, structure, and solutions. For example, industries as different as fast food outlets, medical services, and automobile makers can all be considered to be manufacturers with the same structure. The fast-food industry must maintain an inventory of food and a supply of labor, the medical-services industry must maintain an inventory of beds and medical personnel, and the automobile industry must maintain a parts inventory and a labor pool. When viewed in this light, every piece of inventory carries with it a "bill of material." What goes into a Big Mac? What are the components of a hospital room? What are the parts of a car?

Beyond this conceptual framework, industries differ drastically. In the fast-food industry, personnel-planning may be the biggest nightmare. A hospital may be more concerned with recruiting patients and doctors and managing its work in process (making the patient better) than it is with how fast a new bed can be delivered.

An automobile may have thousands of parts, and the lack of any one part may halt the production of millions of dollars worth of inventory. Each industry has its own concerns and problems, even though each industry is a manufacturer of something. Only in this latter respect is the design of an MIS generic.

Work Flow

The work flow in an MIS can viewed as a series of interlocking feedback loops. At the lowest level, that of the data-entry clerk, feedback must be immediate. Invalid data must be returned to the user as quickly as possible for correction. With each succeeding level in the feedback mechanism, longer delays are both permissible and necessary.

Data, once entered, causes something to happen. If a new order has been entered, a pick ticket must be printed (or something that causes an item to be shipped or a service to be performed). The permitted delay depends on when the item can be shipped or when the service can be performed. In almost all cases (except in a point-of-sale situation), the action taken as a result of new data being entered does not have to take place at the highest priority (or immediately). The action can occur seconds, minutes, or even days later, depending on the situation.

Moving up one level in the system feedback, invoices can be printed and posted to an accounts receivable system. Printing invoices can occur some time after the goods or services are delivered, and posting invoices to an accounts receivable system need only take place in time to print statements or update a general ledger.

 In an MIS system, only on-line data entry need take the highest priority—everything else can "fit between the cracks."

MIS Implemented on a Mainframe

Many operating environments on IBM mainframes can support an MIS, but none can support as many data-entry terminals as CICS. In the mainframe environment, data entry is performed through CICS or off-line with Remote Job Entry (RJE). The structure of most mainframe MISs is to use CICS for on-line data entry and use one or more batch queues for everything else. Because each batch queue runs at a different priority, a well-prioritized system can be developed.

MIS Implemented on UNIX

UNIX is designed to be friendly to on-line users, which is both an advantage and disadvantage in the design of an MIS. The advantage lies in the fact that response to on-line data entry is universally fast. The disadvantage of UNIX is that background processing in UNIX is designed primarily to meet the needs of on-line users.

Specifically, `nice` has very little effect on the actual priority of a process; `at`, `cron`, and `batch` run all commands from all users with equal urgency. Thus, a CPU "hog" of low-managerial priority may block the progress of a more urgent task. It is more difficult to create a well-prioritized system on UNIX than it is in the mainframe environment. The system administrator or MIS manager must take a different kind of control of system resources in UNIX than is required in a mainframe environment.

MIS Implemented with a DBMS on UNIX

The introduction of data base management systems has been both a curse and a blessing to developers of MIS systems. The primary advantage lies in the collection of raw data. Most DBMSs contain screen-generation programs that enable fast prototyping and changes to data-entry screens. Very few DBMS screen-generation programs, however, offer the scope and flexibility of conventional programming (even those DBMSs with fourth-generation languages).

Clever designs can usually mitigate most of the flaws, but most DBMS screen-generation programs do not offer convenient ways of interacting with the UNIX environment. It becomes a trade-off between ease of use and flexibility.

Several other drawbacks may occur when using a DBMS as a programming tool. Report generators, although easy to use, generally lack the sophistication and flexibility of conventional third-generation languages, and although many enable a programmer to link in C programs, many forbid calling 4GL programs from C or any other language.

 Another drawback is that those DBMS systems that do allow linking only allow linking to C programs or to those languages that obey the C conventions. For all practical purposes, this stricture forbids the use of FORTRAN or COBOL.

A final drawback in most DBMSs is their inability to conveniently read and write standard UNIX ASCII files. All DBMSs have an ASCII import and export facility, but this is not the same as being able to integrate ASCII files easily. In many cases, this problem can be overcome, at least partially, by doing the following:

1. Use the DBMS standard report writer to generate field-delimited ASCII output. The pipe character (|) is a good delimiter because it is rarely encountered in data.

2. The report generator output can then be sent to a file or piped into a process by using the standard UNIX utilities or conventional language programs. If the results of

the process are intended to update the database, the final output must be in the database language of your specific DBMS. Today, this language is usually one of the many forms of Structured Query Language (SQL).

UNIX was never originally intended to be a commercial operating system, but the simple economics of UNIX have forced it in that direction, and the current design of UNIX, specifically Release 4, is almost an ideal platform. The following chapters discuss the deficiencies that remain and offer some solutions.

Summary

This chapter explored the concept and design of a typical management information system. Specifically, the use of various languages was explored and the reason COBOL is generally preferred to C for business applications was discussed.

This chapter described a typical management information system as a feedback loop with a natural frequency of months or years. Feedback to management is the purpose of a larger MIS accounting system.

The component parts of a management information system were discussed. The methods of collecting data, verifying it, and distributing it were explored together with issues of timing and data integrity. Finally, the implementation of a management information system as found on a mainframe was contrasted with a UNIX implementation or a UNIX MIS as implemented with a data base management system.

Topics covered in this chapter:

Managing System Resources

Minimizing Overhead with Daemons

Managing Users

Restricting Access to the Shell

**Understanding Limitations of Standard
UNIX**

Chapter 7

Resource Management

The current maxim in the computer industry, "the user is king," has resulted in the creation of many graphical user interfaces (GUIs) to make the task of the user easier. Unfortunately, a great deal of a power is wasted on GUIs if the average user spends most of the time using only one or two full-screen applications. This waste slows down or makes more costly the process of running a MIS.

The goal of a MIS is to aid in the management of a company by providing needed information in a timely fashion. The rule in a MIS environment must be "the process is king," and the management of all system resources, of which the user is only one part, must be paramount.

Managing System Resources

The goal of the system administrator is to keep the system running smoothly. The system cannot become overloaded because the performance of data collection is then degraded. (On-line data collection is, after all, the primary mission of a MIS.) To effectively administer the system, the source and timing of system loading must be known.

On-line users represent a relative constant; system use is directly proportional to the number of users logged in. If a user is logged in, but not active, very little system overhead is required above RAM use. Beyond the minimal overhead created by users that are actually logged in, on-line system overhead parallels the activity of the business day.

 In the normal 9-to-5 business environment, activity rises to a peak about 10 a.m. and again at about 11:30 a.m. Activity then declines over the lunch hour until about 1:30 p.m. Thereafter, activity rises steadily and swiftly to the day's largest peak at 4 p.m., and declines rapidly to minimal levels after 6 p.m.

Determining System Loading

This scenario represents the consistent pattern of activity in a wide range of industries. It is consistent, regardless of measurement technique. The activity-measurement techniques available include the UNIX System Activity Report, `sar`, the number of transactions-per-hour as measured by various DBMS, and the simple expedient of periodically counting the number of running processes by using the `ps` (process status) command.

This information can be used to determine how many terminals are currently connected to the system, which processes are running on each terminal, and how much CPU time has been used by each process.

To count the number of processes currently running on the system, the ps command can be piped through the wc (word count) command:

```
ps -a | wc -l
```

The -a switch causes the ps command to report all processes; the -l switch causes wc to count only lines. The output from ps is a table of data. Each row of the table represents a single process; the columns in each row report different information about the process (see fig. 7.1).

```
$ ps -e
    PID TTY        TIME COMMAND
      0 ?          0:08 Sched       Process scheduler
      1 ?          7:19 init        UNIX state control
      2 ?          0:00 vhand       UNIX "housekeeping"
      3 ?          0:02 bdflush     UNIX "housekeeping"
    129 ?          0:00 lpsched     Printer queue program
    181 ?          0:28 cron        Alarm clock
     72 tty00      0:00 getty       Terminal program
    195 tty01      0:21 sh          Your shell
     51 console    1:33 sh          Console's shell
    197 tty02      0:00 getty       Terminal program
    302 tty08      0:00 ps          This ps
$
```

Figure 7.1:
Output from the ps *command.*

So far, this chapter has only discussed system activity that is generated immediately by on-line users. These users generate considerable background activity in the MIS environment, however. For example, when a data-entry clerk enters an order from a customer, the order does not sit idly in a database. It triggers a series of actions that can include printing a "pick list", an invoice, a manufacturing order, or all of the above.

In essence, an increase in on-line activity can be magnified by the background requirements of the system. For example, if twenty seconds of on-line data entry create the need to run background programs that take over a minute to run, overall system activity can rise exponentially as the on-line activity rises linearly.

 The consequences of the explosive growth in the number of processes can be catastrophic—the system can be quickly pushed into its *thrashing region*. Because most background processing requires the use of temporary files for sorted data, it can literally use up all available disk space when combined with thrashing. UNIX and UNIX applications cannot anticipate how much disk space will be required for temporary files. As a result, applications and the operating system itself will continue allocating space to temporary files and the UNIX swap area until all available disk space is consumed. Inevitably, there will be a system crash.

Such systems complicate capacity planning because no one can accurately predict which resources are needed under these conditions. The only solution is to have more resources available than can be anticipated. Any excess file space will eventually be used for data files and new applications. It is nearly impossible to build "too much" disk space into a system.

A Second Look at Batch Processing

There is a long tradition in the minicomputer industry of ridiculing mainframes' batch queues and block mode terminals. Although mainframes may be considered obsolete by some standards, their architecture ensures that only a limited number of processes run at any one time. Interrupts on mainframe systems are controlled almost entirely by the operating system, not by external events such as user requests.

The design and number of batch queues on a mainframe can be tuned to yield the greatest throughput. By nature, a mainframe cannot enter the "thrashing region" with CICS as the user interface, and all background processes run through a batch queue.

Because of their architecture and immunity from user-originated interrupts, most mainframe systems can be pushed close to their hardware limits without performance degradation. The same cannot be said of UNIX systems. Any UNIX system that simultaneously serves a large number of users is in danger of exceeding its capacity to provide adequate disk space for temporary files, swap space, and data files. Under certain circumstances, it is quite easy to exceed the capacity of a typical UNIX system.

Ideally, any system should operate at maximum efficiency, which is well below the thrashing limit. In the case of an MIS operating on UNIX, this means limiting the number of processes that can be run concurrently. No limit should be (or can be) placed on the processes needed by on-line users (indeed, every effort must be made to accommodate the needs of users). Rather, background tasks, spawned as a result of on-line activity, need to be controlled.

Controlling Background Processes

Ordinarily, a UNIX task is launched into the background, either by using the syntax *command* & or more resolutely with the command syntax nohup *command* &. For instance, the UNIX command sort datafile1 > datafile2 & launches the UNIX sort command in the background, passing it datafile1 and the input file to be sorted, and datafile2 as the output file to receive the sorted data. A process like sort can take many minutes to complete, requiring system resources (CPY time and disk space) until completed.

Normally, there is no way to limit the number of background processes launched by users. Most UNIX systems have an intrinsic maximum number of processes that can be controlled by the CPU at one time. Even if the CPU is capable of running hundreds of concurrent processes, this limit can be exceeded by a large number of users launching background processes.

Fortunately, UNIX provides the cron command that has the capability to control the number of background processes. Because cron runs constantly in the background as a system daemon, it is possible to use cron to monitor and control the number of background processes that are permitted.

The cron daemon offers three ways to control background processes. The first is used for periodic (repeated) programming through the use of a cron table and the crontab command. The second method is the at command. (Neither the crontab or the at command are particularly useful for running ad-hoc commands generated as the result of on-line data collection.) The final commands serviced by cron, the batch commands, are preferable.

All services of the cron daemon are controlled by the queuedefs table, located in /usr/lib/cron in Release 3 and in /usr/

`sbin/cron.d` in Release 4. A typical `queuedefs` table looks like the following:

```
a.10j5n5w
b.5j10n10w
c.10j5n5w
```

It defines, for each job queue, the number of jobs, the `nice` value of each job, and how long to wait before trying to run another job if a new job is blocked. The syntax for `queuefefs` is the following:

*queue.job-count*j*nice-factor*n*wait-seconds*w

In the first example, (`a.10j5n5w`), queue *a* (as explained later, the *a* queue contains all jobs launched with the `at` command) is given a maximum of 10 jobs, each with a *nice* value of 5, and the system is told to wait five seconds before attempting to start another job in queue *a*.

The queues are defined as a = `at` commands, b = `batch` commands, and c = `crontab` commands. In the second line of the example, the `batch` queue is allowed no more than five concurrent jobs executed by `batch` at any one time, and they are run as if executed with the following:

```
nice -10 command
```

In this example, if the maximum number of five jobs are already running, `cron` waits 10 seconds before attempting to run a new job.

Any jobs pending in the *a* queue can be displayed by using the command `at -1` (this is incorporated in a shell script named `atq` on some systems).

The primary drawback of using `batch` for launching background processes is that all jobs are run with equal priority. Once running, a job launched with `batch` must be listed with the `ps` command and terminated with a `kill` command. This is both awkward and dangerous for the average user. The next section introduces methods of controlling the `batch` queue automatically and running background tasks that are both more orderly and easier to use.

Minimizing Overhead with Daemons

Data processing can be viewed either as a series of discrete processes or as a continuous flow. In truth, a combination of views is most practical. For example, when a user logs in and runs a data-entry program, the actions of the system can be viewed from the perspective of the consequences of each discrete transaction. Each transaction can be traced as an individual event, spawning tasks as it goes.

When a data-entry clerk finishes entering a customer order (a single transaction), the event of the transaction may trigger a report program that prints shipping orders. Each transaction causes the system to load a new program from disk, open files, and print the job. To minimize system overhead, each new print job has to run through the `batch` command (or its equivalent) but the operating system still has to load and execute one task for each transaction. Loading and executing generates a lot of overhead.

 Another way to look at the system is as a continuous process, in which data flows from a data-entry screen into a database, then back out as a series of reports. From this perspective, every time a data-entry screen is processed, at least one report is generated (provided, of course, that at least one transaction is completed).

Instead of running reports one at a time, it makes more sense to run a report daemon whenever its corresponding screen program is run. Thus, instead of generating multiple identical processes, only one process is run. If there are many users running the same screen program, the daemon should be made generic (able to run reports for all users).

System Loading during Transaction Processing

If multiple users are running an order-entry screen program, and each completed transaction requires a report, 20 users generating one transaction-per-minute make a total of 1200 reports-per-hour. In the process-per-transaction view of the world, at least 1200 new processes are spawned each hour and each of the 1200 new processes must be loaded and run. Each discrete process must, of course, open and read files, produce the report, and terminate with all the concomitant overhead that is created.

To gauge the overhead of simply loading and running an inconsequential program, run the following Bourne shell script with the *timex* command. For instance, create this Bourne shell with vi, name it test, and run it with timex *test*. The timex command reports the time required to run the test script.

```
x=1
while [ "$x" -lt "100" ]
do
x='expr $x + 1"
done
```

Note that this little program actually loads and runs 202 commands. First, it loads the timex command, then a Bourne Shell, sh, then two commands for each iteration—the test command,

[, and the `expr` command. On a lightly-loaded Intel 386 system with SCO UNIX, the times returned are the following:

real	6.80 seconds
user	0.88 seconds
sys	4.62 seconds

A lot of useful work can be accomplished in this amount of time, which represents almost as much elapsed time as the amount that a full-time data-entry clerk consumes on the same system in an eight-hour shift. Using the example cited earlier, 20 clerks generating 1200 extra tasks-per-hour (or 9600 tasks-per-day) consume the equivalent of 48 additional on-line users, just in the effort required to load and make the system ready to run the tasks.

Using Daemons To Reduce System Loading

Using a single *report daemon* to control transaction processes, the process is loaded once and the excessive overhead associated with launching multiple tasks is returned to the pool of available system resources. (Of course, the efficiency of this approach depends on the design of the daemon.) A daemon that merely mimics the behavior of the one process-per-transaction environment without adding some other service is a waste of time.

The report daemon should be able to process batches of transactions at a time while sleeping intermittently. The overhead associated with keeping a running daemon informed while it waits for system activity is far less than that created by spawning multiple tasks.

For daemons that must execute their tasks quickly upon the completion of a transaction, `signals` and message queues can be used. For less-urgent tasks, such as FIFO queues, *named pipes* can be employed.

Perhaps the most common method used by autonomous daemons is to periodically examine a database for activity, and, if any activity is found, to execute their tasks when enough transactions have accumulated or when an alarm timer expires.

An example of a low-overhead Bourne shell daemon using signals is the following:

```
pgmx()
{
executable instructions
}
trap 'pgmx' 15
while sleep 1
do
  :
done
```

Because this daemon spends most of its time sleeping, its only overhead, after its initial loading, is loading and running the `sleep` command. Although the `sleep` command is running, the shell script is effectively blinded to any incoming signals (except signal 9), and any number of signals may be received while the process is sleeping. As soon as the `sleep` command is finished, the daemon responds as if only one signal was received. Thus, the "granularity" of the daemon's response can be controlled by varying the duration of the daemon's sleep period. Note that the daemon is also blinded when executing the instructions inspired by the signal.

Daemons are most useful when performing tasks that are repeated dozens or hundreds of times per day. Less frequently-run tasks are better left to ordinary processing—they should be run as a background process through `batch` or an equivalent.

There are no rules about what kinds of tasks should be run as daemons or as ad-hoc processes. The balance is determined by average system overhead. Daemons consume system resources, whether or not they perform any services, but they offer the advantage of having a relatively fixed overhead. Processes that are started from the command line, on the other hand, only consume resources when they are actually run. Good system design starts as an educated guess and progresses from there.

Managing Users

The most important function of an MIS is data collection, and data-entry clerks form the backbone of this activity. Because human beings make mistakes, human action is most often the source of direct and indirect system failure. One of the key responsibilities of the system administrator is to protect the system from the aberrant user.

In the financial world, the system administrator cannot count on a fraternal and knowledgeable user base, as can be found in the engineering or academic areas. The minor sources of anxiety found in a "typical" engineering or scientific UNIX environment are magnified when the environment is financial. Security concerns are minimal, for example, when the worst that can happen is the accidental loss of a few days of one individual's work. When the very life of a financial organization is involved, however, security takes on a whole new meaning.

Security Concerns

Security precautions must be balanced by the needs of users to get their jobs done. Excessive security procedures, like multiple passwords, can impose a burden on system users. The goal of a system designer and administrator is to use those security features to be unobtrusive to the ordinary well-behaved user, but to be exclusionary to anyone with malicious or curious intent. For most financial or commercial purposes, enforced but relaxed security is adequate. Relaxed security is far harsher than the security associated with pre-Release 4 versions of UNIX and some Release 3 versions, especially SCO UNIX.

Normal UNIX security consists of very relaxed password protection during login; as well as read, write, and execute protection for the user, the user group, and all others. The enhanced, but relaxed, security features that are found in the current versions of SCO UNIX (Release 3.4) and standard UNIX Release 4, explicitly define which commands a user may access.

Modern UNIX systems are more rigorous in demanding passwords that are unlikely to be guessed (protecting the actual encrypted passwords from all but special eyes). The goal is to pose far greater obstacles to unauthorized access than previous versions of UNIX provided, but not to present insurmountable obstacles to a dedicated and knowledgeable trespasser. Diligence and common sense on the part of the system administrator can usually foil an overt break-in attempt.

> Malicious theft or destruction of data poses a far lower risk, in most cases, than does accidental destruction caused by a wayward but otherwise honest user. Accidental damage should be the system administrator's greatest concern and the system architect's greatest challenge. The source of this danger lies in the user accidentally getting to someplace forbidden and then accidentally doing something he should not do.

It is common on most UNIX systems to have a `root` user (sometimes referred to as the *superuser*) who belongs to a group named `sys` (or an equivalent); ordinary users are assigned to the group `other`. If file and directory permissions are policed adequately, this arrangement prevents ordinary users from accessing important system files (those that are owned by the root user or by the group sys). It does little good to compartmentalize users or groups of users, or to prevent them from interfering with each other, except to deny access to directories not owned by the individual users.

Assigning users to functional groups is an obvious but seldom-used strategy for preventing accidental problems. For example, if all the clerks in an accounts receivable department are assigned to the group ar and a directory is created for keeping common data for the group ar, damage to common data can be limited by giving the common directory the following attributes: it can be owned either by the group's manager or by a non-user, such as bin or sys, while being owned by the group ar. The permissions granted are read and write (but not execute) for the group ar, and all permissions are removed for all others. After creating the directory with the mkdir command, the following series of commands set the right attributes:

```
chown bin ardir; chgrp ar ardir; chmod 0760;
```

Although members of the ar group can read and write data to files in the ardir directory, they cannot peruse the directory manually. Ordinary users that are not assigned to the group ar have no access to ardir. That is, programs can read and write to the files located in the directory, but users (of the group ar) cannot use the cd (change directory) command to move into the directory and, in theory, they cannot even list its contents.

Some versions of UNIX contain a flaw that causes an unauthorized user to acquire the list of files contained in a protected directory. On these systems, UNIX responds to the ls command (for instance, ls ardir) with the message can't stat *filelist*, in which *filelist* is the list of all file names in the protected directory (in our example, the protected directory is ardir). If UNIX returns the names of files in ardir, of course, the whole reason for denying access is defeated.

Another malicious strategy that reveals the contents of a protected directory is with the following command:

```
echo dir/*.
```

This command unambiguously lists the contents of the directory. Thus, the standard UNIX file and directory security does not work.

Although unintended destruction of data can be foiled, intended destruction by a knowledgeable user is harder to prevent. For the average user, ignorance of the system is the best security if the proper precautions are taken against accidental errors.

Preventing Accidental File Removal

The most common problem is the user's accidental destruction of his own data. If given access to the shell, every user (and programmer) sooner or later issues the command **rm** *. This command removes (deletes) every file in the current directory. Normally, on a UNIX system there is no way to retrieve a deleted file (as there is with DOS). Once a file is deleted, the disk space occupied by the file becomes available to the system for storing new files.

Remember that the UNIX file and directory structure is only a logical representation of the files stored on the disk. The data itself may reside anywhere on the physical disk. When a file is deleted, the space becomes available to the system and may be immediately used for temporary files, new data files, or swap space.

Fortunately, disastrous global deletes usually occur only once in a great while, and there is a way to give the user a second chance.

The strategy for preventing the destruction of a directory and its contents stems from two distinct features of the shell. First, if a user attempts to remove a file for which the write permission has been removed, even if the user owns the file, the shell balks with the following statement:

```
file: mode 0 ?
```

If the user owns the file and truly wants it removed, he must answer the query with a **y**.

The second method of recovering from an erroneous rm * relies on the fact that the asterisk, when passed as an argument to a UNIX command like rm, causes the system to process files in ASCII sorting order. This means that the files beginning with the character lowest in the ASCII sorting order are deleted first. If you can force UNIX to stop at the first file in a directory, you get the opportunity to abort the rm command before damage is done.

The trick is to create a file in each directory with the lowest possible ASCII sorting sequence, and then to remove all permissions from it. When UNIX encounters this file (which is the first file to delete), the system stops and ask you if you mean to remove this file.

> When write permissions have been removed from a file, UNIX does not remove it without first confirming the delete.

The lowest non-special character in the ASCII character set is the plus sign. By creating a file named +, and then removing all permissions with the command **chmod 0 +**, the user has a second chance as soon as you type **rm ***.

When rm encounters the file + (the first file encountered due to its sorting order), it responds with +: mode 0 ?. If the user is conscious, he probably realized the mistaken rm * command as soon as he pressed the Enter key. The presence of the file named + gives the user a chance to abort the rm * command before any damage is done.

The easiest way to create a file whose presence has significance, but whose content is irrelevant, is to use the command **>file**. This command creates a file of 0 length. These kinds of files are useful for preventing more than one daemon from running at the same time and for creating a + file in each protected directory.

Restricting Access to the Shell

So far, this chapter has discussed the security concerns when users are allowed access to the shell. A better solution is to prohibit ordinary users access to the shell. Users should be given access to the applications they need, of course, which is where they should spend most of their time.

An easy way to control users and guide them through a maze of different applications is with the use of menus. The next section introduces a simple menuing system that can be used to tie together different applications and, at the system administrator's option, prevent users from having access to the shell. Of course, no menu can prevent the user from gaining access to the shell if the application program permits it, so the system administrator must be cognizant of which applications offer a shell option.

For example, any user that has been placed in a restricted shell can still gain full, unrestricted access on some systems by invoking the vi editor, even if the shell environment variable has been exported. Many DBMS also offer hidden shell escapes that may or may not pass along the shell restriction.

Controlling Data Flow and Ownership

One of the advantages of segregating users into groups is that it is almost impossible for each group to interfere with each other. On the other hand, this same strength imposes obstacles when different groups interact with each other. For example, sooner or later the accounts receivable (ar) group must interact with other groups in the accounting department. With groups that are rigidly segregated by file and directory permissions, interactions between them are impossible.

One way around this dilemma is to use a transient directory with read and write permissions for all. When one group wants to transmit data to another, a file containing that data is placed in the common directory. A member of the receiving group then picks up the data for processing. In most cases, this works well, but the very existence of a common pool of data poses a security threat. One way to avoid this potential quagmire is by using electronic-mail systems to send binary data files or to use daemons.

Although it is certainly easier to move data around with the use of shell scripts, binary programs have the advantage of enabling the system administrator to set the *set user ID (SUID)* bit to on. This setting changes the ownership of the running program from the user who ran the program to the user (or group) who owns the program. Thus, a user can run a program with the status of a user who has the capability to move data from any directory to another.

Because it is easier to accomplish these movements with shell scripts, only a very minimal C program is necessary, as in the following:

```
main()
{
    system("shell script");
}
```

On most systems, a compiled and stripped executable file is fewer than one thousand bytes long and occupies, when running, the absolute minimum number of pages in memory.

On older, less-secure UNIX systems, manipulating the set user ID bit and *set group ID (SGID)* bit were a strategy for illicitly gaining superuser status. A user could make a copy of the Bourne shell; set the set user and set group bits to on; change the mode of the file to full read, write, and execute permission for all; and change the ownership of the file to `root`. When such a purloined shell was run, the user had full superuser status. Most modern versions of UNIX prohibit the illicit manipulation of the SUID and SGID bits.

Moving Data between Groups with a Mailer Daemon

A second way to transfer data from one user group to another is to use a *mailer daemon*. In this case, the daemon can be a shell script run by `root` from within one of the `rc` files or by `cron` from the system administrator's `crontab` file.

This process is simple. The system administrator creates two subdirectories within each common group directory. One of the subdirectories is used for outgoing data and the other is used for incoming data. Because the *mail* directories are within the common group directory, they are protected by the wall of user permissions. A daemon run by `root` has privileges that can surmount any wall of protection, however.

As a result, a daemon can pick up and deliver data "packages" from one group and deliver them to another. Although these daemons only pick up and deliver data, it is still incumbent on the local group to process the data. The data processing can be done by a daemon, but this time the daemon is owned and run by the local group.

Writing a mailer daemon is relatively straightforward. The following sample daemon can be run by `cron` via an entry in the system administrator's `crontab` file. The sample daemon assumes that there are five groups—ar, ap, gl, pr and ic—and that the common directory for each group is a directory named after the group (the ar group maintains a common directory in /usr/ar).

 NOTE In Release 4 systems, the directory is /home/ar.

It is assumed that the directories for incoming and outgoing data are within the common directory, and that they are called in and out. The last assumption is that the files within the transfer directories are named after their destination. In other words, files from ar destined for the gl group have names beginning with gl. A typical file from ar, intended to be sent to gl, has the path /usr/ar/out/glx, and the daemon places it in /usr/gl/in/glx. The following is the sample daemon in Bourne shell script:

```
:
umask 0; # give all moved files rwx permission
for k in gl pr ic ap ar
do
    for i in gl pr ic ap ar
    do
        x='echo /usr/${k}/out/${i}*'
        if [ -n "$x" ]
        then
            for j in $x
            do
                if [ -s $j ]
                then
                    cp $j /usr/${i}/in
                    rm $j
                    chgrp $i /usr/${i}/in/$j
                fi
            done
        fi
    done
done
```

Conceptually, this process looks like the diagram in figure 7.2, in which data is picked up from one bin and dropped into another.

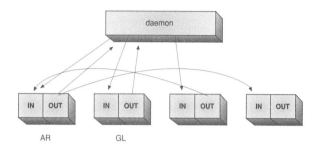

Figure 7.2:
The data mailer daemon.

Using daemons is better than using binary mailers because they give the system administrator full control of both the flow of data and the ownership of that data. Note too that any shell daemon that is owned and run by `root` has the capability to "substitute user" with the `su` command without having to know any passwords.

Because they are the targets for mischief, these daemons must be well protected, with read, write, and execute permissions for `root` only (and no permissions for anyone else).

Similar daemons can be used for intersystem communications. If communications daemons are used blindly (byte-for-byte), transfers can be used between systems on a local area network.

The system administrator should be aware of the potential security problems posed by routing sensitive data over public channels, such as X.25, the Internet, or by `uucp`.

The next section offers a simple encryption and decryption system, designed to code ASCII text for automatic transmission over public media.

Understanding Limitations of Standard UNIX

UNIX possesses few of the features that are considered standard and almost mandatory in the world of the mainframe MIS. Raw UNIX consists of nothing more than a multitasking platform with excellent networking utilities, reasonably fast disk I/O, and a standard programming toolkit, with which an MIS system can be fashioned. It is up to the UNIX programmer to provide some semblance of these services, when needed, from the collection of tools at his disposal. There are limitations, however, which can only be resolved by the designers and distributors of the UNIX family of operating systems.

Security Limitations

This chapter has mentioned several strategies for maintaining relatively good security on standard UNIX systems. Good security depends entirely on the vigilance and competence of the system designer and administrator, however. The result is that the security of a system is problematic and time-consuming. What is usually required is automatic enforcement of security provisions. Automation causes other problems, however.

On some versions of UNIX, notably SCO UNIX and Release 4, the system administrator may choose either relaxed or enforced C2 security. The C2 designation for system security is a U.S. Government standard that indicates a medium level of "trust" (normal UNIX systems are not considered trustworthy). With C2 security in force, an *authorization administrator* can define exactly which programs any user is entitled to run, and any user can define directories that are secure from programs that change the effective user ID. The login ID of a user is maintained separately from the effective user ID, which ensures that a logged-in user cannot execute programs that are forbidden by the authorization administrator, even if the user's effective ID has become `root`.

The major drawback to C2 security is the added burden placed on the superuser. For C2 security to be effective, audits must be run and checked, authorizations must be maintained, and the system administrator must use the system administration program (`sysadm` on Release 4 or `sysadmsh` on SCO UNIX).

It was common practice, with older versions of UNIX, for the superuser to manually update system tables. This is no longer allowed because one of the security checks performed on system tables is the synchronization of the date and time of file updates. For example, the system administrator cannot manually update the `uucp Systems` file without signaling that the `uucp` system has been tampered with. Once tampering has been detected anywhere in the system, the system is *crashed* by the security subsystem. Clearing such a tampered system requires about as much effort as clearing a real crash.

The system administrator must also realize that maintaining audit and other log files on a C2 system requires a conscious effort, and that un-policed logs will grow and eventually consume all available disk space.

Process Control

This chapter has stressed in great detail the need for a very tight control of processes that are spawned by users. Put simply, the larger the system, the greater the variability in demand for resources. At off-peak hours, the system may be very lightly used; at peak times any system can easily reach its *thrash point*, and, given the need for temporary storage, almost any system can easily run out of disk space.

Engineering applications, as a rule, have little need for sorting data. As a result, capacity planning is relatively straightforward and limited mostly to providing adequate disk space for anticipated data-file needs.

In a typical commercial or financial MIS, however, sorting is one of the primary tasks and the use of temporary disk storage is immense. As a result, there is an overwhelming need to control user-spawned processes, both to reduce the threat of thrashing and to provide temporary storage.

Standard UNIX offers only marginal control of background processes, but the tools are available to the system administrator to correct these defects. The next section introduces several systems, using the standard UNIX tools, that help gain control of background tasks.

System Toolkit Limitations

The fundamental *unit* of an MIS is a transaction that consists of accepting data from some source and updating any number of files. If the transaction aborts for any reason, the database must be rolled back to remove any incomplete transactions in order to maintain the integrity of the system. Systems that are written in shell script cannot guarantee the integrity of data and, without considerable effort, the same applies to programs written in C.

Although a complete MIS can be written in C, or even in shell script, it would be difficult to support and maintain. In this respect, the standard UNIX toolkit is unequal to the task. Indeed, any third-generation language, by its nature, cannot perform true *transaction processing* without the services of a transaction-processing monitor. This service is usually performed by most modern database management systems (a DBMS is considered a mandatory component of any MIS).

Unfortunately, besides the ill-defined Structured Query Language, there are few standards in DBMS. Although dozens of benchmarks are performed each year on DBMS, there is no reliable and independent source for performance and integrity information. Let the buyer beware.

Summary

This chapter surveyed some of the primary concerns regarding resource management. At the same time that sufficient data security must be provided, user access to resources must be easy and trouble-free.

The number of background processes spawned by users must be monitored. It is easy to drive a UNIX system into the thrashing region if too many background processes using temporary files are running simultaneously.

Most data loss on UNIX systems occurs by accident or oversight, rather by than malicious intent. Through the simple expedient of carefully controlling user and group access to data files, most accidental data loss can be prevented. A scheme was presented using a mailer daemon to transfer files between groups needing to share data. The mailer daemon runs as a `root` process, enabling it to create the data files in directories that are not accessible to normal users.

Resource planning can be difficult for management information systems. Because of the need to frequently sort large data files, it is difficult to predict the disk-space requirements of the typical MIS.

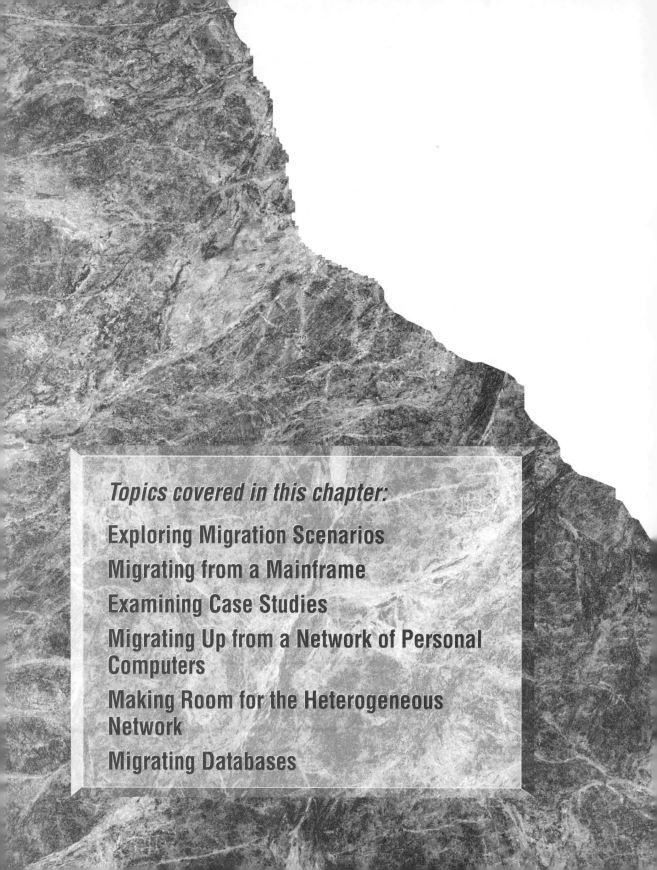

Topics covered in this chapter:

Exploring Migration Scenarios

Migrating from a Mainframe

Examining Case Studies

Migrating Up from a Network of Personal Computers

Making Room for the Heterogeneous Network

Migrating Databases

Chapter 8

Migration Strategies

Unless you are building a system from scratch, you must migrate an existing system from somewhere else. This means either migration down from a mainframe or midrange computer, or migration up from a personal computer or network of personal computers. In each case, there are constraints that govern the design of a UNIX-oriented management information system (MIS). This chapter discusses the concerns, concepts, and methods required to perform this migration.

Exploring Migration Scenarios

The only migration scenario that is ideal from a design standpoint (and one of the worst from an equipment and expense viewpoint) is that of replacing a small mainframe or midrange system with a single UNIX system. In this case, all hardware and software is replaced, and users are retrained.

In an ideal world, the long-term costs are lower than that of other scenarios—in fact, the cost of converting to a UNIX-based system may be lower than the cost of replacing an aging small mainframe or midrange system. The design advantage stems from the fact that single UNIX systems can support as many as three or four hundred dumb terminal users, hundreds of megabytes of RAM, and dozens of gigabytes of disk storage. Such processors are currently falling below $100,000 in cost, and dumb terminals are falling below $200, for a cost-per-user of under $600. At the same time, an equivalent small mainframe or midrange system costs more than triple that of a UNIX system, and a network of personal computers costs at least $1000 per user.

Ironically, creating larger or smaller systems both pose the same problem. Replacing large mainframes requires networks of UNIX systems; enhancing and eventually replacing a network of personal computers requires the same skills, although the aggregate number of users may be fewer. The problem with both design alternatives is the limited bandwidth of most networks.

Network Issues

In the case of Ethernet, the maximum theoretical throughput is 10 megabits-per-second, which translates to about one megabyte-per-second. Unfortunately, Ethernet can never reach its true transmission speed potential because each node on the network is free to transmit messages whenever it chooses. If a collision between two data packets occurs, each transmitter backs off and waits a few milliseconds before attempting to retransmit its packet. As the network becomes more and more loaded, the chances of packet collisions increase until the network equivalent of thrashing takes place.

Whatever the actual thrashing point of an Ethernet really is ("experts" claim it is anywhere between 1/3 and 1/2 of the 10-megabit theoretical maximum), it is well below the throughput of modern small computer system interface (SCSI) disks on a UNIX system.

The other popular network technology, token ring, is more efficient than Ethernet because the only inhibition to its maximum bandwidth is the overhead associated with passing the token. Still, the maximum speed of most token-ring networks is only 10 megabits-per-second. Newer technology offers a maximum throughput of 100 megabits-per-second, but because the technology is still new, it is both expensive and not widely known, relative to Ethernet. Device drivers or interface hardware for FDDI and CDDI may not be available for all platforms.

Examining Migration Issues

The major technical problems encountered in migrating to a UNIX-oriented system are the problems inherent in porting databases and programs, as well as the design of data flow within the networks. Porting databases and programs is relatively difficult, yet straightforward.

Designing networks is another matter. In view of the limited bandwidth available on most networks, a network designer must go to great lengths to avoid transmission bottlenecks. Network routers and gateways can only go so far in limiting data traffic, so a conscious effort must be made to analyze and properly design the use and function of each node on the network with a goal of limiting, as much as possible, unnecessary data traffic.

Migrating Down from a Mainframe or Midrange System

The concept of migrating "down" from a mainframe to a UNIX system is a funny statement. After all, the standard mainframe in 1970 could support 20 or 30 users, and today's personal computers have far more power than most minicomputers of that era. Today, midrange systems vary from a four-user IBM System 34 through a 40-plus-user IBM AS400, and the concept of a mainframe varies from a dozen-user low-end IBM 4341 to networks of IBM 3990 systems supporting tens of thousands of users. "Big" systems from other vendors fall somewhere within this broad range.

The actual process of migrating from any one system to any other system, UNIX or not, is the same. It is painful and only to be attempted if there is some compelling reason to do so. In the case of UNIX, the major reason to migrate is cost. Because UNIX runs on almost every type of computer hardware, it is the most inexpensive system to purchase, operate, and program. UNIX is more or less uniform on all systems, and it is the first operating system available on new equipment. Another advantage of migrating to UNIX is that, once installed, no retraining is necessary, even if a further migration to a different manufacturer's equipment takes place.

The next section covers porting data and programs from a midrange system to UNIX. These steps also are necessary when migrating from a mainframe, but with the added complication of planning the flow of data over networks.

Migrating from a Midrange System

As a general rule, midrange system capacities fall within the capabilities of single UNIX systems (systems that do not require the use of networks). In these cases, hardware problems should be minimal when performing a migration from these mid-size computers to single UNIX computers. The bulk of the migration headache consists of moving and converting the data and programs from the originating computer's operating system to UNIX. This process can be more problematic if the system being migrated is commercial software. If this is the case, seek the help of the package's software vendor. Software vendors who have ported their products to UNIX are often willing to help you with your migration because future upgrades and compatibility issues become easier. It is assumed for the remainder of this discussion that the porting task involves data of known format and available source code for all programs.

Migrating from one system to another (unless it is from one UNIX system to another) always involves deciding where to start. The very first task begins on the system being migrated from: binary data must be converted to ASCII or EBCDIC. This process is repeated several times while the transfer is rehearsed.

 Remember that one of the goals of a successful migration is to have as little impact on users and on operations as possible.

Planning the Data Transfer

The first step in the migration task is to determine what data transfer mechanism you should use to physically move data and programs. Each midrange computer uses different formats for storage media. For instance, magnetic-tape formats differ, as do floppy-disk formats. Older midrange systems use nine-track reel-to-reel tape formats; newer systems use cartridge tapes and can read and write MS-DOS floppies. It often takes some experimentation and innovation to come up with a successful strategy to bridge these incompatibilities.

The most obvious problem and one of the easiest to deal with is the conversion from EBCDIC to ASCII. After you find a reliable transmission media, the UNIX dd command performs the conversion of data from EBDIC to ASCII. The major problem is to find fast and reliable transmission media.

The following presents a list of alternative methods for data transfer:

❖ **Nine-track tape.** Most UNIX systems support nine-track reel-to-reel tape, but they are relatively uncommon on small UNIX systems and are generally expensive add-ons offered by third-party vendors. One solution is to hire a service bureau to perform the transfer because they generally have one of every storage device. The midrange computer also might have a nine-track tape drive attached, which solves the transmission issue. If no tape drive is attached, the migration project manager must decide on a vehicle to perform the transfer. Because the tape will be relatively useless after the migration has taken place (faster cartridge tapes are more useful), the migration manager must weigh the cost of purchasing or renting a tape drive ($3,000 to $10,000) against the cost and delay involved in using a service bureau.

❖ **Cartridge tapes.** Several dozen magnetic-tape cartridge standards exist. By accident, the QIC 120/150 format has become a de facto standard on small UNIX systems. In the future, digital-audiotape formats may become UNIX standards, as may helical-scan tapes from companies like ExeByte. The point is that cartridge tapes do not offer much as an exchange medium, except between UNIX systems. A service bureau may be able to convert your midrange tape into a tape format that is readable.

❖ **Floppy disks.** Thanks to the widespread use of personal computers (PCs), the MS-DOS 5 1/4-inch and 3 1/2-inch disks have become standard media for data interchange. Most midrange systems can read and write these disks, as can many UNIX systems, especially those based on the PC architecture. Even for those situations in which neither system can directly read MS-DOS disks, the market has demanded and received inexpensive ways to connect PCs. Thus, an inexpensive IBM PC or clone can serve as a bridge between almost any two systems. (Of course, it is daunting to move several hundred megabytes of data one high-density floppy—or 1.2 megabytes—at a time).

❖ **Hard-wired connections.** Cabling the originating computer to the new system is another means to affect data transfer. The shortcomings of this method are its speed and capacity. The volume of data can be prohibitive or the cost of making the connection can be too expensive to use this media.

For direct data transfer to work, the originating system must already be able to "speak" ASCII. In some cases, this requires additional hardware and software to translate and control the data being transferred from the originating system to the new system, which may be expensive.

Although a direct transfer, called an *ASCII dump*, from a midrange system can be used, a better idea is to use one of the many file-transfer programs, such as `Term` or `MLINK`, as an intermediary. These applications are available for most UNIX and midrange systems and implement transfer protocols to enhance data exchange. Using a protocol transfer instead of a straight ASCII dump ensures data integrity during the transfer.

Because of the overhead imposed by the transfer protocol, these applications are, by nature, slower than dumping data. Yet, because these transfers use software handshaking between blocks of data being transferred, this technique can almost guarantee that buffers on the UNIX system are not overflowed and that any data-transmission errors are caught and corrected.

Possible Complications of a Hard-Wired Transfer

In theory, any system that can emulate an ASCII teletype interface will respond to the start and stop transmission signals (Ctrl-Q and Ctrl-S). In addition, most systems recognize the hardware signals on the *request to send* (RTS) and *data set ready* (DSR) pins of the RS-232 interface. In practice, however, many systems do not respond fast enough to a stop transmission signal to prevent data from overflowing the buffers on the UNIX system. When an overflow occurs, data is inevitably lost.

Even with proper hardware or software handshaking, data transmission over serial data lines may be painfully slow. Transferring 40M at 9600 baud, for example, takes more than 11.5 hours. Because UNIX systems are generally "tuned" to receive uninterrupted data at a slower rate (over serial lines), it may be necessary to execute the transfer at an even lower rate. At 2400 baud, the same 40M transfer takes about 46 hours.

Translation Issues during Porting

Regardless of the language used by the originating data and applications (even if they are based upon UNIX), implementations differ, and it is indeed rare for source code that runs flawlessly on one system to compile or run on another system. It also is unreasonable to expect programmers that are conversant in one system to converse instantly and flawlessly in another. A programmer's learning curve for any new programming language is always steepest at the beginning. The porting period also is the best time for programmers to become proficient in UNIX.

 Be patient. The migration from any system to UNIX is revolutionary; after that, it becomes evolutionary.

Before porting begins, a good strategy is to examine the originating system. Is the old system's native language worth maintaining or can the functionality of the old system be more easily created and maintained with a new language or DBMS? Most languages have been ported to UNIX, but some languages are now obsolete or exist with other more-modern standards. Finding and keeping experienced personnel to maintain these systems can be costly. On the other hand, migrating to a new language or DBMS requires retraining or hiring personnel. If you plan to simply port the old software, is that software well-designed and structured to efficiently run under UNIX?

The least-portable programs are usually data-entry screens, which often contain embedded screen-control codes. Because these programs must be reworked (often by writing and linking in C functions), it is easier to replace these programs with commercially available screen-design programs or with the data-entry programs of database management systems.

Screen-design programs generate portable C code that performs the screen painting and field parsing required by data entry on dumb terminals. That is all they do, however. File access must still be performed by other code, written either in C or in some language that can be linked to C.

The latter is often not easy to do because many languages are implemented as p-code. That is, the language compiler only reduces source code to an intermediate and transportable binary code (p-code). This binary code cannot be executed directly on any system; it must be interpreted by a run-time program (also called an *interpreter*). Some of the most popular business-oriented languages, such as RM-COBOL and Business BASIC, are implemented as p-code.

Many languages that use p-code implementations also can use programs written in C by calling these programs with a `system` function call or by relinking the run-time program with the required C routines. This last approach can cause some problems, though. Relinking a run-time program is not always easy, and the fact that C programs must be incorporated within the run-time program limits the C code's usefulness. You must either incorporate all needed C routines into one very large run-time program or create many different run-time programs.

Programming languages that can be directly linked to C routines often pose minor problems for novice programmers because the languages have added complexity due to those linkages. Problems in converting such programs are caused by the way the programs pass variables to their functions and subroutines. FORTRAN, CO-BOL, and most conventional languages pass function or subroutine arguments by address. Programs written in common business languages, such as COBOL or FORTRAN, use a format in which the arguments `a,b,c` in a command called `pgm(a,b,c)` are transferred automatically, bypassing the address of the variables. In C, however, arguments are often passed by value. For example, simple variables are passed by their values, whereas more complex arrays and strings pass their arguments by address. Knowing what is being passed and its inherent format is very important in C, but it is irrelevant in most other high-level languages.

The last danger in direct porting source code from one environment to another, specifically from an EBCDIC to an ASCII environment, is that binary string matches can fail. Programs that count on the binary value of specific characters fail because the ASCII- and EBCDIC-character sets are different. Because an "a" in EBCDIC has a different binary value than an "a" does in ASCII, programs that depend on the sorting order of EBCDIC have problems when the data is converted to ASCII.

If the difficulties involved in directly porting old source code appear insurmountable, an alternative can be found in a fourth-generation language or even in a simple database language. The primary distinction between a fourth-generation language and a third-generation language, such as COBOL, is that, in addition to the normal programming syntax of a third-generation language, fourth-generation languages usually incorporate a true database as well as screen-generation and report-generation extensions. These extensions have file and record access provided by some version of Structured Query Language (SQL).

Modern fourth-generation DBMSs offer several advantages over third-generation languages. For instance, after the database tables (files) have been defined, a DBMS utility can load properly prepared ASCII files very quickly. Expeditious loading is important if the migration is to proceed smoothly and quickly. After the data has been loaded into the database field, any modification, such as expanding the size of a field, can usually be done quickly and painlessly. These modifications can often be accomplished without having to recompile application programs. Finally, most DBMSs have data-entry screen subsystems that enable a programmer to quickly prototype screens while file access, field verification, and transaction management processes are handled automatically. Work that takes weeks of effort using a conventional programming language can often be accomplished in hours with a DBMS language.

Testing and Rehearsals

Migrating from a non-UNIX system to a UNIX system is an evolving process. After you find a way to transfer data and programs from one system to another, the second task is to transfer the functionality of the old system to the new system. This process involves porting the old software or writing totally new software. The migration cycle involves repeating the transfer of data, formatting and loading a database or data files, testing the software, and testing the new hardware.

The goal of the migration effort is to use the old system through the close of business on Friday and have the new system ready for operation at the start of business the following Monday morning. For a midrange system, the goal of a weekend migration can be accomplished, but only by repeated rehearsals of the switchover, by exhaustive testing of the new software before switchover, and by adequate training of users.

Milestones for the testing period are as follows:

- ❖ Functional review of the existing system, compared closely to the new system
- ❖ Data and program-porting methodology adopted and tested
- ❖ Design, writing, and testing of the new system
- ❖ Installation and testing of the new cabling system
- ❖ User and administrator training
- ❖ Practice migrations, including unloading the old system and loading the new system

Use a migration shell script to write the procedures for the migration. In the heat of the actual switchover, things can be forgotten or overlooked. If all the procedures are incorporated into a shell script (complete with prompts as to what should happen on the old system as well as the new), and a successful rehearsal is accomplished with that script, very little should go wrong during the actual transition.

Migrating from a Mainframe

The definition of a mainframe has been blurred for some time. Systems that used to be classified as minicomputers have far more power today than do many modern low-end mainframes. For this discussion, a *mainframe* is considered to be a system that supports more users and has more resources than are today available on a single conventional UNIX system.

What, then, is a conventional UNIX system? A *conventional UNIX system* is a minicomputer or super-microcomputer that runs UNIX and requires a network of UNIX-based computers or minicomputers to perform the same work as a single mainframe.

This section describes two migration scenarios used to move data from a mainframe to a UNIX environment. The first method is a two-part process, moving from the originating software to mainframe UNIX and from there to a conventional UNIX system. The second method takes a more direct approach by moving from the originating mainframe system to the new UNIX system.

Mainframe UNIX as an Interim Migration

Several good versions of UNIX run on mainframes, and migrating to these versions of UNIX as an interim step is not a bad idea. Amdhal's UTS is a version of UNIX System V Release 3 that is modified for EBCDIC and supports conventional mainframe block-mode terminals. One of the advantages of migrating to this kind of UNIX is that the life of the mainframe hardware can be extended while programmers learn UNIX. Also, UNIX can coexist on the same hardware platform with classic mainframe-operating systems such as MVS.

If you select an interim migration to a mainframe-based UNIX, the mainframe can be divided into multiple virtual machines using partitioning systems. At the beginning of the migration process, all virtual machines will be running a proprietary operating system, such as MVS. When the migration begins, one of four virtual machines can be converted to run UTS; the remainder will still be running MVS.

As programs are migrated, each virtual machine is switched over to UNIX in turn. This migration path was chosen by at least one of the "Baby Bell" operating companies for its telephone billing systems. The design goal was to complete the migration to UNIX on the mainframe and then to begin to migrate to smaller and faster UNIX systems as the design life of the mainframe and its components came to a close.

Direct Data Transfer

The second migration path confronts the replacement of the mainframe directly and is the next logical step in the migration path just described. Before any physical migration can take place, however, a psychological migration must first occur. Programmers and system managers must realize that, under UNIX, much of the tight control they previously held over an MIS process is lost, and that the process itself requires different controls than programs required under a centralized mainframe-based organization.

 The migration process resembles the dismembering of an onion—each successive layer of the MIS is removed from the mainframe and placed on successively more remote and smaller systems until the core of the system, the mainframe, becomes an empty shell that performs little or no work.

The concept of this second migration path is easier to grasp than it is to execute. Mainframes that have vast resources can support hundreds or thousands of files and can support as many or more application programs. Before any migration can take place, these files must be sorted into functional groups. Ideally, these functional groups consist of the following:

- ❖ Stand-alone or communications-dependent applications
- ❖ Data-entry programs with limited database querying
- ❖ Secondary (or summary) batch programs
- ❖ Secondary database programs (communications-oriented)
- ❖ Tertiary batch programs

The goal of such functional groupings is to determine where applications can eventually be placed in the new UNIX-based system and to determine the potential volume of data communications that lies between the new functional groupings.

Examining Case Studies

If you select the direct approach, the next step is to begin the migration process. As mentioned in Chapter 1, begin the porting process by replacing block-mode terminal controllers with UNIX systems that are capable of emulating terminal controllers. Users and programmers can then get used to the UNIX environment while stand-alone and communications programs are migrated.

After replacing the communications interface, move the data to the new platform. Ideal candidates for initial migration are word processors, spreadsheets, and electronic mail.

Moving data-entry programs is more problematic than migrating word processors. Verification of the data may involve searching any number of files of almost any size on the mainframe. Data entry must be fast, and one reason to migrate to a UNIX system is to provide more computer power per user for this task. As a result, it is necessary to fragment the corporate database. Fragmenting goes against the grain of most mainframe programmers and system architects, whose instincts tell them to consolidate data rather than disseminate it. In the structure of an MIS, however, only highly abstracted data is needed at the top.

 If data verification takes "forever" on the mainframe, serious consideration should be given to redesigning the application.

The data-entry clerk, for example, needs to use customer names and account balances, but the chairman of his company is only concerned with the overall health of the company—names and balances of individual accounts are irrelevant.

WARNING Another danger in the design of a UNIX-oriented MIS is to push too much data and processing to the periphery.

The onion analogy serves well here. Each ring in an onion is a sphere of (more or less) uniform thickness. By analogy, the surface area of each sphere represents the number of users who input or receive data contained in the volume of each ring.

As figure 8.1 illustrates, each successive inner sphere receives its data abstracted from the next sphere external to it. Thus, although the outer sphere (that of data collection) contains the greatest surface area of any individual ring, it is dwarfed by the volume of data contained within its particular ring.

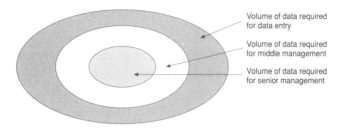

Volume of data required
for data entry

Volume of data required
for middle management

Volume of data required
for senior management

Figure 8.1:
Data required by successive levels of management.

The object of a successful UNIX system design is to balance the needs of each successive class of users with the accessibility of data, keeping in mind that the greatest limitation in any system is the bandwidth of the networks required to carry intra-system data.

Order Entry Systems

The design of an order-entry system for a large corporation is a good example of the usefulness of data fragmentation on UNIX systems. Assume that the order-entry department is localized in one building and supported by one large UNIX system with 200 users. What information do the users need and how is it going to be delivered to them?

For an order-entry system to work, clerks need access to basic customer information—in this case, a very large file. If the accounts-receivable department (in another building and on another system on the network) also needs customer information, how should the information be shared? The choices are the following:

❖ The master customer file can reside on either the order entry or accounts receivable system and can be shared by using NFS over the network.

❖ The master customer database can reside at the source (order entry), and a duplicate can be kept on other systems, with any changes or updates made by messages over the network. This obviously involves a duplication of data.

❖ The master customer database can be kept anywhere on the system that has available disk space, and a network-oriented DBMS can be used to synchronize queries over the network.

Each of these options has advantages and disadvantages. The first option appears to be the cleanest and easiest to control, but if the network is based on Ethernet or any other 10 megabit-per-second network, the network presents a potential bottleneck (modern SCSI disks can read data at a rate approaching 10M-per-second.)

Thus, whichever system reads the file over the network is very slow, and the network quickly reaches saturation.

 If the network is based on one of the new 100-megabit media such as FDDI, the saturation problem is somewhat reduced. Even with a 100-megabit network, however, there is still network saturation because a 100-megabits-per-second network has about the same bandwidth as a single SCSI disk. If there are 10 systems on the network, and each has at least one SCSI disk (each capable of delivering 10M of shareable data), a 100-megabit network is still too slow. Network file-sharing only works if the files are small or rarely accessed.

The second option is preferable to the first. If the source database is duplicated, the data is accessible whenever it is needed, and the only network traffic are periodic updates sent from the master file. Duplicating data, however, is a curse to the data-processing profession—there must be a better way.

The third option may be the best choice. Many modern DBMSs support networked databases, which means that, with file servers running on all relevant systems, only the immediate query and the matching data is passed over the network using NFS.

In terms of network traffic, this option represents a compromise between the other two options. Option two represents the least possible data traffic on a network (as well as the most secure and least network-dependent solution), whereas option one requires a program to read and write entire files over the network.

The only drawback to option three is that the database manager is required to keep all *tables* (database files) synchronized, and the data dictionary for a particular database must be accessible to all systems on the network. This requirement implies the interdependency between the systems on the network: if any system on the network goes down, all remaining dependent systems on the network go down as well. When deciding on a DBMS, be aware of how that DBMS uses the network.

As stated earlier, the design of a system is always a compromise between many imperfect alternatives. In truth, the design of a UNIX network as a replacement for a mainframe inevitably results in an imperfect use of all three options, specifically when lower-speed networks, such as T1 or fractional T1 data lines, X.25, ISDN, and ordinary modem lines enter the system in support of remote locations.

Migrating Up from a Network of Personal Computers

Personal computer networks have been so well-marketed that people normally consider migrating to a UNIX system only after a

PC-based network reaches saturation, and they realize that more horsepower is needed at the back end rather than at the front end of the data-processing cycle. Remember the onion analogy: as a PC network grows and assumes more functions, its sphere continues to grow. Eventually, the system balloons into a thin sphere that supports lots of users but with a lot of empty volume inside.

For any new business or any business beginning to automate, adding personal computers is a natural evolutionary process. As that company grows, its PCs also proliferate. Eventually, the MIS function, which began as a simple accounting system, expands beyond the capabilities of a few users and their PCs.

Because most business users dread learning a new system or changing software, networking the PCs together to form a larger system is the only answer. This PC network typically is designed as a client-server architecture with data files and programs residing on a centralized PC designated as the server, and data dispersed to the client PCs using the equivalent of a Sun Network File System (NFS).

Processing Data on a PC Network

When a client PC runs a program, it retrieves the binary file from the server as if the file name is locally mounted. Every byte of the program must be transported across the network before it can be executed. When the program executes, all of the required data also must be read across the network from the server. The only function of the server in this design is to deliver data; thus, no processing other than I/O management takes place.

This scheme works fine when only two or three systems are on the network and if the data traffic is only a few hundred thousand bytes-per-second. Networks, however, continue to grow as long as the company does. Fortunately, most PCs use disk-access technology that can access data at rates of only a few hundred thousand bytes per second. With such relatively low access rates, if there is only one server on a PC network, the network never becomes saturated. As I/O requests increase, however, the response to each user becomes sluggish.

Eventually, users and management complain that the network's response is too slow. If management does not want to abandon programs based on MS-DOS, the only solution is to have a faster file server or to have more file servers. The network quickly becomes saturated, and no amount of added hardware alleviates the problem except by partitioning the network with gateways and routers.

As soon as gateways and routers enter the network, so does the problem of dividing the company's database to run on multiple servers, with each server hosting a limited number of users. When this strategy stops working, as it does eventually, the only other choice is to run applications programs on the server.

Applications programs can run on the server (instead of on client machines) in one of two ways. The first is to rely on the very limited multitasking capabilities of DOS-compatible network operating systems, such as Novell NetWare, and to use network-oriented databases. The second alternative is to use a good multitasking system as a file (or process) server. At this point, UNIX enters the picture.

Using UNIX as a Network Server

Although companies such as Sun, DEC, Hewlett-Packard, and others have successfully sold network-based workstations and "diskless" workstations for years without running into the performance and capacity issues covered in this chapter, these UNIX-based workstations have been primarily used for engineering applications. There is a fundamental difference between most technical applications and most management-oriented applications.

Technical applications are CPU-intensive; MIS applications are disk- and I/O-intensive, and it is the intensity of I/O that kills networks. It takes, for example, a lot of computing horsepower and very little I/O to read a CAD/CAM file of a solid model of a widget and then to rotate the widget on a bit-mapped screen in real time. On the other hand, it requires a lot of I/O bandwidth and very little computing horsepower to generate statements from an accounting file that might be as large as 30M or more because each record must be read and written several times, each requiring an I/O interrupt.

Many multitasking systems can be used as a file server or process server, but, for economic reasons, UNIX-based systems are the logical choice. How then is a UNIX system to be integrated into a network of personal computers? Most of the popular networking systems, such as Novell, Banyon VINES, and TCP/IP-NFS, are supported by both the personal computer and by many versions of UNIX, so compatibility with existing systems is not an issue. Also, you can use applications software without requiring conversion because most of the better MS-DOS software has been ported to UNIX or can be run under one of the several commercial DOS-emulation packages.

Does UNIX reduce network traffic? With conventional network file-sharing, UNIX cannot do this, but if the application is run on the UNIX system through terminal emulation programs on PCs, it can dramatically improve system throughput.

If, for example, generating financial statements requires searching and sorting a 20M file, this task may generate 50M or more of data traffic on a network. In other words, it consumes two or three minutes of network bandwidth over a seven- or eight-minute period. If the network contains just two or three clients and a server, the network can easily handle the traffic, but if there are 30 or 40 systems, each trying to get its fair share of access, the network becomes saturated.

The same program, run exclusively on the server, still manipulates a similar number of bytes, but it runs over a higher-speed disk bus and in local memory instead of through the network. The only data traffic over the network in this arrangement is the program start-up commands, passed through a terminal-emulation package to the server (at most, a few hundred bytes).

For database operations, which is the bulk of most MIS work, networked personal computers perform as little more than dumb terminals. This is a letdown from the technological promise of a computer on each person's desk, linked by high-speed networks. Without faster networks, however, the goal of fully-distributed processing remains a mirage.

Eventually, as this fictitious company grows, the abbreviated network of personal computers becomes a burden that gives way to dumb terminals. The network is then free to support the more important task of communications in a growing "mainframe" UNIX network. The assumption is that Ethernet will remain the predominant network architecture over the next few years. This may or may not occur—breakthroughs happen all the time, and the true limit of fiber optical cables has yet to be found.

 If a 500 or 600 megabit-per-second fiber optical system can be delivered at the cost of contemporary Ethernet, all bets are off as to Ethernet remaining the dominate network architcture.

Making Room for the Heterogeneous Network

So far, UNIX-based systems have been presented as if this were a black-and-white issue, UNIX or nothing. Because nothing is ever that simple, this section addresses the vices and virtues of a heterogeneous network.

Every hardware and software system has its good and bad points, and UNIX is no exception. When you introduce a UNIX-based system into a company, users soon discover that UNIX is not a panacea. Mainframes that run conventional mainframe operating systems outperform all current UNIX-based systems in I/O performance, as do many midrange and minicomputer systems. Although almost any mainframe can be replaced by a network of UNIX systems, it requires a deft system designer to replicate mainframe reliability and performance.

Except when migrating from a small, obsolete midrange system, every migration path discussed includes a network connected to the original host system. In fact, migrating from a modern midrange system more closely resembles the migration to UNIX from a mainframe. Each computer in these heterogeneous networks performs the function for which it is best suited. UNIX systems handle all interaction with users and any communications chores; the midrange computers and mainframe systems handle the massive batch jobs, for which they are so well suited. Thus, only when the economic life of the midrange or mainframe system comes to a close do most rational businesspeople contemplate abandonment.

At the other extreme, some applications work best on a personal computer, workstation, or microprocessor. Although engineering applications, graphics arts applications, and process control are not strictly part of a management-information system, they are integral parts of many companies and contribute to the MIS.

In a highly automated manufacturing environment, for instance, product design can be performed on engineering workstations and downloaded to numerical-control systems on the shop floor. Bills of material can be uploaded to the MIS system for material requirements planning.

As products are manufactured, the automated equipment on the shop floor reports production information back to the MIS system. At the executive level, the same terminals used to control operations are used to send and receive electronic mail; reports from the MIS system can be used to create marketing material on PCs. In short, a heterogeneous environment is probably the norm rather than the exception, and an integrated enterprise-computing system encompasses far more than the traditional MIS function (namely, accounting and control).

The heterogeneous system is already a reality. Mainframes, midrange systems, UNIX mainframes, UNIX workstations, UNIX file servers or terminal servers, personal computers, and microprocessors all have a unique place in this type of system and, by means of routers and gateways, interpreted into a comprehensive whole. It seems only natural that the form and command structure of UNIX will find its way into larger and more powerful systems, as well as find its way down into sub-PC microprocessors. From this point of view, UNIX is the ultimate open system because it is nonproprietary and thus able to reside on machines at each computing level.

Because of the acceptance and standardization of the "UNIX way" of doing things, UNIX concepts will find their way into many different and specialized operating systems. For instance, at the high end, Amdahl's UTS is recognizably UNIX, even though it must pass through mainframe block-mode terminals. Its character set is

EBCDIC, and you cannot run some UNIX favorites such as the `vi` or `EMACS` editors. At the low end, operating systems such as OS-9 and QMS have recognizable UNIX features, as does MS-DOS. If Microsoft's soon-to-be-released operating system NT is to succeed in the market, it will probably look and feel like UNIX. The Open Software Foundation's OSF/1 is, for all practical purposes, UNIX.

 It is unlikely that the heterogeneity of enterprise networks will disappear soon. The tools are currently available to make the integration of heterogeneous components simple and easy.

There are two basic requirements to make integration of hetrogeneous components simple: the full standardization of languages at the source level and the standardization of communications between systems and between applications. From the MIS viewpoint, the major requirement for a heterogeneous system is the capability of transferring data between systems and between applications.

Migrating Databases

Whether the goal of a migration to UNIX is to replace the original system or to add power and functionality to the MIS environment, the most important consideration is the portability of the MIS database. In some cases, this portability must go both ways. The database migration method can take one of two tactics: you can port the DBMS as "flat" ASCII text files or as delimited ASCII files.

Most UNIX-oriented DBMSs enable the importation of *flat* ASCII files (text files without formatting or word-processing codes). If the DBMS does not accept the first method, you can port it using the second method. In this case, the files can or must be fixed-format files that conform to the database scheme, or, in other cases, they can be ASCII-delimited files with some known character delimiting the fields.

If you choose a field delimiter, use a character that does not conflict with the data. In most cases, the pipe symbol (|) is the best choice because it is seldom used in most data.

Moving DBMSs from a Mainframe

The most popular DBMSs found on mainframes only run on mainframes. Many of the popular UNIX DBMSs also run on mainframes, midrange systems, PCs, and many proprietary minicomputers. This leads to a curious problem. If the goal of the migration is to use the mainframe or midrange system as a file server, the mainframe database must be converted to a UNIX database on the mainframe before a network can be built.

With network-oriented DBMSs operating from a mainframe, queries are performed and tokenized on the UNIX system or client, and then passed to the mainframe or midrange system over the network. Relevant data is then passed back to the client over the network. In most cases, if the requested data is spread over a number of database tables, the `join` of multiple tables is performed on the client. Whereas this process may cause more data to flow over the network than is absolutely necessary, it is a lot less than with NFS.

Using a mainframe as a file server is unlikely because of the bandwidth limitations of most networks. Use the mainframe's power as a back-end data cruncher and pass data from a front-end processor to the mainframe and back over conventional communications media. In this case, much of the mainframe database must be migrated to UNIX DBMSs running on UNIX front-end processors. If the mainframe or midrange system is to play a significant role in the network, data must flow from the UNIX DBMS to the mainframe.

One of the easiest standard mainframe communications methods to implement on a UNIX system is Remote Job Entry (RJE). Logically, RJE resembles the old punch-card readers. Data on a UNIX system can be gathered into a standard ASCII file that resembles card images (in individual fixed-length records). After enough data has been collected, it is passed to the mainframe with a few header cards that tell the mainframe what to do with the data. Similar utilities "talk" to midrange systems.

Because of the batch-oriented nature of most mainframes (and midrange systems), a continuous data stream from the UNIX system(s) to the mainframe is not necessary or even desirable. Data should be present on the mainframe only when a batch program that needs that data is ready to run. From this perspective, standard mainframe communications methods are extremely effective. The data-transmission medium can be Ethernet, hard-wired RS-232, or IBM's own SNA, depending on your network topology and the volume of data to be passed.

Migrating from a Network of Personal Computers

Moving from a PC to UNIX is perhaps one of the easiest UNIX migrations to accomplish. First of all, most PC database managers also are offered on small UNIX systems. For example, dBase is available, as is FoxBase under SCO UNIX. Thus, migrating programs between MS-DOS and UNIX is simply a matter of recompiling programs.

Tip

Because data formats on PCs and UNIX systems may differ, it is usually a good idea to convert the actual data in the DBMS to ASCII before importing it to UNIX.

Both UNIX systems and personal computer systems understand ASCII. When transferring data between the two systems, however, it is important to remember that MS-DOS uses a carriage return plus a new line character to delimit the end of a line of ASCII text, and UNIX text files use only a new line character. These minor discrepancies can occasionally create problems.

Summary

Migrating to UNIX can be relatively easy. UNIX is not a hard operating system to learn when compared to many proprietary systems. Even though UNIX runs on the widest variety of hardware platforms, it does not run on all of them. In fact, it currently runs least on the biggest systems. Porting an entire mainframe MIS to UNIX is not something you should undertake lightly or quickly. It is unrealistic, for example, to expect to migrate to UNIX in six months and then turn the mainframe off.

Migrating from a minicomputer or midrange system to UNIX is a lot easier than migrating from a mainframe because most midrange systems fall well within the power and capabilities of available UNIX replacements, and the migration strategy is about as straightforward as one could expect.

Migrating from a network of personal computers to UNIX is conceptually the easiest task of all, but it is one of the hardest to implement in practice because of the natural reluctance of network users and administrators to centralize their work.

It is difficult to imagine how replacing a powerful PC on everyone's desk with an old-fashioned dumb terminal will improve the throughput of the MIS. The goal of any MIS design, however, is to provide sufficient computational horsepower at the right place and at the right time. In some cases, this can be accomplished on a single UNIX box. In other cases, multiple processors on a carefully designed network are required. Careful thought and a strategic design should precede implementation.

This chapter gave you an overview of UNIX, a glimpse into how an MIS system might work under UNIX, and strategies for migrating from a variety of systems to UNIX. The next section is designed to give the engineering-oriented UNIX "guru" an overview of the issues and designs of an MIS.

Part Three: UNIX Enhancements for Management Information Systems

Designing a Management Information System with UNIX

Menus for Security and Simplicity

Data-Entry Screens: Mimicking the Mainframes

Program Spooling (Batch Spooling)

Useful System Administration Commands and Utilities

Topics covered in this chapter:

Segmenting Tasks
Understanding Designing Strategies
Developing a Toolkit

Chapter 9

Designing a Management Information System with UNIX

As an operating system, UNIX is not much different than other operating systems, except that it runs on many different hardware platforms. Like all operating systems, UNIX has its peculiarities and idiosyncrasies; therefore, some techniques work better under UNIX than they would under another operating-system philosophy. Indeed, as multiprocessor versions of UNIX become commonplace, many of UNIX's concepts and methods will work even better. This chapter looks at some of the tactics and strategies that you should consider when you design a management information system under UNIX.

287

Segmenting Tasks

Textbooks have long advocated the use of structured programming; it encourages efficient design and reusable parts. UNIX takes the concept of structured programming one step further by encouraging the use of separate programs and by using the power of the shell to bind these detached parts into a coherent whole at execution time. You can achieve far greater flexibility and reusability through this arrangement than if the separate parts were linked into one executable program from a library. On multiple-processor architectures, each element in a command pipeline can run on independent CPUs; in a networked environment, elements of a pipeline can run on different machines, as shown in figure 9.1

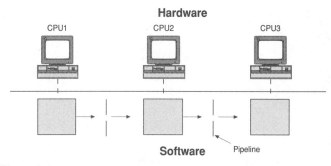

Figure 9.1:
Multiple-processor architecture.

This design strategy implies far more task segmentation than is common or even practical on a mainframe or midrange system. Although a mainframe system designer might balk at the idea of fragmenting programs into their component parts, the exercise proves fruitful in the long run.

A normal COBOL program, for example, might contain code to paint and edit a data-entry screen, and can contain more code to handle file access. Normally, file-access code is written as part of subroutines and linked as one large program. As a result, executable code is duplicted at runtime as many users log in and execute commands.

UNIX provides two ways around this problem of duplicating code. The first solution is to place common code in a shared library so that only one copy of the shared library is brought into memory, as shown in figure 9.2.

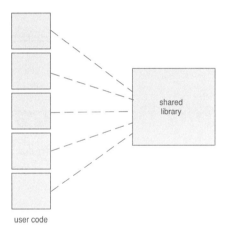

Figure 9.2:
A shared library system.

The second—and most flexible—solution, illustrated in figure 9.3, is to place the shared code into a separate program and run that program as a daemon or a pipeline element using one of the interprocess communications methods (see Chapter 4) to connect the elements. By using a separate program for each element of a command, you create code that is immediately reusable and that can take advantage of multiple processors and network architectures.

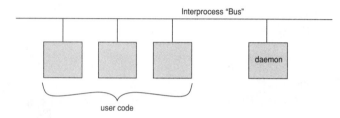

Figure 9.3:
Interprocess communications.

Understanding Design Strategies

With the concept of task segmentation in hand, you can begin the design of a viable MIS. The main strategic goal of any good system design is flexibility. If the company grows, for example, can the MIS system also grow by migrating to a larger and faster system or by adding systems to the network without a great deal of trouble? If programming tasks have been properly segmented so that data is easily merged or dispersed, the answer to this question should be yes.

If the system has been properly designed, it can easily balance the demands of the system against the available computing power. As the system changes, so does the mix of system hardware components. Adding discrete systems would be easy if there were no network bandwidth limitations.

The relatively low speed of current networks should not pose a great obstacle to the design of a network-oriented, distributed management information system. The limitations of networks have been emphasized in this book because if improperly used, they quickly become a primary bottleneck in the system. To illustrate this concept, Table 9.1 lists the true maximum throughput speeds of various networks.

Table 9.1
Maximum Throughput of Various Raw Network Media

Network Media	Bytes/second
FDDI	10,000,000
Ethernet	600,000
Token Ring	900,000
ARCnet I	700,000
T1	100,000
X.25	5,600
9600 Baud Modem	960

The raw speed of a network is tempered by the overhead of data-framing software such as TCP/IP and the speed of disks delivering data over the network. For disks, the raw access speed varies from several hundred thousand bytes-per-second (for a PC-oriented disk) to as much as 10M-per-second for a SCSI or SMD disk array.

When a user queries a database with an index of 10M for a single data record, about .5M of data needs to be delivered to search the index. If the search is performed on a file that is accessed by NFS, then, on average, .5M must be transferred over the network to affect the search. If the search is performed on the server, however, only the record in question is transferred.

To put this in greater perspective, assume that one hundred data-entry clerks are performing substantially the same query at roughly the same time. With an NFS approach, as much as 50M are transferred over the network during the index search process. This process takes over one minute on an Ethernet running at full capacity or five seconds on an FDDI network. If, however, the queries are run on the server, only the resulting 100 records of data are transferred. It might still take a long time for the server to deliver the data, but the network is no longer the bottleneck.

More realistically, each data-entry clerk might make as many as three queries-per-minute, so one hundred clerks on average make five queries-per-second. An NFS network must deliver 2.5M of data-per-second, which is well beyond the capacity of Ethernet. Thus, the strategic placement and use of data and network-oriented database servers can either enhance or destroy the effectiveness of an MIS design.

Developing a Toolkit

Developing a specialized programmer's toolkit is the essence of programming in UNIX. The conventional UNIX programmer's toolkit, although necessary for MIS development, is not sufficient. Other tools must be developed, and in the absence of a standard business-oriented toolkit, the development of new tools falls on the system designer and developer. The tools listed in the remainder of this book are a start in this direction.

The design of a toolkit implies the reusability of the tools developed. Your toolkit by no means is limited to commands that you can use directly in shell scripts. Source and object libraries, as well as preprocessor programs, all contribute to the concept of a toolkit. The object of a toolkit is to standardize the approach to programming and the manipulation of data by simplifying each programming task.

Most private toolkits simply evolve, as did the standard UNIX toolkit, but there are advantages to planning your toolkit in advance. Tool design targets, for example, include standardized approaches to human interfaces, standardized data formats, I/O routines, and any other commonly executed chore. New tools are fashioned from existing tools. In the case of a business-oriented toolkit, the standard assortment of UNIX tools and the C language might not always yield the best results. It is often more important to choose the right language for the task than it is to economize by simply using the tools supplied with UNIX.

Languages

You can write business applications in FORTRAN, just as you can write scientific applications in COBOL. Doing so, however, makes as much sense as using a pair of pliers to change a tire when the lug wrench is in the trunk. You only use the wrong tool when you do not have any other choice.

Supporters of C and C++ might argue that you can write any application in these languages, and that they would be right. The C language was designed, however, as a language to create UNIX and other operating systems. It also is great for creating word processors, spreadsheets, and database-management systems. Do not consider it for highly specialized UNIX applications, however. As their names suggest, FORTRAN (*FOR*mula *TRAN*slator) is much better suited for scientific applications and COBOL (*CO*mmon *Business-Oriented Language*) remains the preeminent language for business applications.

In the process of migrating from one system to another, designers often have to tolerate what is generally considered obsolete code. After the migration is complete, you can redesign the system with considerable ease if you choose the right tools—the right language compilers—at the beginning of the migration process.

 Designers should realize that the object of migration is not the complete redesign of an existing system, no matter how gratifying that might be, but rather the simple migration from one platform to another.

Almost every language that has been used to write business applications has been ported to UNIX, from BASIC to COBOL to RPG. Implementations of these languages vary dramatically, however. To take full advantage of UNIX, the specific language compiler you choose should be able to call and be called by programs written in C.

This sounds obvious, but it is surprising how many languages are written as P-code (semi-interpreted languages). If the language compiler you choose can be linked to native C programs, the designer can use all the UNIX system calls in the standard UNIX library, as well as the vast library of commercially available C programs. These programs perform every function, from data-entry screen design to transaction-oriented database updates and queries.

If distributing the processing and I/O load across a network reduces the need for high disk throughput, can you integrate the advantages of a modern database management system using obsolete programs? The answer is yes, but only if the language allows linking in the C libraries that accompany most modern DBMSs.

Databases

The major advantage of UNIX-based DBMSs is that they are relatively simple to use and manage. Unlike their mainframe cousins, these DBMSs do not usually require a dedicated DBMS manager unless the database has grown across multiple platforms. If it has, you might need a DBMS manager to coordinate database changes; even then, it is rarely a full-time occupation.

For example, using a conventional language to add a single character to a field in a fixed-length record is a major task. First, you must modify and recompile all relevant programs under temporary names. Then you must write a program to convert the old file format into the new format and test it against all the recompiled programs, to make sure that all programs are correctly modified. After verification—a process that might take some time—you must convert the old files once again, then change the new programs to their old names before the system can go back on-line.

In contrast, most modern DBMSs offer a superset of the Structured Query Language (SQL) called a Data Dictionary Language (DDL), which automatically modifies, indexes, or deletes fields in a table. Rather than writing an entire program in COBOL, RPG, or whatever to modify a file, the DBMS manager needs to give a command resembling `alter table` *table-name* `modify` *field-name new-data-type*;. If, for example, you have a table called `addrs` in a database with a field named `company`, which has a 30-byte field length, you can use the following command to easily alter the table so that `company` is 50 bytes long:

```
alter table addrs modify company char(50);
```

If the table `addrs` is a large one, the conversion can take considerable time. The DBMS reads the old table, writes out a new table with the modified field length, then renames the new table and updates any relevant indexes.

Generally, the only remaining chore is to recompile data-entry screens (modifying them for field changes as necessary) and report programs (again, modifying fields if necessary). Using a DBMS to accomplish this task is far simpler than using a conventional language. In a *mixed environment*—an environment in which database commands are embedded within conventional languages—the results are mixed. You can easily change the database, but you still have to modify the conventional language source to accept the new field sizes.

In most cases, you can accomplish this program modification by changing the data-definition statements in the source, then recompiling. By using the UNIX program maintenance toolkit— Source Code Control System and `make`, as well as the preprocessors—makes that task considerably easier.

Embedded SQL statements, used in third-generation languages, do not add as much overhead as you might expect. In most cases, the SQL statements are tokenized at compile time, so the overhead (both in runtime and the size of executable code) is minimized when the program runs.

Fourth-generation languages, used with embedded SQL, are more problematic. Most of the existing fourth-generation languages are excellent; however, they are as verbose as COBOL. In addition, these languages do not yet have any standards regarding language syntax or SQL. Although SQL has been defined as an ANSI standard, that standard is incomplete. As a result, each manufacturer has improvised, using extensions to the standard SQL, to make the language usable. After you select a database management system, you must adhere to its structures and strictures.

 At the time of this writing, there is no standard fourth-generation language suitable to replace COBOL as the standard for business applications.

Human Interfaces

The only goal of a management information system is to improve the efficiency of the company. No matter how much programmers might love UNIX, the only reason to consider migrating to UNIX from a proprietary architecture is because it is more efficient—both in terms of actual cost and in personnel training. After you decide to migrate to UNIX, you must also decide which human interface to present to users. UNIX is unusually rich in this respect.

Unadorned, standard UNIX offers three different shells with services that are at least as powerful as those found on midrange and mainframe systems. Also, with the addition of graphic display terminals and X-Window software, you can make UNIX's graphical user interface (GUI) at least as "friendly" as a Macintosh or Windows interface. Every system designer must ask if the increased efficiency for the average user is worth the cost and added power required to offer a GUI. Is one of the standard shells sufficient to guide the user and keep her out of trouble? The answer to both sides of the question is probably no.

No matter how easy a GUI is supposed to be, it consumes an inordinate amount of computer horsepower in exchange for a minimal improvement in efficiency. This primary improvement comes in reduced training costs for novice users; however, they still must be trained to use the applications. Because most users in an MIS environment spend most of their time in a few data-entry applications, a GUI's usefulness is questionable.

A different complaint is raised regarding standard shells. With a standard shell, you can execute any valid UNIX command as long as the PATH environment variable points to the standard executable directories. Although you can limit access to these directories, permitting novice users to operate under one of these shells invites trouble. A reasonable compromise between a GUI and a standard shell is a menu for the average user.

Menus

Menus have all the advantages of GUIs because they present the user with a limited and easy-to-select set of options—a virtue that does not exist with standard shells. Another advantage of menus is that you can use them as shells. Because menus perform far less work than full-fledged shells, they consume far fewer resources than even the Bourne shell. On an Intel-based system, for example, the Bourne shell generally requires about 80K bytes to run; a simple menu program that uses printf can run in less than 40K bytes. If extreme economy is wanted, you can run a simple menu in less than 10K bytes by using getchar and putchar. Because the user spends most of her time in applications and not in menus, menus do not have to be very complex or pretty.

Because UNIX has no standard menu system, a menu is one of the first tools required in a commercial toolkit. To help you avoid "reinventing the wheel," Chapter 10 provides a simple but adequate menuing system.

Regardless of the user interface, the average MIS user primarily enters or retrieves data from data-entry screens. Data-entry screens resemble simple template forms in which the user fills in the blanks. A dumb terminal can display a form as well as an X-Window terminal, and at far less cost.

All of the currently popular DBMSs have data-entry screen systems, as do most of the current third-generation commercial languages like COBOL, RPG, and many "Business BASIC" compilers. If C-linkable data-entry screens are required for application development, several excellent stand-alone screen-design systems are available.

System Services

Although UNIX is one of the best operating systems, no one operating system can be all things to all people. For engineering applications, very little in the way of system services is required beyond providing a fast and unencumbered CPU and a large address space. Everything else is up to the application.

Business applications are different. In the business environment, many users' needs must be addressed; various communications methods and speeds must be supported; large volumes of data must be stored, served, and saved; and the entire system must be kept in safe operation.

Raw UNIX addresses all these concerns, but in a manner that would be considered primitive by the standards set on mainframes and operating systems designed for MIS. Consider the following examples:

❖ UNIX offers several methods of running programs in the background, but none address the issue of priority or truly address the potential problem of thrashing.

❖ UNIX also offers several very good methods of backing up data; however, it is devoid of facilities to manage a tape library.

❖ For software development, the UNIX utility `make` is excellent for recompiling dependent programs, but this utility has no facility for running dependent programs.

❖ UNIX offers utility programs that manage nearly every aspect of the system, many of which must be used by ordinary users to control communications, printers, and background tasks. Unfortunately, these utilities are so inclusive in their control of their respective tasks that they appear completely incomprehensible to the ordinary user.

Summary

This chapter just barely touches the surface of the concepts needed to design an MIS under UNIX, such as the segmentation of tasks (a job made easier by the richness of the UNIX environment) and the concept of pipes and generalized I/O redirection. You learned about the limitations of networks and suggested ways to use the resources of a network wisely.

In this chapter, you also explored the concept of software tools and the importance of developing a toolkit, as well as what belongs in that toolkit and how to use it. The chapter reminded you of the limitations of the standard interfaces of UNIX and looked at some of the underlying deficiencies in UNIX as an MIS environment. In the following chapters, solutions to these problems and concerns are addressed.

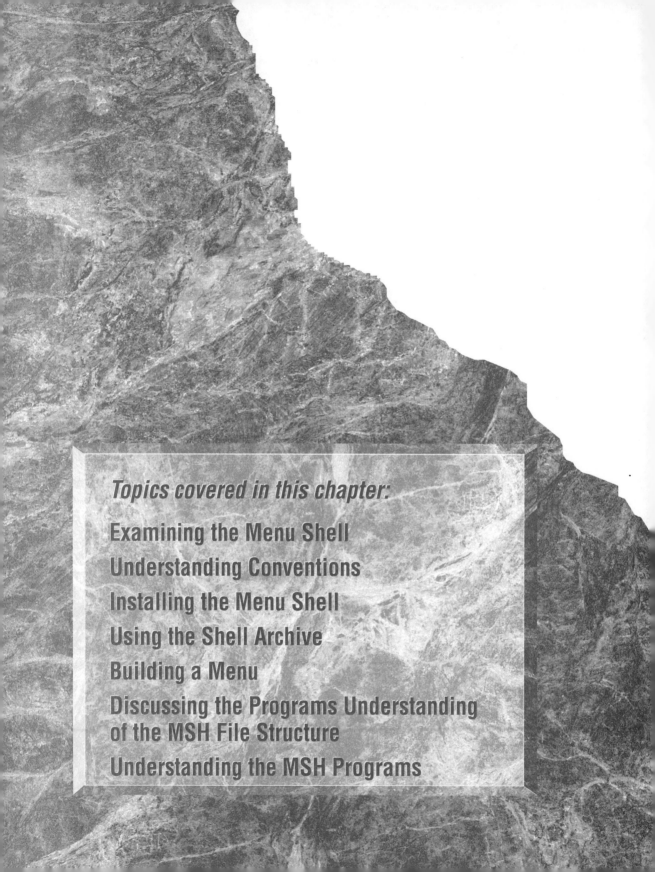

Chapter 10

Menus for Security and Simplicity

This chapter presents the concept behind (and the source code for) a simple menuing system called the *menu shell* or MSH. The source code is written entirely in shell script—specifically, the Bourne shell, the `awk` language, and several other utility programs such as `sed` and `csplit`.

Examining the Menu Shell

The Menu shell consists of three parts. The first part is a compiler, which translates a simple menuing language either to Bourne shell script or to highly transportable C. The second part consists of a front-end shell script called `msh` and several useful utility programs that are used throughout the remainder of the programs listed in this book. The final part of the Menu shell is a menu-interpreter program that can be embedded in shell scripts.

Menus offer a simple way to guide the average user around the UNIX system. Using menus, the UNIX system administrator can limit the user's contact with the UNIX system, freeing the users to learn application programs, rather than UNIX. Menus also protect the UNIX system from adventurous but uninformed users.

The Menu shell offers a consistent user interface that is both easy to use and learn. In addition to the simplicity of the user interface, the creation of a menu script created by the system administrator also is very simple. (A menu system with five embedded menus can be generated and compiled in less than an hour.)

Another feature of MSH is the execution of menus that are user-dependent, user-group dependent, and system-wide. Thus, all users may be assigned the msh shell, but the menus they receive are dependent upon their login and group ID.

 The system administrator can easily segregate users into functional groups and allow each group to run only those programs permitted.

The system administrator, for example, may set up several groups such as payable, receivable, or payroll. Each user is then assigned a specific group in the usual UNIX fashion. All that remains is to set up corresponding group menus.

A menu is provided that enables the administrator to quickly set up specific groups and to generate the appropriate menus. Individual menus also may be set up to override any defaults. The order of processing is as follows: local menus first, followed by group menus, then system-wide menus.

The startup menu is always the Main menu, but the msh shell first tries to execute the user's private Main menu. If this is unavailable, the program then tries to execute the Main menu assigned to the user group. Failing that, `msh` executes the system-wide Main menu. Thus, the system administrator has a great deal of control over the presentation of available options to the user.

 A number of hidden options also are embedded in each menu. Each menu provides access to an editor, the UNIX mail system, a calendar function, listing functions, and the UNIX Bourne shell. Control over these functions is exercised by setting environment variables.

The command `ccm` is the Menu shell compiler that generates menus from a simple command script. The compiler itself is a UNIX shell script that uses `awk` and `sed`. It can be modified to produce any format the user desires.

 Modifying the compiler script is difficult and should not be attempted by a novice.

Two different compilers are included in the `ccm` package. The first generates UNIX Bourne shell scripts; the other generates and compiles C code. The `ccm` script detects whether or not you have a C compiler on your system by searching for `cc` in the `/bin` directory. If you have a C compiler, `ccm` generates C code; if not, it generates shell scripts. The resulting output can be intermixed and looks the same on the screen. The shell script version executes more slowly, but this is only a matter of degrees.

The Menu shell is designed to minimize the use of system resources. With the compiled version, a single menu uses only 40K of RAM on an Intel-based system. The ordinary Bourne shell uses 72K of RAM. Thus, two running menus occupy as much space as one normal Bourne shell. (Because the shell script version uses the Bourne shell, no savings are found with that implementation).

The compiled version uses only the standard I/O functions to minimize overhead. If the `curses` library were used, each executable menu would use over 100K, but screen painting would be faster.

The `ccm` compiler was developed on an Altos series 1000 running UNIX System V.3 (Altos version 5.3dt1). It works on this version and should work on all UNIX System V machines. The C code has been designed to be very generic. It does not, however, run on any XENIX System 3 machine because UNIX and XENIX are different.

Understanding Conventions

All conventions are arbitrary, but they are useful for keeping the system manageable. It is recommended that you follow the conventions described here:.

❖ Menu names should begin with a capital letter.

❖ The first menu executed is always Main—after that, you can express yourself as you wish.

❖ All system-wide menus should be placed in the `/usr/lib/menu` directory.

❖ All menus to be executed by a specific group should be placed in the `/usr/lib/menu/group/groupname` directory. `Groupname` is a directory with execute permission, whose name is that of the group. `Root` is usually assigned to the group `sys`, so all menus specific to the group `sys` would be placed in `/usr/lib/menu/group/sys`. The MSH installation script determines the group ID of the root user and renames the `sys` directory to the proper group name. The installation script creates the `/usr/lib/menu` and `/usr/lib/menu/group` directories with the proper permission.

If you execute `msh` with the `-a` option, a menu displays that will help you to create a group-specific menu system.

❖ All local menus (menus executed by specific users) should be placed in a directory called `menu` in the user's home directory. The `menu` directory must have execute permission.

 If you create the `menu` directory with `mkdir`, you also must change the directory mode using `chmod +x menu`.

❖ The `msh` command is the start-up shell script that executes the Main menu. It is located in `/usr/bin`. If you want to have `msh` execute as the primary shell, change the shell field in `/etc/passwd`. The password file has an entry for each user that looks like this:

```
prospect:i34Jx1:prospect:/usr/prospect:/
usr/bin/msh
```

Notice that the last field is `/usr/bin/msh`, which automatically executes the Menu shell as soon as the user logs in.

 UNIX systems with security options enabled balk if you edit the `/etc/passwd` file. Use the system-management program instead (such as `sysadmsh` on SCO UNIX systems).

❖ The order of precedence is to execute the user's private Main menu first. If that is not found, `msh` executes the user group's Main menu. If the group has no Main menu, the system-wide Main menu executes. Other menu systems can be created that correspond to specific functions.

❖ The ccm compiler creates two files in the C compiled version and one file in the shell script version. Both versions create a file called M.*Filename*, in which *Filename* is the name of the menu script. In the C version, it also creates an executable version called m.*Filename*. In the shell script version, all executable code is placed in the M.*Filename* script. In the C version, a start-up script called M.*Filename* is generated; the C is compiled into a binary file called m.*Filename*. The M.*Filename* script executes the m.*Filename* program.

❖ When creating menu scripts, menus must be executed by calling M.*Filename*. For example, the executable version of the Main menu is M.Main, and it must be called that. In its simplest form, the M.Main program contains one line of executable code: exec m.Main. This system is necessary to keep the C and script versions compatible, as well as to offer a way to execute setup code, such as setting environment variables.

❖ There also is a menu interpreter that reads the menu source file and displays a menu with functions that are more limited than a fully compiled menu. The command menu can be run by using the syntax menu *Filename*, in which *Filename* is a file containing the source for menus that can be compiled using ccm. The menu program is the slowest and uses the most memory of the three options.

Installing the Menu Shell

The Menu shell requires the following utilities to work: awk, sed, vi (or ex), and, if you are using the C version, a full C compiler and cb, the C beautifier. The command ccm checks to see that the C compiler exists in the /bin directory. If it is not there, ccm automatically compiles the Bourne shell version. The awk program must be the "new awk." To be sure, the ccm compiler calls nawk.

Users should be aware that the old awk will be fully replaced by the new awk command, and that someday the nawk command may not work. When this happens, make a link between awk and nawk or change the code in ccm. To create a link between awk and nawk, first find the location of awk (it should be in the /bin or /usr/bin directory). Then create the link by typing **ln awk nawk**, which enables ccm to compile your menus.

The Menu shell programs are contained in the file MSH on the disk that accompanies this book. The disk is a 360K MS-DOS disk, which is by far the most universally accessible. The file MSH itself is a shell archive that contains all programs in the MSH system. A shell archive is self-executing— by running the shell archive as a Bourne shell script, it automatically splits up the files it contains. Thus, by running the command sh MSH, the constituents of the archive are released.

Using the Shell Archive

The structure of a shell archive is simple, and only the most basic UNIX utilities are used to execute it. Although forms of shell archives differ, the basic structure remains the same. For example, to extract a program named program.c, the following shell archive can be used:

```
if test -f "program.c"
then
echo "File program.c already exists, will not overwrite"
else
sed 's/^    #//' << \SHAR_EOF > 'program.c'
    #main()
    #{
    #/* insert body of program here /*
    #}
SHAR_EOF
if test 41 -ne "`wc -c < 'program.c'`"
then
echo "SHAR: Error in transmitting 'program.c' should have been
41 characters"
fi
fi
```

The shell archive first tests for the existence of the file in the archive. If the file exists, it is not overwritten. Otherwise, the sed command is used to separate the text of the file. Finally, the wc (word count) command is used to count characters to be sure the new file matches the original.

This last test of file integrity can cause problems. The archives were created on a UNIX system as text files, then copied to an MS-DOS disk. In the process of moving the files from a UNIX system to the MS-DOS disk, MS-DOS replaced the UNIX end-of-line character, a new-line character, with a combination new-line/carriage return which is used in MS-DOS.

If the added carriage return is removed during the file transfer from MS-DOS to your UNIX system, the archive may be executed as it stands. If not, the carriage return character must be manually stripped, or the character count tested after each sed command will be wrong.

The process of stripping carriage returns is easy with the `vi` command `:1,$s/^v^m//` (`^v` means "press Ctrl-V," and `^m` means "Press Ctr-M"). After the archive has been prepared, it can be run with the Bourne shell by using the following dialog:

```
Login as "root"
Type: umask 0;sh MSH
```

Your Menu shell self-installs, and you are placed in the default menu for the group `sys`, of which `root` is a member (or whatever group MSH determines that the root user belongs to).

Type **q** to exit the default menu.

To update MSH or to replace an existing copy, run `update`, rather than `MSH`. `Update` deletes the old version and runs MSH.

Building a Menu

Creating menus is easy. Each menu has three parts, although only two parts are necessary to run. The first part is called the *start-up script*, which consists of Bourne shell commands to be executed before the menu itself is run. The second part is the *menu title*, which is required although it can have a null value. The final part is the menu itself. A typical menu script is the following:

```
PATH=:$PATH:$HOME/bin;export PATH
#Main System Menu
Word Processing!uniplex;;
Call another system!cu 'prompt Enter System Name';;
Kill a task!(ps -f;kill -9 'prompt Enter PID to be
killed';
Printer Status!lpstat -t;
Kill Print Job!cancel 'prompt Enter Print Job id';
```

The line containing the PATH variable is the start-up script. The line beginning with a # is the menu title; the remaining text is the menu itself. The # can be on a line by itself if no menu title is desired.

Start-up Scripts

This section of text can contain any Bourne shell script commands except the initial # as a comment. Typical uses are to set the PATH, EDIT, CALENDAR, and MAILER environment variables. For remote users, the TERM variable can also be prompted for. This section of the menu is placed in the M.*Menuname* file and is executed before the menu itself.

The MSH system has a number of defaults that can be changed by setting environment variables. The default editor can be changed by setting the EDIT variable, and CALENDAR changes the default schedule system. The default CALENDAR is $EDIT $HOME/calendar.

By running calendar at night using cron, each user receives in the system mail a listing of the day's activities. If another schedule system is to be used, set CALENDAR to the name of your preferred program. The same is true of MAILER. The system default is to prompt for the name of the user you wish to send mail to, and, using the standard mail utility, send mail or retrieve your mail. MSH always prompts Send mail to who >, even though some mail utilities do not accept parameters.

Menu Title

The title line of a menu always begins with a #. The title can be up to 30 characters long, but it should be kept short for ease of reading. There can be only one line in the menu containing a # . The title line must be present, even if there is only a # . All text following the title line must be in menu text format because the compiler assumes that the title line is the divider between the start-up text and the menu proper.

Menu Entries

Each menu entry consists of two parts, delimited by an exclamation mark (!). The first part is called the `menu` and the second is called the `executable`. Each entry has the following form:

```
menu ! executable
```

There can be no more than nine (9) menu lines per menu because MSH expects only a single character. Menus can be nested to any depth, however. The rules for creating menus are as follows:

❖ Menus are numbered in the order in which they occur in the menu script.

❖ Menus must be called by M . *Menuname*. A menu called Admin would be called by another menu as M.Admin. (M.Admin is the executable name for Admin.)

❖ If MSH is to repaint the menu after execution of a menu choice, the executable portion of the menu script must be followed by double semi-colons (; ;) or else the menu will not be repainted. For example, if the user wants to display a list of other users that are currently logged in, and does not want the screen cleared after executing the `who` command, the executable portion of the menu reads `who`. If `who; ;` is used instead, the screen is cleared, the menu is repainted immediately after execution, and the user cannot see the results of `who`.

❖ If compound statements are to be executed, they must be enclosed in parentheses (). Otherwise, MSH executes only the first statement in the list, and then returns to the menu. Pipes are not compound statements. For example, the following two statements work:

```
Who is on the system!who|more
Write to a user!(who;write 'prompt Write to who')
```

❖ Lines that are too long may be continued by the use of the \ character.

❖ If you wish to prompt the user for some data, use a command called `prompt`, which takes the following form:

```
prompt prompt-text
```

You can use `prompt` to set an environment variable or to prompt for positional parameters. When prompting for an environment variable, use the following form:

```
TERM='prompt Enter Terminal'
```

For positional parameters use the following form:

```
vi 'prompt Filename'
```

`Prompt` then displays `Filename` >. Answer the prompt and press a carriage return.

`Prompt` has one flag in the compiled version. If it takes the form `prompt - prompt-text`, `prompt` collects exactly one character. In the shell version, the – flag has no effect; all prompts (in the shell version) must be terminated with a carriage return.

❖ The menu compiler is `ccm`. To compile a menu, type the following:

ccm *Menu*

The `ccm` command informs you if it is compiling to binary or to shell script. If you want to force a compilation to shell script, use the `-s` flag (`ccm -s` *Menu*). If you do not have a C compiler, `ccm` automatically compiles to Bourne shell script.

Sample Menu Scripts

This book includes a large number of MSH scripts as part of the MSH system. Specifically, there are two MSH scripts that enable the system administrator to manage parts of the system and manage and install the MSH system itself. During installation, the install script determines to what group the root user belongs and assigns these management scripts to that group. On most systems, `root` belongs to the group `sys`, thus the following MSH script becomes the default script for the group `sys` (or whatever group `root` belongs to).

The following MSH script was designed to show all possible ways of writing a script. Strictly speaking, the setup portion of this script is not necessary, but it is included to show how it is used. The calling program `msh` is located in the `/usr/bin` directory. When invoked, `msh` first determines the group name of the calling user, then it searches for an executable Bourne shell script named `M.Main`. It docs this by rcsctting the `PATII` environment variable to:

```
PATH=$HOME/menu:/usr/lib/menu/group/group-name:$PATH
```

Thus, the program first searches for `M.Main` in a directory called `./menu` in the user's home directory. If `M.Main` is not found here (or if the directory does not exist), a search is made in the proper group directory. The installation program automatically sets up the proper directory for the `root` user's group, so `msh` finds a `M.Main` in its proper place. The installation program also compiles the

MSH script into pure Bourne shell script or, if your system has a C compiler, into a `M.Main` Bourne shell script, a `Main.c` file, and a `m.Main` executable file, which results from compiling the `Main.c` file.

As delivered, the MSH script used as a main menu for system administration looks like this:

```
PATH=:$PATH:$HOME/bin;export PATH
#Main System Menu
Update Your Cron table!(crontab -l>$HOME/crontab;\
   $EDIT $HOME/crontab;crontab $HOME/crontab);;
Who is on the system!who -u -T -H|more
Kill a user!kill -9 'prompt Enter process id'
Write to all users!/etc/wall
Write to a specific user!(who -u -T -H;write \
   'prompt Write to who')
Run Menu Setup Menu!M.Menuadmin;;
HELP!echo press \"h\" for help
```

You notice that the title, indicated by the line beginning with a pound sign (#) is `Main System Menu`. The executable portion of the MSH script consists of all lines after the title and takes the form *menu-list* ! *executable-text*. The first executable line uses two distinct features of the MSH system:

```
Update Your Cron table!(crontab -l>$HOME/crontab;\
   $EDIT $HOME/crontab;crontab $HOME/crontab);;
```

The display portion of this menu script is:

```
Update Your Cron table
```

The executable portion (the script that is executed when this item is selected) is:

```
(crontab -l>$HOME/crontab;\
   $EDIT $HOME/crontab;crontab $HOME/crontab);;
```

The display and executable portions of this command are separated by an exclamation mark. The first feature of this executable command is the use of the continuation character \. If a command requires more than a single line of text, the continuation character must be used to tell the compiler that the next line is a continuation of the first. The second feature of this command is that it is a compound command—it consists of three separate commands, delineated by a semi-colon, and enclosed within parentheses.

You also notice the use of the environment variables $HOME and $EDIT, which are set automatically by msh and passed on to M.Main. Finally, the command is terminated with double semi-colons, which indicate to the compiler that when the command is completed, the screen should be cleared and the menu repainted.

The second line of the executable script demonstrates the use of pipes within the MSH system. Note that a pipe is not a compound command; rather, it is considered by the shell as one command. Note also that the command is not terminated with double semi-colons. This instructs the compiler to leave the results of the command visible, that is, not to clear the screen. This is because the command who -u -T -H|more displays a list of users and their process ID numbers and is designed to be used in conjunction with the third command. The third command is as follows:

```
Kill a user!kill -9 'prompt Enter process id'
```

This command demonstrates the use of the prompt command. The prompt command is discussed in depth later in this chapter.

The next-to-last line in the menu demonstrates how to execute other menus, as follows:

```
Run Menu Setup Menu!M.Menuadmin;;
```

In this case, the menu `Menuadmin` is provided to aid the system administrator in managing the MSH system. The file `Menuadmin` is compiled into `M.Menuadmin`; it is compiled into `m.Menuadmin` if there is a C compiler on the system.

After a menu has been compiled with the `ccm` command, it may be executed directly by running the `M.Menuname` shell script or through the menu shell itself, `msh`. In the latter case, all initial menus must have the name "Main" because `M.Main` is the only command `msh` will execute.

Navigating through a Menu

The Main menu provided with MSH for the `root` group looks like this on the screen:

```
        Mon Sep 18 11:52:37 AM EDT 1989

        Main System Menu
        /usr/adm
    1   Update Your Cron table
    2   Who is on the system
    3   Kill a user
    4   Write to all users
    5   Write to a specific user
    6   Run Menu Setup Menu
    7   HELP
      >
```

The main components of the displayed menu are the date/time line, the menu name, the current directory, the menu itself, and the prompt line.

The date, time, and current directory are recalculated each time the menu is redisplayed. The menu also checks to see if any new mail has arrived. If it has, a `Messages` flag displays. A menu with pending mail looks like this:

```
        Tue Sep 19 11:33:18 AM EDT 1989
        Messages
        Main System Menu
        /usr/lib/menu
    1   Update Your Cron table
    2   Who is on the system
    3   Kill a user
    4   Write to all users
    5   Write to a specific user
    6   Run Menu Setup Menu
    7   HELP
      >
```

To access the mail (and a number of other functions), use one of the following "hidden" functions:

- ❖ c. Changes directories relative to your current directory. For example, at the prompt, type .. to go back up the directory tree or give an absolute path name such as /usr/prospect or $HOME.

- ❖ e. Invokes the system editor (the default is the vi editor)

- ❖ h. Displays HELP file.

- ❖ l. Lists files in the current directory in ls -F format.

- ❖ m. Invokes the mail system (the default is the UNIX mail command).

- ❖ q. Exits the current menu (or logs out from the Main menu).
- ❖ s. Invokes the schedule system (the default is to edit $HOME/calendar).
- ❖ !. Invokes the Bourne shell (or csh if SHELL=/bin/csh).

To make a selection from the menu, press the number displayed next to the item you want to run. In the compiled C version of MSH, the prompt command expects a single character; in the Bourne shell version a carriage return after the selection is required. For example, if item one is desired, press the number **1** or press one of the hidden command characters (followed by a carriage return in the shell script version).

The menu interpreter, menu, responds to all of the hidden functions except c and s—in all other respects, it acts the same as a compiled menu.

Running the Menu Shell

The Menu shell may be run in three ways. First, it may be run from any standard shell by typing **msh**. Second, it may be placed in the login file as the standard shell to be run when a user logs in. The password file (for UNIX System V Release 3) has an entry for each user and looks like this:

```
prospect:i34Jx1:prospect:/usr/prospect:/usr/bin/msh
```

Notice that the last field is /usr/bin/msh, which automatically executes the Menu shell as soon as the user logs in. Most current versions of UNIX (and all versions of Release 4) require the use of a system-administration program to create or alter the passwd file for a user. Some versions require the shells to be defined, so msh must be installed as a shell. Your manual can instruct you on this.

Finally, the menu administration menu may be run by running `msh -a` from the shell. The administration menu enables the system manager to create groups, group menus, `.profile` files for groups, and menus for everyone. Only the superuser should run `msh` in this manner. Ordinary users can invoke `msh -a` and the menu will still be displayed, but none of the commands will execute properly.

Discussing the Programs

The development of MSH was one of evolution and necessity, rather than of revolution and insight. The necessity was the result of developing and maintaining diverse applications on many different UNIX machines.

Some UNIX system manufacturers offered menuing systems as additions to their particular versions of UNIX, but these were not universally available or portable. In other cases, applications programs included menu systems, but these were not portable either. Because learning UNIX was so hard, becoming familiar with a dozen different menu systems and maintaining them on a haphazard basis was impossible. It was easier to write menus in portable shell script than it was to use any one proprietary menu system, but keeping menus graphically consistent (important in business applications) was difficult.

As a result of necessity, the first menu generator was developed with the intent of generating only an approximation of a working shell script. It was used successfully for several years in several small UNIX installations. To ensure portability across systems, only the Bourne shell scripts `awk` and `sed` were used.

The first menu scripting language was awkward at best, and its redesign necessitated a rewrite of the menu generator. This redesign of the menu scripting language resulted in the Bourne shell version of the MSH system. The only major departure from that original MSH Bourne shell compiler has been the creation of the `prompt` program, which has proved useful as a stand-alone command and the addition of the hidden functions described above.

 The C version of the MSH system resulted from the need to improve the speed of the MSH system and the security of the menu shell itself. The `menu` command was developed last as a useful afterthought.

Understanding the MSH File Structure

The MSH install program creates a number of directories and installs several front-end programs in `/usr/bin`. This section is intended to acquaint you with the names, locations, and functions of the programs in the MSH system.

The front-end programs placed in `/usr/bin` are the following:

* ❖ `ccm`. The first stage of the menu compiler, it calls the program `/usr/lib/menu/bin/CC` if there is a C compiler present in the system, or `/usr/lib/menu/bin/MM` if the menu is to be compiled into Bourne shell script.

* ❖ `getwho`. This small program generates the login name and group name of the user and is called by `msh`.

* ❖ `menu`. This program is an interpreter for MSH source files. It displays menus that look exactly the same as compiled menus, but it misses several hidden functions.

This command is useful for embedding menus within shell scripts.

❖ `msh`. This program is actually a Bourne shell script that is called as a shell. Its function is to search for a `M.Main` menu in the correct order, and then to execute that menu.

❖ `prompt`. This program displays a prompt line and requests input from the user. It is delivered as both a C program and a conventional Bourne shell script. If the system has a C compiler, `/usr/bin/prompt` is a compiled executable C program. If not, it is the Bourne shell script version. The source code for `prompt.c` is located in `/usr/lib/menu/src`, and the Bourne shell source code is found in `/usr/lib/menu/bin/prompt.old`.

The install script creates the following directories (if these directories already exist, the install script balks):

```
/usr/lib/menu
/usr/lib/menu/bin
/usr/lib/menu/group
/usr/lib/menu/group/sys
/usr/lib/menu/lib
/usr/lib/menu/src
```

The main directory, `/usr/lib/menu`, contains several subdirectories. It also contains the MSH source for the menu administration menu (named `Menuadmin`), which is called by the command `msh -a`. The installation script compiles both of these menus, so that there is at least one additional file named `M.Menuadmin`. If there is a C compiler on the system, two additional files are found: `Menuadmin.c` and `m.Manuadmin`. The `.c` file is the C source code generated by the `ccm` command, and the `m.` file is the binary executable version of the `.c` file.

The directory `/usr/lib/menu/bin` contains all subsidiary programs used by the MSH system. This directory is appended to the environment `PATH` variable to be searched for executable programs by the `msh` and `ccm` commands. This directory contains the following programs:

❖ `CC`. This program is the shell script that generates a C source from an MSH menu script. Once the C source is created, it is compiled and named m.*Filename*, in which *Filename* is the name of the MSH script and *Filename.c* is the name of the C source file.

❖ `MM`. This program generates Bourne shell script from an MSH script file.

❖ `ccm`. This program is the first stage of the MSH compiler. A copy of this program is placed in `/usr/bin`.

❖ `cgroup`, `dgmenu`, `dgroup`, `egmenu`, `egroup`, `emenu`. These Bourne shell script programs are called by the `Menuadmin` menu. Their functions are to create groups (`cgroup`), delete group menus (`dgmenu`), edit group menus (`egmenu`), edit groups (`egroup`), and edit menus (`emenu`).

❖ `getwho`. This program generates the login name and group name of the user. A copy of this program is placed in `/usr/bin`.

❖ `menu`. This program interprets MSH source scripts and displays menus in the same format as compiled menus. A copy of this program is placed in `/usr/bin`.

❖ `msh`. This program is the front-end shell that searches for an executable menu named `M.Main`. A copy of this program is placed in `/usr/bin`.

❖ `prompt.old`. This program is the Bourne shell script version of the `prompt` program. If no C compiler is found on the system by the installation script, this program, `prompt.old`, is copied to `/usr/bin` and renamed `prompt`.

❖ `xplit`. Both CC and MM use the standard UNIX command `csplit` to separate the three parts of an MSH menu script. Some earlier versions of UNIX do not have `csplit`, so `xplit` was created to perform the same function.

Whenever a user presses **h** from a compiled menu, a help screen is displayed through the filter pg. This help screen is a file named `/usr/lib/menu/lib/HELP`.

The `prompt` command is the only part of the MSH system that is written in C. If the install script detects that there is a C compiler on the system, `/usr/lib/menu/src/prompt.c` is compiled and copies of the resulting `prompt` command are placed in `/usr/bin` and in `/usr/lib/menu/bin`.

The MSH source script for the default Main menu for the `root` user group is located in `/usr/lib/menu/group/sys/Main`. If the install script detects, through the `getwho` command, that the group name of the `root` user is something other than `sys`, the `/usr/lib/group/sys` directory is renamed to that group.

In addition to the directories and their contents, the `/usr/lib/menu` directory contains three other files: `Menuadmin`, `install`, and `update`. The `Menuadmin` file is the MSH source for the menu administration menu. The `install` and `update` files are Bourne shell scripts for installing and updating the MSH system, respectively.

Understanding the MSH Programs

The heart of the MSH system consists of seven programs. Three of these programs are utility programs that are used outside the Menu shell proper: `prompt`, `getwho`, and `menu`. The `msh` command is invoked as a standard shell; `ccm`, `CC`, and `MM` are components of the MSH compiler.

The remainder of the programs are not part of the MSH system; they are part of the "demo" package that contains the `sys` group, the Main menu, and the `Menuadmin` menu. The order in which the programs are presented represents a logical order of use rather than the traditional alphabetical ordering. The utilities are discussed first.

The `prompt` Program

Within the MSH system, the `prompt` command is called only from within Bourne shell menus (from within menus compiled into Bourne shell scripts). The `prompt` command has a far wider use than just to simplify the MSH system, however. The `prompt` command can be used within shell scripts to prompt the user to enter data. This data can, in turn, be used to set environment variables or positional parameters.

The `prompt.old` Program

Functionally, the `prompt` command does very little. How little it does can be seen in the following source code for the Bourne shell version:

```
if [ "$1" = "-" ]
then
shift
```

```
fi
echo "$*  >\c" >/dev/tty
read x ; echo $x
```

Because the `prompt` command is used with a prompt line such as `prompt` *Enter data*, the `echo "$*  >\c"` command echoes the data to the screen, appends a >, and leaves the cursor positioned just after the prompt. When executed, the command displays the following:

```
Enter data  >
```

Anything typed in response to the prompt is echoed back. This is useful when used in command substitution. For example, to set an environment variable with the `prompt` command, enter the following:

VAR='prompt Enter value for VAR'

The `prompt` command also is useful when setting positional parameters, as in `pg 'prompt Enter File Name'`. In both cases, the string entered in response to the prompt is substituted for the command.

Note that in the fifth line of the `prompt` program, the output of the `echo` command is redirected to `/dev/tty`. The `tty` device is a pseudonym for whatever device the user is connected to. If the `echo` command were not redirected, the string produced by the `echo` command would be placed on the standard output (substituted for the command). Instead, the prompt line should go to the terminal (`/dev/tty`), and what is typed in response to the prompt should be placed on the standard output.

The `if` statement at the beginning of the `prompt` command is used to make the Bourne shell version of `prompt` conform to the compiled version. In the compiled version, the – flag indicates that the `prompt` command accepts exactly one character in `raw` mode. (Only a single character is accepted and it is not necessary to enter a carriage return to enter the data.) The Bourne shell version ignores the flag and a carriage return is necessary to terminate the entered string.

The prompt.c Program

If the system has a C compiler, the install script compiles the prompt.c program, located in /usr/lib/menu/src, and places copies of the executable prompt program in /usr/bin and in /usr/lib/menu/bin. In almost all respects, the prompt.c program does the same thing as the shell script version, with one exception. If the prompt command is invoked with a flag, that is, as prompt - *prompt string*, the prompt command reads exactly one character and returns it without the user having to enter a carriage return. This makes the Bourne shell version of a menu much faster and makes it behave exactly like the compiled version.

The source for prompt.c is written in portable and minimal C. This section has used system calls to stty, rather than using ioctl, in order to make the program smaller and more portable.

If speed is important, use ioctl.

The following is the source code for prompt.c (note that comments have been added that are not included in the source on the disk):

```
#include <stdio.h>
char *cpyrit = "#@ Prompt -- Copyright (C) 1992 S.R.Glines";
```

The preceding lines include a comment that will print when the executable file is scanned with the strings command.

```
char x;FILE *fpt;
main(argc,argv)
int argc;char *argv[];
```

```
{
    int a, y=1;
    if (strcmp(argv[1],"-") == 0 ){
        y=2;
    }
```

The preceding lines test `argv[1]` for a flag character. If present, it signals the input of just one character.

```
fpt=fopen("/dev/tty","w");
```

The preceding line opens `/dev/tty` for writing, just as the Bourne Shell script version.

```
for (a=y;a<argc;a++){
    fprintf(fpt,"%s ",argv[a]);
}
fprintf(fpt," >");
fclose(fpt);
```

Print out the `prompt` string, starting with `argv[2]` if `argv[1]` is a flag character. You then print the `prompt` character and close `/dev/tty`. The prompt has been displayed.

```
if (y == 2 ) {
    system("stty raw");
    x=getchar();
    system("stty cooked");
    printf("%c\n",x);
}
```

If the flag character was present on the command line, the preceding lines show where you collect a single character. By setting `"stty raw"`, you can read every character typed by the user, instead of waiting for the user to press Enter before reading. Because you do not want to leave the terminal in a `raw` state, set `"stty cooked"` as soon as you get a character. Then print that character on the standard output.

```
else {
    char w[80];
    gets(w);
    printf("%s\n",w);
}
```

If the flag character was not present on the command line, you want to read a string that is terminated by a carriage return. For this, leave the terminal in normal cooked mode and read the string with gets. When you have received the string, print it out on the standard output.

```
exit();  /* This is superfluous but "correct". */
}
```

The getwho **Program**

The getwho command is used by msh to get the login name and group name of the user. It does this by passing the output of the id command through sed to strip extraneous characters. The source for getwho is kept in /usr/lib/menu/bin, and a copy is placed in /usr/bin. The getwho shell script is:

```
id|sed -e 's/[0-z]*(//g; s/)//g'
```

The output for id, if run by the root user, looks like this:

```
UID=1(root) GID=2(sys)
```

The sed command strips away everything but root sys. It does this by using two commands. The first sed command, s/[0-z]*(//g, removes all characters between the characters 0 and z (including the equal sign, using the ASCII character set) and terminates with (. Note that this regular expression does not include the space character. The output of the first sed command is:

```
root) sys)
```

The second `sed` command, `s/)//g`, removes all `)`s, so that the output is `root sys`. The `g` that is appended to each of the commands instructs `sed` to perform the command on multiple occurrences of the test string.

The `menu` Program

As UNIX programs go, `menu` is not very big because it is a primitive language interpreter. Any language interpreter contains two parts. The first part (the *parser*) splits up the source code according to rules of grammar and presents the parts in a normalized form to the second half of the language interpreter (the *interpreter*), which actually executes the instructions. Fortunately, the rules of menu shell script grammar are simple.

A menu shell script consists of three parts: a start-up Bourne shell script, a menu title, and the menu itself. The third part of a menu script also consists of three parts: the display item, the execution script, and a flag (or absence of a flag) that indicates whether or not to redisplay the menu before prompting the user for input. The redisplay flag consists of two semicolons appended after the execution script.

Sample Menu Script

A simple menu script might look like this:

```
echo "this is part of the start-up Bourne shell script"
read x
#The Menu Title
first!echo "first";;
second!echo second;;
```

The job of the parser is to split the source into two components. The first component, which must be isolated for later use, is the

Bourne shell start-up script, if it exists. In the case of the sample menu, the start-up script consists of two lines, which generically consist of all the lines in the menu script, up to, but not including, the line beginning with a pound sign (#):

```
echo "this is part of the start-up Bourne shell
script"
read x
```

In the compiled versions of MSH, this startup script, together with some additional code, is placed in M. *Filename*. In the menu interpreter, the startup script is placed aside for later execution as an inline shell script by using the dot command, so that its execution affects the environment later in the menu program. In the menu program, this shell script is placed in /tmp/m.$$, in which $$ is replaced by the process ID of the menu program.

What remains after this first step is:

```
#The Menu Title
first!echo "first";;
second!echo second;;
```

The parser now has a few remaining chores. First, the leading pound sign can be stripped. Second, any lines containing the line-continuation character must be merged with the following lines. Finally, the repaint flag must be dealt with.

The process just described is called *normalizing* the data: all the data in the file is made consistent by simplification.

The normalized data is placed in a file named /tmp/M.$$, in which $$ is the process ID of menu. The normalized (fully-parsed) menu now looks like this:

```
The Menu Title
first!echo "first"!0
second!echo second!0
```

The actual interpretation of the normalized menu is performed by another interpreter, `nawk`. Before `nawk` can perform, however, the start-up shell script must be executed. This is performed by using the dot command, as follows:

```
.  /tmp/m.$$
```

Any environment variables that are set in the start-up script are in force when `nawk` performs its interpretation of the menu.

 There is an important difference between compiled menus and menus interpreted by `menu`. In menus run by the `menu` command, environment variables must be exported if they are to have any effect. They need not be exported in compiled menus because the compiled menu is either the inline Bourne shell script or the executable file, m.*Filename*. This is run by the `exec` command, which replaces M.*Filename* as the executing task, and does not require variables to be exported because they inherit the same process environment as the calling program.

The `nawk` program that interprets the menu uses the exclamation mark as the field delimiter. Thus, the menu title can be distinguished because it is the first line in the data. All of the remaining records in the data have either two or three fields in each record.

Records that have three fields in each record are, by definition, records indicating that the menu is to be repainted on the screen after execution. In the following sample, both records repaint the screen after execution. The sample menu, when run, looks like this on the screen:

```
Tue Jun 22 11:52:37 PM EDT 1992

The Menu Title
/usr/srg
1  first
2  second
>
```

The menu Program

Now that you know how menu works in general, the next sections discuss the specifics. As with prompt.c, comments are included here that are not present in the source code on the disk. The following is the source for menu, a menu interpreter:

```
:
if [ $# -eq "0" ]
then
cat >/tmp/X.$$
set 'echo "/tmp/X.$$"'
fi
```

Check to see whether a menu name has been provided on the command line. If not, assume that a menu script is to be piped into the menu command, either from a genuine pipe or through inline text redirected with the use of the << symbol.

 Menus that run from within a pipe disconnect the standard input, so applications like vi cannot be run.

The set command is used to put the temporary file into $1:

```
if [ -f "$1" ]
then
```

Check to see if the menu source file exists. If it does, proceed.

```
nawk 'BEGIN{x=0;}
/^#/ {x=1;print ;next}
{if(x == 1){print}
else print > TEMP }
END{
print "EDIT=${EDIT:=vi};export EDIT" > TEMP
print "MAILER=${MAILER:=mail};export MAILER" > TEMP
}' TEMP="/tmp/m."$$ $1|
```

The preceding step splits the start-up script from the rest of the menu script. The loop looks for a line beginning with #, which separates the start-up script from the body of the menu. Until a # is found, all lines of the menu are placed in a temporary file.

As soon as a # is found, that line and all remaining lines are passed unaltered to the next step through a pipe. After the last line of the menu script has been processed, the END section appends the EDIT and MAILER lines to the temporary script. Note that the name of the temporary file is passed as a parameter, and the name is derived from the shell variable "$$," which reduces to the process ID of the menu program.

```
sed -e '
/^$/D
/\\$/ N
/\\\n/ s/\\\n/ /
s/"/\\"/g
s/\\\\"/\\"/g
/^#/,$ {
s/! */!/
s/:;;/: ;;/
/[\ -9,A-z];;$/ s/;$/!0/
s/^#//
} ' >/tmp/M.$$
```

The following describes the effects of each line in the `sed` program:

- ❖ `/^$/D.` Deletes any empty lines

- ❖ `/\\$/ N U.` Places any lines ending in \ in the hold space to be concatenated

- ❖ `/\\\n/ s/\\\n/ /.` Converts any lines that contain a \, followed by a new line, into a space—effectively concatenating two lines that are intended to be continued

- ❖ `s/"/\\"/g.` Converts a quotation mark to an escaped quotation mark

- ❖ `s/\\\\"/\\"/g.` If the user escaped the quotation mark already, you have just double-escaped it, so this line converts it back to a simple escaped quote

- ❖ `/^#/,$ {.` An address range that performs the instructions between { and } on the range between the line that begins with a # and the last line

- ❖ `s/! */!/.` Removes any extra space after the exclamation point

- ❖ `s/:;;/: ;;/.` Removes any ambiguity from the next command

- ❖ `/[\ -9,A-z];;$/ s/;$/!0/.` Converts any line ending in ; ; to a line ending in ! 0, which yields three fields in lines that must be repainted

- ❖ `s/^#//.` Deletes the # from the menu title. The text of the title record is now just the title as it will be displayed

The `sed` program ends with the } to enclose those instructions operating on the address range.

The menu has now been fully parsed and is ready for interpretation.

```
if [ -f "/tmp/m.$$" ]
then
. /tmp/m.$$
fi
```

If the shell script worked correctly so far, there should be a Bourne shell script ready for running in /tmp/m.$$. This tests for its existence; if it is there, the script is run with the dot command, which effectively includes that script within this program. Any environment variables that are modified in this temporary file affect the rest of this program, but only if they have been exported.

```
nawk 'BEGIN { FS="!"}
NR == 1 {title=$0;}
NR > 1 {count=NR-1;A[count]=$1;B[count]=$2;
if(NF==3){C[count]=$3} else {C[count]=1}}
```

Start by defining the exclamation point as the field separator. The first record is the title; you detect it in line 2. All other lines in the menu are instructions. You know that there will be either two or three fields in the remaining records. They are defined as follows:

❖ What is to be displayed

❖ What is to be executed

❖ A flag, saying that the menu should be redisplayed

These fields are placed in arrays A, B, and C, using the record number minus one for the index. Because records requiring redisplay have three fields, no other records are marked for no display after execution. The "if" statement sets up the redisplay array in C.

Now that the menu is safely in memory, you can proceed with the interpretation:

```
END{
r=0
```

The r is set to the redisplay setting of the last command run. The first time through, you want the menu displayed, so r=0:

```
while(1){
if(r==0){
```

The loop is runs perpetually unless a command that generates a break is encountered. Then r is tested; if r=0, the menu is displayed, as follows:

```
printf("%s\n%26s",cls," ");system("date")
if(! system("test -s $MAIL")){
printf("\n              Messages\n")}
else printf("\n\n")
printf("%25s %s\n"," ",title);
printf("%26s%s\n\n"," ",pwd)
```

The menu header is displayed, along with the menu title. The first thing that is displayed is the string contained in the variable cls, which is the clear screen string set externally (see the last line of the program). It consists of cls=`clear`. Using it this way only requires that the clear program be executed once. The next line uses the return from a system call to test for any mail in the mailbox. If the user's mailbox contains one or more characters, the Message line is displayed. After that, the title and the current working directory are displayed. Because there is no easy way to change directories from within nawk, the current directory is passed to nawk in the same fashion as the clear screen string.

```
for(i=1;i<=count;i++){printf("%22s %1u  %s\n"," ",i,A[i])}
}
```

In the preceding lines, you actually display the menu and terminate the `if` statement.

```
printf("\n%26s",">");
x=""
getline x <"/dev/tty"
```

The preceding displays the prompt `">"`, sets *x* to the null string, and reads *x* from the user using `"getline"`.

```
if(x == "" || x == "r") {r=0;continue}
if(x == "c" || x == "s") {r=1;print "Not
available";continue}
if(x == "!") {system("exec sh");r=0;continue}
if(x == "l") {system("ls -F -c");r=1;continue}
if(x == "e") {system("$EDIT `prompt
File`");r=0;continue}
if(x == "m") {system("$MAILER `prompt To
who`");r=1;continue}
if(x == "h")
{system("pg -n -c -s /usr/lib/menu/lib/
HELP");r=1;continue}
```

Because there is no `case` or `switch` statement in nawk, you have to use the old fashioned "`if`" statement, as in FORTRAN or BASIC. In the previous section, you tested for all system defaults and executed the appropriate command by using a `system` call. Note also that you must explicitly define the redisplay flag, `r`, to 0 for redisplay or 1 for no redisplay. Note also how easy it is to add or change these defaults.

```
if(x == "q"){break}
if(x > 0 && x <= count ){system(B[x]);r=C[x];}
else
{printf("\007\n\nNot Found -- press \"h\" for
help\n");
r=1;
}}
}´ cls='clear'  pwd='pwd'  /tmp/M.$$
```

In the preceding lines, test for a q, which indicates "quit," and you use the `break` command to exit the `while` loop. If you fall through to the default, you test the value of x to be sure it falls within the correct number range. If it does, execute the command found in `B[x]` using the `system` call, and update the repaint flag from the `C[x]` address in the array. If all else fails, print an error message that begins with a beep, `octal 007`, and remind the user that help is available. Notice, on the last line, that you have "fed" nawk with the values of `cls`, `pwd`, and the name of the parsed file.

One way to pass the entire environment to a `nawk` program is to append a `'set'` command before naming the data file, as in the following:

```
"nawk '{program}' `set` filename"

rm /tmp/[XMm].$$
fi
```

After you exit from the `nawk` program, the preceding lines clean up the temporary files you create and exit the "`if`" statement that tested for the existence of the original menu source file.

The msh Program

There is nothing special about a shell—it is a program that takes input from an ordinary user and does something with it. Writing shells in UNIX is a lot easier than in other operating systems because there are a number of processes that happen automatically.

First, in UNIX a shell inherits open inputs and outputs from the `login` process, so no complex programming is required on that task. Second, if the UNIX kernel detects that the file listed as a shell is executable, but is in fact a text file, it is (by default) run as a Bourne shell script. Because the Bourne shell is the internal UNIX standard, its shell script can be used as a login shell.

A C program (or any binary executable program) that transforms itself into another program with one of the `exec` system calls can transmute itself into either another binary executable command or a Bourne shell script. If the command is a shell script, the Bourne shell is called first in the form `sh -c ´exec command´`. The `msh` program is a Bourne shell script.

 Only shell scripts written in the Bourne shell can be used as shells in themselves. All other forms of shell scripts fail because shells must be binary executable files or Bourne shell scripts. (All `exec` commands are executed by the kernel as `sh -c 'exec command'`.)

The `msh` shell script is very simple—its only function is to set up the execution of a menu. More specifically, the `msh` program sets up required environment variables and searches for a Main menu in the required order: a private menu first, followed by a group menu, and finally a system-wide menu. It executes the first Main menu it finds. (Again, comments have been added that are not found in the source on the disk):

```
:
. /etc/profile
```

Run the `/etc/profile` start-up script just like the Bourne shell. Note that it is run with the dot command, so it will affect the rest of the script.

```
EDIT=${EDIT:-vi}
MAILER=${MAILER:-mail}
CALENDAR=${CALENDAR:-"$EDIT $HOME/calendar"}
```

Set up the environment variables used later on in a menu and accessed by "hidden" functions.

```
#stty intr 'echo "\003"'
#tset -Q
```

It is usually expedient to set the interrupt key to something other than the Del key, which is usually the default. In this case, you have set the interrupt key to Ctrl-C. To enable this feature, disable the comment on the `stty` line.

The `tset` command sends the terminal initialization string, as found in the terminal's `termcap` or `terminfo` definition.

 Most of these definitions are wrong or play havoc with dial-up terminals. It is the user's choice to use the `tset` command. In general, it is better left commented out.

```
X=$*;
set 'getwho'
```

You save any and all command-line parameters in the variable X. You do this so that you can place the user's login name and group name the environment with `getwho`. The `set` command places the login name in `$1` and the user group name in `$2`.

```
if [ -r "/usr/lib/menu/group/$2/.profile" ] ;
    then . /usr/lib/menu/group/$2/.profile; fi
```

In the preceding lines, if a `.profile` file has been defined for the user group, execute it with the dot command.

```
if [ -r "$HOME/.profile" ] ; then . $HOME/.profile;
fi
```

If the user has a private `.profile`, execute it also with the dot command.

```
PATH=$PATH:$HOME/menu:/usr/lib/menu/group/$2:/usr/
lib/menu
```

Update the PATH variable, so that `msh` searches for menus in the right order. Note that the search path is the user's `./menu` directory first, followed by the user's group directory, and finally by the system-wide menu directory `/usr/lib/menu`.

```
export PS1 PS2 EDIT PATH CALENDAR MAILER
```

Now you export everything you have set in the environment.

```
if [ "$X" = "-a" ]
then
shift
exec M.Menuadmin
else
exec M.Main
fi
```

The only valid parameter used on the command line when calling `msh` is `-a`. This is intended to be used by the system administrator to manage and create menus by using the `Menuadmin` menu included as part of the demonstration package. All other command-line parameters (or the absence of any parameters) cause `msh` to exec to the first executable `M.Main` file found in its search path, as defined by the `PATH` variable.

The `ccm` Menu Compiler

There are purists who claim that `ccm` is not really a compiler—that it is a code generator. This book, however, defines a *compiler* as a program that takes human-readable, non-executable code, and transforms it into a program that can run on a given machine.

It does not matter whether the code is Bourne shell script or compiled C; both run on any standard UNIX system and produce exactly the same results. The `ccm` program is only the first step in the compiler; its function is to determine if the menu is to be transformed into Bourne shell script or into C. Having made that decision, it sets up the proper environment and calls one of the two code-generation programs. Programs are compiled using the following syntax:

```
ccm [-s] [-g] [-c] Menu_name
```

If the system has a C compiler installed as /bin/cc, the default for ccm is to compile a menu from generated C code. The -s flag overrides the default and produces Bourne shell script instead. The -g flag generates menus, without any of the "hidden" features, for security-conscious installations.

The -c flag overrides the default of prompting the user in raw mode. That is, in raw mode the user need only type a single character instead of a character and a carriage return for the menu selection to take effect. In the absence of a C compiler, the menu can only prompt in cooked mode.

The following is the code for ccm (comments are added that are not in the source on the disk):

```
:
echo "Menu Compiler V 3.0 --  Copyright (C) 1992
S.R.Glines   "
X=1
GUT=NOGUT
COOKED=RAW
for i in $*
do
case $1 in
"-c") COOKED="";shift;;
"-s") X=0;shift;;
"-g") GUT=GUT;shift;;
esac
done
export COOKED GUT
```

The default menu is to be compiled C with all hidden functions enabled with prompting in raw mode. To change any of these defaults requires the use of one or more flags.

The `-c` flag sets the `prompt` command to cooked, which means that a carriage return must be entered to continue. The `-s` flag (and hence the *X* variable) means that the menu is to be compiled to shell script. The `-g` flag indicates that the menu is to be compiled with all hidden options removed (the menu is "gutted").

```
if [ -r "$1" ]
then
```

The file to be compiled must exist and be readable or an error message is printed.

```
if [ -x "/bin/cc" -a "$X" = "1" ]
then
echo "compiling to binary "
/usr/lib/menu/bin/CC $1
```

The preceding lines check to be sure that a C compiler exists on the system and that you wanted the menu compiled to binary. If so, run the CC compiler.

```
else
echo "compiling to shell script"

/usr/lib/menu/bin/MM $1
```

Otherwise, compile to Bourne shell script with the MM code generator.

```
fi
else
```

This is the end of the inner loop.

```
echo "$0: $1 not found"
fi
```

This is the end of the outer loop. If the file to be compiled cannot be found, print an error message.

The bulk of the "real" work of compiling a menu is performed in the two shell scripts CC and MM.

The MM Program

Technically, the MM program is really a code generator; however, it generates Bourne shell script that performs the same way as its compiled counterpart (even to the point of respecting the gut and cooked flags).

Sample Menu

The sample menu used in the menu program was the following:

```
echo "this is part of the start-up Bourne shell
script"
read x
#The Menu Title
first!echo "first";;
second!echo second;;
```

When compiled with the command ccm -s *Menu*, the MM program generates the following output (the menu script is annotated with comments that do not appear in the actual M.*Menu* file because it is generated by MM):

```
:
echo "this is part of the start-up Bourne shell
script"
read x
```

This code is common to all versions of the start-up file "M.Menu".

```
clear='clear'
pwd='pwd'
EDIT=${EDIT:=vi}
MAILER=${MAILER:=mail}
```

Set the environment variable `clear` to the string that clears the screen. Set `pwd` to the current directory. Set `MAIL` and `MAILER` if they have not already been set.

```
while true
do
echo $clear"

                                'date'"
if [ -s "$MAIL" ]; then echo "
            Messages" ;else echo "";fi
echo   "                              The Menu Title
                        $pwd

                     1   first
                     2   second
       "
```

You start the perpetual loop here. The only way out is with the interrupt key or with an `exit`. The `echo` commands contain the variables `clear` and `pwd`, which are substituted before the full string is echoed to the screen. The `if` statement tests for existence of mail.

```
while true
do
CMD='prompt - "                          "'
```

You enter a second loop that does nothing but loop on the prompt routines. To exit and redisplay the menu, a `break` is required.

```
case $CMD in
r) break;;
q) echo "";exit;;
h) pg -n -c -s -p"(page %d):" /usr/lib/menu/lib/
HELP;break;;
 1) echo "\n";echo "first";break;;
 2) echo "\n";echo "second";break;;
 !) echo "\n";sh ;break ;;
```

```
e) echo "\n";$EDIT `prompt "filename "`;break;;
s) echo "\n";$CALENDAR ;break;;
m) echo "\n";$MAILER `prompt Mail to who`;read
x;break;;
l) echo "\n";ls -C -F|pg -e -n -s -p"(page %d)" -;;
c) echo "\n";cd `prompt "Change to
"`;pwd=`pwd`;break;;
*) echo "\007\r\c";;
esac
done
done
```

In the preceding lines, the `case` statement is used to test for the entered value. If the user did not make a valid entry into the `prompt` command, a `bell` is sounded. Note the "hidden" commands.

Inside the MM Program

The MM program performs the same parsing operation as the `menu` command. Instead of displaying a menu immediately, however, it generates Bourne shell script that, when run, displays a menu. It is actually easier to display an interpreted menu than it is to generate the code that does the same. Here is the annotated version of the MM program:

```
:
trap 'rm M$$ MSH0[0-3]' 0 1 2 3 4 5 6 7 8
```

If you press the interrupt key while MM is running, trap that interrupt and clean up the mess you have created.

```
if [ ! -r "$1" ]
then
echo "ccm: file not found"
exit 1
fi
```

The preceding lines are redundant because the existence of the file is checked in the ccm program. Leave it here, though, so that MM can be run as a stand-alone program for debugging during changes.

```
echo ´:´ >M$$
```

This line places a colon at the beginning of the file, which ensures that if the menu is invoked from a C shell, a Bourne shell will actually be run.

```
sed -e ´
/^$/D
/\\$/ N
/\\\n/ s/\\\n/ /
/^#/,$ {
s/! */!/
/[\ -9,A-z];;$/ s/;$/break;;/
/[\ -9,A-z]$/ s/$/;;/
/[\ -9,A-z];$/ s/$/;/
/^#/ s/;;$//
}´ $1>> M$$
```

This sed script performs exactly the same function as it did in the menu program, so you do not have to perform a line-by-line analysis as you did for menu. Note that you have appended the parsed file in M$$.

```
if [ -x /bin/csplit -o -x /usr/bin/csplit ]
then
csplit -f MSH M$$ /#/  /./ >/dev/null
else
/usr/lib/menu/bin/xplit M$$
fi
```

The csplit command is usually a standard part of UNIX, but it is not always included in older versions of XENIX. When it is found, its location wanders. If you find it, use it;, if it is missing, use a little awk program called xplit.

Using `csplit` is faster. You use this to parse the three segments of a menu script into three separate files named MSH00, MSH01, and MSH03.

```
mv MSH00 M.$1
```

You know that the first file created by `csplit` is MSH00 and that it contains the Bourne shell start-up script, if any, so you can move it to the executable menu file.

```
sed 's/^#//' << \XXXXX >>M.$1
## MSH compiler V 3.0 Copyright (c) 1992 S.R.Glines
#clear='clear'
#pwd='pwd'
#EDIT=${EDIT:=vi}
#MAILER=${MAILER:=mail}
#while true
#do
#echo $clear"
#                              'date'"
#if [ -s "$MAIL" ]; then echo "
#              Messages" ;else echo "";fi
XXXXX
```

You append a standard Bourne shell code to the file after the start-up script. Note that you have used `sed` to insert text exactly as it would appear. The # is used to ensure that the shell considers the text to be comments while `sed` is running.

```
sed 's/^#/echo  "                                /'
MSH01>>M.$1
echo '                              $pwd'>>M.$1
echo "">>M.$1
```

With the preceding lines, you remove the leading # from the menu title found in MSH01 and use `sed` to insert the proper space. The menu title is appended to the executable shell script, as is the command that prints the working directory.

```
awk 'BEGIN{FS="!";i=0}
{i++;print "                            "i"  "$1}'
MSH02>>M.$1
echo '"'>>M.$1
```

In the preceding lines, you scan the executable portion of the menu script now in MSH02 and, using ! as a field separator, pick out the display items and format them. Finally, you close the echo command by appending a double quote to the executable file.

```
sed 's/^#//' << \XXXXX >>M.$1
#while true
#do
XXXXX
if [ "$COOKED" = "RAW" ]
then
sed 's/^#//' << \XXXXX >>M.$1
#CMD='prompt - "                           " '
XXXXX
else
sed 's/^#//' << \XXXXX >>M.$1
#CMD='prompt   "                           " '
XXXXX
fi
```

You determine if the input to the prompt command is to be in cooked or raw mode and append the correct version of prompt.

```
sed 's/^#//' << \XXXXX >>M.$1
#case $CMD in
#r) break;;
#q) echo "";exit;;
#h) pg -n -c -s -p"(page %d):" /usr/lib/menu/lib/
HELP;break;;
XXXXX
```

In the preceding lines, you append the beginning of the case statement that determines what is to be run from the user's input.

You also append all hidden functions that are still valid if GUT was defined. Note that a break exits the while loop and redisplays the menu.

```
awk 'BEGIN{FS="!";i=0}
{i++;print "  "i") echo \"\\n\";"$2}' MSH02 >>M.$1
```

You rescan the executable portion of the menu script to detect what is to be run for a given menu item and append the proper case statements.

```
if [ "$GUT" = "NOGUT" ]
then
sed 's/^#//' << \XXXXX >>M.$1
#!) echo "\n";sh ;break ;;
#e) echo "\n";$EDIT `prompt "filename "`;break;;
#s) echo "\n";$CALENDAR ;break;;
#m) echo "\n";$MAILER `prompt Mail to who`;read
x;break;;
#l) echo "\n";ls -C -F|pg -e -n -s -p"(page %d)"
-;;
#c) echo "\n";cd `prompt "Change to
"`;pwd=`pwd`;break;;
XXXXX
fi
```

In the preceding lines, if NOGUT is defined (with the absence of the -g flag), you append all the remaining "hidden" functions to the file.

```
sed 's/^#//' << \XXXXX >>M.$1
#*) echo "\007\r\c";;
#esac
#done
#done
XXXXX
chmod +x M.$1
```

Finally, you append the default for the `case` statement, which is to ring the bell, `octal 007`. Then you end the `case` statement and the two `while` loops, and finally make the menu file executable. Note that the `trap` command includes 0, which forces the `trap` command to execute when the program has finished. Thus, there is no need to remove the residue.

The xplit **Program**

As mentioned earlier, some versions of UNIX (notably, some versions of XENIX) are missing the `csplit` command. The `csplit` command is easy to use, and it is fast. The `xplit` command is an `awk` program that performs specifically what is required for the MM and CC programs. Because it is an `awk` program, it is slower (but not by much) and hard-wired (it does not have the flexibility of `csplit`). It is mimicked in the `menu` program. The following is the annotated source:

```
awk 'BEGIN {y=""}
{y=substr($0,1,1)}
```

With the preceding lines, pick out the first character and place it in y.

```
NR==1,/#/ {if(y != "#" ) print $0>"MSH00" }
```

From the first record, up to but not including the record containing a #, write to `MSH00`, the start-up file.

```
/#/ {print $0>"MSH01" }
```

The previous line prints the menu title to `MSH01`.

```
/#/,/END/ {if(y != "#" ) print $0>"MSH02"}
´ $*
```

Print the remainder to `MSH02`, the executable portion of the menu.

The CC Program

The CC program performs exactly the same function as MM, except that the output is standard C, which is then compiled. Some effort is made to determine on which variety of UNIX the MSH system has been installed, so that the standard C can be adjusted to actually run on it.

XENIX is different; it requires slightly different code to run. HP-UX also resembles XENIX more than it does UNIX System V. If the generic code produced by CC does not work on your machine, check the ifdef in the C output and change the code in CC accordingly. (Future versions of HP-UX will conform more closely to System V.)

In many respects, the CC program is much simpler than MM. In the MM program, there are several if statements that are absent in the CC program. This is because you have made use of the C preprocessor to handle both the raw/cooked code and the gut/nogut code.

There also are some programming decisions made that may be considered "bad form" among C programmers. These decisions include using the system("clear") function instead of using the curses library. (If the curses library is included, the executable size of a menu leaps from 40K bytes to over 100K bytes, with only a marginal improvement in performance.)

The ioctl function is used instead of system("stty raw") and system("stty cooked") because of the better terminal control it offers and because it adds only a small amount of RAM to the run-time requirements of each menu.

Sample Menu

The sample menu used in the menu program was:

```
echo "this is part of the start-up Bourne shell script
read x
#The Menu Title
first!echo "first";;
second!echo second;;
```

When compiled with the command ccm *Menu*, the CC program generates three files: an M.*Menu* start-up file, an *Menu.c* C-source file, and an m.*Menu* compiled binary executable file. The M.*Menu* file generated for the sample menu is as follows:

```
echo "this is part of the start-up Bourne shell script"
read x
exec m.Menu
```

The actual menu is contained in the generated C program, which is annotated:

```
#define NOGUT
#define RAWMODE
#include <stdio.h>
#include <sys/types.h>
#include <time.h>
#include <sgtty.h>
char x;
long xx;
#ifdef XENIX
char tmpcl[30], *xclock=tmpcl;
#else
char xclock[64];
#endif
char pwd[64];
char *cpyrt="MSH compiler V3.0 Copyright (c) 1992 S.R.Glines";
```

The results of the `gut` and cooked flags can be found in the previously discussed definitions. The standard `include` files are listed, including `<sgtty.h>`, which enables you to use `ioctl`. XENIX is not defined, so this is a UNIX system. Note the differences in getting the current time and date.

```
main()
{
    struct sgttyb oldparam, newparam;
    ioctl(0, TIOCGETP, &oldparam);
    newparam = oldparam;
    newparam.sg_flags |= RAW;
    newparam.sg_flags &= ~ECHO;
```

You start out by getting the current `stty` parameters, using the `ioctl` function, and setting the new parameters if you need them.

```
start:
    while ( 1 ) {
        system("exec clear");
        time(&xx);
#ifdef XENIX
        xclock=ctime(&xx);
#else
        cftime(xclock,"%a %b %e %r %Z %Y %n",&xx);
#endif
```

Getting the time is one of the few incompatibilities between UNIX and XENIX.

```
        getcwd(pwd,64);
        printf("\n%22s     %s"," ",xclock);
        system("if [ -s \"$MAIL\" ]; then echo \"
Messages\" ;else echo \"\";fi");
```

In the preceding lines, finding out if there is mail can be accomplished without resorting to the `system` function, but only at the expense of writing more code.

```
printf("%26s%s\n","","The Menu Title");
printf("%26s%s\n\n"," ",pwd);
printf("%22s%2d  %s\n"," ",1,"first");
printf("%22s%2d  %s\n"," ",2,"second");
printf("\n");
```

This is as simple as it gets.

```
      while( 1 ) {
#ifdef RAWMODE
        ioctl(0, TIOCSETP, &newparam);
#endif
        printf("\r%22s   %s"," ",">");
        x = getchar();
        ioctl(0, TIOCSETP, &oldparam);
```

The preceding lines enter the user prompt loop. If `raw` mode is defined, set `stty` to `raw` using `ioctl`. After prompting the user and getting a single character, set `stty` back to cooked, even if `RAWMODE` has not been defined.

```
        switch(x) {
        case '1':
          printf("\nloading...\n");
          system("exec echo \"first\";");
          goto start;
        case '2':
          printf("\nloading...\n");
          system("exec echo \"second\";");
          goto start;
        case 'q':
          goto end;
```

Instead of using a `goto end`, you should have copied the two functions at the end of the program: `printf("\n")` and `exit(0)`. It is better to just `goto end`.

```
case 'l':
    printf("\n\n");
    system("ls -C -F|pg -e -n -s -p\"(page
%d):\"");
    break;
```

If you do not want to repaint the screen, use a `break` to return to the loop.

In the following, you use the C preprocessor to sort out the GUT flag. If the `ccm` command was used with the `-g` flag, the following would not be included in the compile:

```
#ifdef NOGUT
        case '!':
            printf("\n\n");
            system("exec sh");
            goto start;
        case 'e':
            printf("\n\n");
            system("exec ${EDIT:=vi} `prompt What
file`");
            goto start;
        case 'm':
            printf("\n\n");
            system("${MAILER:=mail} `prompt Mail to
who`");
            break;
        case 's':
            printf("\n\n");
            system("$CALENDAR");
            goto start;
        case 'c':
```

```
            printf("\n\n");
            printf("%s\n",pwd);
            printf("Change to what directory > ");
            gets(pwd);
            chdir(pwd);
            goto start;
#endif
        case 'h':
            printf("\n\n");
            system("pg -n -c -s -p\"(page %d):\" /
usr/lib/menu/lib/HELP ");
            goto start;
        case 'r':
            goto start;
            default:
            printf("%c",7);
            break;
```

Again, as in the Bourne shell version, if the command falls through to the default, there is an error. Ring the bell, `octal 7`.

```
            }
        }
    }
end:
    printf("\n");
    exit(0);
}
```

Close all open brackets and end with a carriage return and an `exit` function.

Inside the CC Program

The CC command is actually simpler than MM because some of the "thinking" is performed by the C preprocessor. Here is the annotated CC program:

```
:
trap 'rm MSH*  $1.x' 0 1 2 3 4 5 6 7 8
if [ ! -r "$1" ]
then
echo "ccm: file not found"
exit 1
fi
echo ':' >MSH$$
sed -e '
/^$/D
/\\$/ N
/\\\n/ s/\\\n/ /
s/"/\\"/g
s/\\\\"/\\"/g
/^#/,$ {
s/! */!/
/[\ -9,A-z];$/ s/$/@;break;/
s/:;;/: ;;/
/[\ -9,A-z];;$/ s/;$/@;goto start;/
/[\ -9,A-z]$/ s/$/@;break;/
/^#/ s/@;break;//
} ' $1>> MSH$$
```

To this point, the CC and MM programs are almost exactly the same, except that to repaint the screen with CC, you use a `goto` to save a few lines of code. You insert an at symbol (@) before terminating each command. It is used as a field separator that splits the executable portion of the menu.

In the `menu` command, you used another exclamation point and searched for three fields instead of two. There are many ways to do things in UNIX, and all of them are correct.

```
if [ -x /bin/csplit -o -x /usr/bin/csplit ]
then
csplit -f MSH MSH$$ /#/ /./ >/dev/null
else
```

```
/usr/lib/menu/bin/xplit MSH$$
fi
mv MSH00 M.$1
echo "exec m."$1>>M.$1
```

The preceding lines are almost identical to the MM code, except that you append an exec m.$1 command to the Bourne shell start-up script.

```
what='uname'
if [ "$what" != "unix" ]
then
what=XENIX
echo '#define XENIX'>$1.x
fi
```

In the preceding, you use uname to find out what version of UNIX is being run. Most current versions of UNIX return unix; most non-standard versions return XENIX, xenix, or HP-UX.

 If uname returns unix, you know you are safe. Most other versions of UNIX will work if the XENIX flag is turned on. If your version does not work, this is the first place to look.

```
if [ "$GUT" = "NOGUT" ]
then
echo '#define NOGUT'>>$1.x
fi
if [ "$COOKED" = "RAW" ]
then
echo '#define RAWMODE'>>$1.x
fi
```

In the preceding, you insert the definitions for RAWMODE and NOGUT if you need to. In the following, insert the entire first half of the program. Note the insertions of ifdef to correct for the differences between UNIX and XENIX. You use the shell archive

format and sed to remove leading # . The leading # is to prevent
the shell from thinking that it should interpret any of the data.

```
sed 's/^#//' << \XXXXX >>$1.x
##include <stdio.h>
##include <sys/types.h>
##include <time.h>
##include <sgtty.h>
#char x;
#long xx;
##ifdef XENIX
#char tmpcl[30], *xclock=tmpcl;
##else
#char xclock[64];
##endif
#char pwd[64];
#char *cpyrt="MSH compiler V3.0 Copyright (c) 1992
S.R.Glines";
#main()
#{
#struct sgttyb oldparam, newparam;
#ioctl(0, TIOCGETP, &oldparam);
#newparam = oldparam;
#newparam.sg_flags |= RAW;
#newparam.sg_flags &= ~ECHO;
#start:
#    while ( 1 ) {
#        system("exec clear");
#        time(&xx);
##ifdef XENIX
#        xclock=ctime(&xx);
##else
#        cftime(xclock,"%a %b %e %r %Z %Y %n",&xx);
##endif
#    getcwd(pwd,64);
#    printf("\n%22s    %s"," ",xclock);
```

```
#         system("if [ -s \"$MAIL\" ]; then echo \"
Messages\" ;else echo \"\";fi");
XXXXX
```

The following creates a `printf` statement to print the title from the `MSH01` file. This is accomplished with `sed`:

```
sed 's/^#/printf("%26s%s\\n","","/
s/$/");/' MSH01>>$1.x
echo 'printf("%26s%s\\n\\n"," ",pwd);'>>$1.x
```

Parse and build the display portion of the menu:

```
awk 'BEGIN{FS="!";i=0}
{i++;print "printf(\"%22s%2d  %s\\n\",\"
\","i",\""$1"\");"
}' MSH02>>$1.x
```

You insert `printf` functions to display the actual menu items on the screen:

```
sed 's/^#//' << \XXXXX >>$1.x
#       printf("\n");
#       while( 1 ) {
##ifdef RAWMODE
#           ioctl(0, TIOCSETP, &newparam);
##endif
#           printf("\r%22s    %s"," ",">");
#           x = getchar();
#           ioctl(0, TIOCSETP, &oldparam);
#           switch(x) {
XXXXX
```

You use `sed` to insert the prompting portion of the menu. Use the C preprocessor to insert an `ioctl` statement that puts the terminal into `raw` mode, if so defined. You still reset the terminal to whatever mode you found it in after reading the prompt character. This helps if an application changes something, and when you exit, you know that the terminal is in exactly the same state you found it in.

```
awk 'BEGIN{FS="!";i=0}
{i++;
print " case @" i "@:"
print "printf(\"\\nloading...\\n\"); "
split($2,x,"@")
if(substr(x[1],1,1) == "(" )  print
"system(\""x[1]"\");"
else
print "system(\"exec "x[1]"\");"
print x[2]}' MSH02 |sed -e "s/@/\'/g
s/^;//" >>$1.x
```

You parse the executable portion of the menu and insert the correct case statement. Note that you search for a (at the beginning of the executable string. If you find one, the string represents a compound command that must be executed within a subshell, so you execute it. If the string is a simple command, use the statement: **system("exec command")**, which forces the subshell created by the system command to exec into the executable statement. It is the difference between the sh command and sh -c 'exec command'. The exec version spawns one less shell.

In the following, you append all of the remaining commands. Note that you use the C preprocessor to handle the GUT/NOGUT issue. In MM, this logic had to be in the MM program itself.

```
sed 's/^#//' << \XXXXX >>$1.x
#    case 'q':
#        goto end;
#    case 'l':
#        printf("\n\n");
#        system("ls -C -F|pg -e -n -s -p\"(page
%d):\"");
#        break;
##ifdef NOGUT
```

```
#    case '!':
#        printf("\n\n");
#        system("exec sh");
#        goto start;
#    case 'e':
#        printf("\n\n");
#        system("exec ${EDIT:=vi} `prompt What
file`");
#        goto start;
#    case 'm':
#        printf("\n\n");
#        system("${MAILER:=mail} `prompt Mail to
who`");
#        break;
#    case 's':
#        printf("\n\n");
#        system("$CALENDAR");
#        goto start;
#    case 'c':
#        printf("\n\n");
#        printf("%s\n",pwd);
#        printf("Change to what directory > ");
#        gets(pwd);
#        chdir(pwd);
#        goto start;
##endif
#    case 'h':
#        printf("\n\n");
#        system("pg -n -c -s -p\"(page %d):\" /usr/
lib/menu/lib/HELP ");
#        goto start;
#    case 'r':
#        goto start;
#        default:
#        printf("%c",7);
#        break;
```

```
#    }
#    }
#    }
#end:
#    printf("\n");
#    exit(0);
#}
XXXXX
```

You finish up by making the start-up script executable, and then you run the C code through cb to "beautify" it. Then you can compile it with the optimize and strip flags on, with output going to m.Menu. Some versions of the HP-UX C compiler do not render the compiled output executable, so you take care of it. Note, too, that the trap command at the beginning of this program takes care of deleting residue.

```
chmod +x M.$1
cb $1.x>$1.c
cc -O -s $1.c -o m.$1
if [  "$what" = "XENIX" ]
then
chmod +x  m.$1
fi
```

The Demonstration Menu System

Included in the MSH package are two menus. As the installation script installs MSH, it determines the group name of the installer (who must be the root user). It then creates a Main menu for the root user group, which is usually sys. Thus, there will be a file named /usr/lib/menu/group/ sys/Main installed on your system. This menu is compiled, and the install script places the installer in that menu. The text for this Main menu is as follows:

```
#Main System Menu -- UNIX System V (only)
Update Your Cron table!(crontab -l>$HOME/crontab;\
$EDIT $HOME/crontab;crontab $HOME/crontab);;
Who is on the system!who -u -T -H
Kill a user!kill -9 'prompt Enter process id'
Write to all users!/etc/wall
Write to a specific user!(who -u -T -H;write \
'prompt Write to who')
Run Menu Setup Menu!M.Menuadmin;;
HELP!echo press \"h\" for help
```

$EDIT and $HOME are exported environment variables. The default value for EDIT is vi, so the first command places your current system crontab table in $HOME/crontab. If this represents a conflict, exit the menu immediately and edit the sys Main menu.

 This demonstrates the use of compound shell statements, as well as the use of the continuation character \. The menu item Write to a specific user demonstrates the use of compound statements and an embedded prompt command.

Of more interest is that this menu calls another menu, the Menuadmin menu. Notice that it is called by its executable name, M.Menuadmin.

The menu script for Menuadmin is:

```
cd /usr/lib/menu
umask 0
#Menu System Administration
Edit Menus!/usr/lib/menu/bin/emenu;;
Create Group !/usr/lib/menu/bin/cgroup;;
Delete Group!/usr/lib/menu/bin/dgroup;;
Edit Group .profile!/usr/lib/menu/bin/egroup;;
Edit Group menus!/usr/lib/menu/bin/egmenu;;
Delete Group menus!/usr/lib/menu/bin/dgmenu;;
```

What this menu does is self-explanatory; how the menu does it is shown in the following shell scripts.

Editing a Menu with emenu

There is nothing difficult about editing menus because they are nothing more than normal text files. Here is the source for /usr/lib/menu/bin/emenu:

```
:
X='prompt Menu Name'
$EDIT $X
ccm $X
```

Creating Groups with cgroup

Creating groups for MSH purposes is accomplished with /usr/lib/menu/bin/cgroup, which is a simple Bourne shell script:

```
:
cd /usr/lib/menu/group
ls
umask 0
mkdir 'prompt Group name'
```

Deleting Groups with dgroup

Deleting a MSH group is performed with /usr/lib/menu/bin/dgroup:

```
:
cd /usr/lib/menu/group
ls
umask 0
rm -r 'prompt Group name'
```

Editing a Group `.profile` with `egroup`

In the normal execution of the `msh` command (or shell), the `/etc/profile` shell script is executed with the dot command, followed by a `.profile` command for the user's group, followed by any `.profile` defined for the user in the user's home directory. All three "profiles" (if they exist) contribute to the user's environment before `msh` searches for a menu to run.

Having a `.profile` for a group may seem superfluous because of the existence of a start-up script at the beginning of a group menu. A user may, however, belong to a group with a `.profile` defined and still have a personal menu that is executed first. A group `.profile` shell script influences all the members of a group from within the MSH system, even if they have their own personal menus.

Here is the source for `/usr/lib/menu/bin/egroup`:

```
:
cd /usr/lib/menu/group
ls
X='prompt What Group'
cd $X
$EDIT .profile
chmod +x .profile
```

Editing a Group Menu with `egmenu`

This little shell script is as straightforward as the others. The source for `/usr/lib/menu/bin/egmenu` is as follows:

```
:
cd /usr/lib/menu/group
ls
X='prompt Which Group'
cd $X
/usr/lib/menu/bin/emenu
```

Note the use of emenu in this shell script. Remember that only the initial menu must be named Main. This shell script enables you to create and edit as many menus as you like.

Deleting a Group Menu with dgmenu

This last shell script is as simple as the rest. The source for /usr/lib/menu/bin/dgmenu is as follows:

```
:
cd /usr/lib/menu/group
ls
umask 0
cd  'prompt Group name'
ls M.*|sed -e 's/M\.//g'
X='prompt Delete which menu'
rm -r M.$X m.$X $X $X.c
```

All valid menus are listed by their start-up names, deleting the leading M. with sed, and finally removing all traces of the menu, including any C source.

Summary

In this chapter, you learned about the Menu shell, which is a shell script-based menuing system. Using msh, a system administrator can easily provide a consistent user interface that can present appropriate menu systems to different users depending on their requireent and security levels.

Chapter 11 builds on the msh techniques you have learned in this chapter by introducing you to different methods of creating data-entry screens.

Topics covered in this chapter:

Integrating Data-Entry Screens

Examining Stand-Alone, Data-Entry Screen Programs

Understanding SCREEN

Chapter 11

Data-Entry Screens— Mimicking the Mainframes

Many "high-tech gadgets" are available today— such as X-Window terminals, high-performance personal computers, and graphic-output devices. The bulk of the work of an MIS department, however, remains the dull task of collecting and dispersing data by using dumb terminals. If dumb, block-mode terminals and mainframe hardware were as inexpensive and as easy to use as UNIX systems, UNIX would never have become as popular as it is today.

Because UNIX systems save money and are easy to use, many companies are now downsizing from mainframes to UNIX. Central to the downsizing concept is the idea that a UNIX system should provide all the functionality of a mainframe or midrange computer or a network of microcomputers, but at a lower cost and with better performance. Although data entry is mundane, it is costly and time-consuming. Improved performance is therefore crucial.

The data-entry screen is an essential tool of any management information system. Virtually every DBMS and commercial language has, as part of the package, some kind of data-entry screen generator (see fig. 11.1).

```
        Accounts: edit, add, delete, query

Account No. [02178]

   Name [John Doe                              ]
Address [                                      ]
        [                                      ]
   City [                  ] ST [ ] Zip [      ]

  Phone [                 ]

Edit/Add/Delete/Query [ ]


```

Figure 11.1:
A typical data-entry screen.

These screen generators are thoroughly integrated with their software and are completely separate from the UNIX environment, except through system calls from the native language. This means that all data-entry activity must take place within the context of the language or DBMS. This is normally a small burden because most MIS activity takes place within the confines of an application program; however, it also makes integrating UNIX applications with data-entry programs much more difficult.

If data must be shared between two separate applications—for example, a DBMS and a COBOL program—a number of options must be considered. You can enter data in either of the applications, or you can write programs to export the data from one application and import it to the other. In both cases, data is converted from ASCII (in data entry) to binary (in the first application), converted back to ASCII, and finally converted back to binary form in the second application.

At some point, one of the applications must interact with the shell through a system call by having the application buried within a shell script, or by exiting the application altogether and giving an instruction from the shell. Figure 11.2 illustrates this sharing of data.

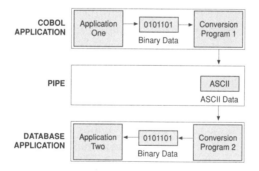

Figure 11.2:
Sharing data between two applications.

 A better way to handle an application's interaction with the shell is to capture the data in ASCII in the first place, and then insert it in the appropriate application files by using a program or database utility.

Integrating Data-Entry Screens

In the IBM mainframe universe, the standard data-entry system is built on the CICS (Customer Information Control System). No similar standard exists in UNIX. Each DBMS, each fourth-generation language, and each third-generation language used for commercial purposes has its own data-entry screen-generation system. It is no use to pretend that applications written in different languages can be seamlessly integrated into a single coherent system. On the other hand, most users generally spend most of their time in one application or another (the larger the organization, the more true this becomes). Truly seamless integration of applications is seldom necessary.

Screen-design systems are all different, both in conception and execution. Some of these systems generate code to be embedded in programs and compiled later; others generate stand-alone program files for later interpretation by a run-time module or by libraries linked to the application.

Manufacturers have different ideas of the way data-entry screens should behave. (In fact, screen behavior sometimes varies among different products from the same manufacturer.) The objective, though, is to capture the data by having the user enter it on the screen and save it to a file. Once a system is chosen and users are trained in its use, that system becomes easy and natural, regardless of how awkward it may appear at first.

Examining Stand-Alone, Data-Entry Screen Programs

Stand-alone screen-design systems can be useful. They also can be a hindrance. In fact, they are rarely needed. Because most data entry takes place within an application, stand-alone data-entry screens are not used very often. On the other hand, most database management systems can accept some form of ASCII input, even if the input is written in Structured Query Language (SQL). Because everything else in UNIX is based on ASCII files and access to the UNIX toolkit, stand-alone data-entry screen programs have their place and can surpass the built-in data base programs in overall usefulness.

Because stand-alone data-entry screen generators are not as useful as full-fledged database management systems, there are more DBMS than screen generators on the market. Most screen-generator systems generate portable C code, which must then be integrated in an application program, or screen interpreter, which cannot be integrated into applications developed with the C programming language.

Most commercial screen generators require a thorough knowledge of C. Furthermore, they are generally priced too high for casual purchase (they are used in only the largest installations). The output of the better screen generators, however, is versatile—many menu formats are available, as are pull-down and pop-up windows, field editing, and many other options.

There are no current data-entry screen systems that are as simple as the Menu shell (MSH) because manufacturers believe that they must offer bells and whistles to sell products—even if only a few of the "bells" are needed or ever used. The need for a simple data-entry system led to the creation of SCREEN.

Understanding SCREEN

 The origins of SCREEN match those of MSH, as described in Chapter 10. To maintain and support a variety of UNIX-based systems, a simple menuing system and an equally simple data-entry screen system were required. Building

MSH was easier than SCREEN conceptually because it does not do as much; building the SCREEN system was a lot harder. The first version of SCREEN used a C template that could be quickly modified to represent the required screen display. A preprocessor was written to create the specific code, but many of the systems did not accept a C compiler (or did not have disk space for one).

The overriding philosophy of UNIX maintains that the shell binds applications together, permitting shell scripts and applications to pass data between each other. Thus, all applications should be integrated in the UNIX environment and shell variables passed transparently from application to application. Because the shell environment is the only means of transmitting information within a shell, any screen-generation system should pass its data to the shell's environment. The screen-generation language should resemble a simple Bourne shell script, to facilitate communication within the shell.

At first, it was thought that writing a screen-generation system in Bourne shell script would require a Bourne shell compiler, as well as a parser and code generator for the presentation portion of the screen. Because necessity is the mother of invention, it proved simpler to first write a screen generator that generates pure Bourne shell script, and then compile the script with a Bourne shell compiler. Unfortunately, the Bourne shell compilers that were available proved inadequate, so the first version of SCREEN was born.

 The SCREEN package only works on UNIX System V or systems that support the tput command.

The screen compiler, ccsc, generates a pure Bourne shell script from a simple screen-scripting language. The only C program in the SCREEN system is readf which, like the MSH prompt command, reads a specified number of characters from the terminal before it prints it to the standard output file. The only difference between `readf` and `prompt` is that `prompt` reads either one character in `raw` mode or an unlimited string in `cooked` mode. (On the other hand, `readf` reads a specific number of characters in `raw` mode.)

In *raw* mode, characters typed at the keyboard are passed directly to the application by the device driver. In *cooked* mode, characters are trapped and processed by the device driver and released to the application only when an end-of-line character is detected, usually a carriage return.

One unexpected benefit of using the Bourne shell is that data-entry screen programs are small. For example, on an Intel 386 system running SCO UNIX, a screen program consumes about 76K of memory when running. In contrast, a UNIX C program has to load the `curses` library and, although it executes considerably faster, it consumes more than 100K. Likewise, data-entry programs for database management systems typically require nearly 500K of memory to run.

SCREEN **Conventions**

The file-naming conventions used in SCREEN match those of MSH. Source-code files begin with an initial capital letter, which helps to distinguish ordinary text files and shell scripts from specific source files. Just as C code files can be found using `ls *.c`, MSH and SCREEN source and executable files can be found with `ls [A-Z]*`. The other conventions are that compiled MSH start-up files take the form M.*Menu* and compiled SCREEN files take the form S.*Screen*. For example, a SCREEN source file named `Accnts` is compiled with the command `ccsc Accnts`, and the resulting executable file is named `S.Accnts`.

As with all conventions, the ones adopted for SCREEN are arbitrary, and you are free to change them. Try to be consistent, however; UNIX is forgiving but dumb.

Before learning the ways that SCREEN programs are used, it is useful for you to understand the structure of a program. A SCREEN program is relatively simple. It consists of only two parts; in contrast, an MSH script contains three parts. The two SCREEN parts are the display and command sections. The *display section* of a SCREEN script is a text representation of exactly what the screen will look like on the terminal. The *command section* is a Bourne shell script that enables you to manipulate the data entered on the screen.

Data is collected from the display in order of presentation; data-entry fields are collected from top to bottom and from left to right, as shown in figure 11.3. After the data-entry screen has been completely filled, the data collected is placed in the positional parameters with the set command. Thus, data from the first field is found in $1, the second field in $2, and so forth. This is the state of the SCREEN program when it enters the command portion of the script. In the absence of a command section, data is left in the positional parameters, and the SCREEN program ends.

SHELL
VARIABLES

[(field $1)]   [(field $2)]

[(field $3)]   [(field $4)]

Figure 11.3:
Data collection.

SCREEN programs can be used in two ways. Because they are stand-alone Bourne shell programs, they can be used by themselves. (This makes little sense unless a command section is present.) On the other hand, SCREEN programs, with or without command sections, can be used as in-line commands in Bourne shell scripts with the "dot" (.) command. In this case, any commands in the command section are executed, and when the SCREEN program ends, the data collected from the display is left in the shell script's positional parameters for further processing. Thus, even a SCREEN program without a command section can prove useful.

If a SCREEN program is called with command-line parameters, each parameter is taken to be the default for its respective field in the display. It for example, if, for example, the S.Accnts program just noted is called S.Accnts 02178 "John Doe", the first two fields of the screen are filled with "02178" and "John Doe," respectively. This data becomes the default for those fields in the absence of any input.

Creating a SCREEN **Program**

A SCREEN program's display section begins with the word screen on the first line of an ASCII file, and it ends with a right curly brace (}) on a line by itself. Between these two markers is an ASCII representation of the way the image will appear on the screen. Data-entry fields are delimited by a pair of opposing square brackets ([]). The display section for a typical data-entry screen program looks like this:

```
screen

            Accounts: edit, add, delete, query
Account No. [      ]

       Name [                                    ]
    Address [                                    ]
            [                                    ]
       City [                    ] ST [  ] Zip [   ]

      Phone [                 ]

Edit/Add/Delete/Query [ ]
}
```

When compiled and executed with the `S.Accnts` command, the
screen appears as follows:

```
            Accounts: edit, add, delete, query
Account No. [      ]

       Name [                                    ]
    Address [                                    ]
            [                                    ]
       City [                    ] ST [  ] Zip [   ]

      Phone [                 ]

Edit/Add/Delete/Query [ ]
```

If the program is run as `S.Accnts 02178 "John Doe,"` the
screen shows the default values for the first two fields and looks
like the following:

```
                Accounts: edit, add, delete, query

Account No. [02178]

       Name [John Doe                        ]
    Address [                                 ]
            [                                 ]
       City [                    ] ST [  ] Zip [    ]

      Phone [                ]

Edit/Add/Delete/Query [ ]
```

When the screen is first displayed, the cursor is placed on the first
position of the first data-entry field. If there is default data, a carriage return confirms the acceptance of the default. Otherwise, the
user enters data up to the limit of the field imposed by the right-
hand square bracket (]).

If the field has been completely filled by the user or if the user enters a carriage return, the cursor jumps automatically to the next
field. The process continues until all fields are filled. When the last
field has been filled, the display section ends by placing all the
fields in the environment (the first field is placed in $1, the second
field in $2, and so on). Because there are nine fields in the preced-
ing example, $1 through $9 are defined, although some fields can
contain a null value.

If the SCREEN script contains a command section, the data from the screen is handled as if it were a normal Bourne shell script that accepts positional parameters. A full SCREEN script, named X, might look like this:

```
screen

Display Section data [                        ]
}
# Command Section
echo $1
```

In this example, there is only one data-entry field, and the only command in the command section echoes the data back to the screen.

Simple SCREEN programs that do not contain a command section may be used (for instance, in-line commands within a Bourne shell script). In that case, the positional parameters are used to pass data. If, for example, the preceding sample screen program X is used in a shell script, the syntax can be the following:

```
#Bourne shell script
. S.X
echo $1
```

The result is that the first parameter, $1, is echoed twice—once from within the screen program and once in the shell script. In the following, all nine positional parameters are available for use:

```
#Bourne shell script
. S.Accnts
#more Bourne shell script
```

The cursor is left "dangling" (wherever it was when the last field was filled). Use the cursor command to position the cursor at a more convenient site. The syntax of cursor is as follows:

```
cursor x y
```

The *x* and *y* variables stand for the terminal's row and column, respectively, beginning with column zero and row zero.

A built-in command, `respawn`, redisplays the screen with any data that has been entered. This feature of the command section is not available as a Bourne shell command, but it is useful for editing data.

The following example shows a more complete version of the `Accnts` script that enables the user to confirm data entered:

```
screen

           Accounts: edit, add, delete, query

Account No. [      ]

        Name [                                        ]
     Address [                                        ]
             [                                        ]
        City [                    ] ST [  ] Zip [     ]

       Phone [                ]

Edit/Add/Delete/Query [ ]
}
cursor 16 0
echo $1
echo $2
echo $3
echo $4
echo $5" "$6" "$7
echo "\n"$8
echo "COMMAND:"$9"\c";X=`prompt "Is this correct
(Y/N)"|toupper`
# Note: "prompt" and "toupper" are little commands
found
# elsewhere in this book
```

```
if [ "$X" = "Y" ]
then
# echo "data accepted"
set -f
# to prevent file name expansion on the command
line
case $9 in
[Ee] ) do_edits $*;;
[Aa] ) do_add $*;;
[Dd] ) do_delete $*;;
[Qq] ) do_query $*;;
*) respawn;;
esac
else
respawn
```

The case statement shows how to use the data collected—the do_. . . commands are programs that perform the desired information. For the purpose here, they are "dummy" commands. If you know the Bourne shell, you probably understand this usage.

With the exception of respawn, all commands in the command section are normal Bourne shell script—including prompt and toupper, which are part of MSH and BATCHQ—and cursor, which is part of SCREEN.

Before looking at an actual SCREEN program, it is helpful to learn about the two utility commands that are included in the SCREEN package.

The cursor **Command**

The cursor command positions the cursor at a specified row and column on the terminal. This feature would require a complex C program involving the `curses` library, if not for the `tput` command. The `tput` command is available only on UNIX System V machines or systems that support the `terminfo` database as opposed to the `termcap` database. All the capabilities of a terminal are defined within the `terminfo` database in the form of *tcap_name=escape_string*.

 A list of capability names can be found in UNIX's *System Administrator's Reference Manual*.

The `tput` command enables a shell access to the `terminfo` database by passing, as a parameter or series of parameters, the information needed to complete a call to the `curses` library. Clearing the screen and moving the cursor are capabilities that are useful here. Clearing the screen can be accomplished with the `tput clear` command or by calling the `clear` command.

Moving the cursor is accomplished with the `cursor` command, which is designed to be as simple to use as the `clear` command. Its syntax is `cursor` *row column*. The `cursor` command is a simple Bourne shell script containing the following line of code:

```
tput cup $1 $2 >/dev/tty
```

By convention, the upper left hand-corner of a screen ("home") is location 0,0 or `cursor 0 0`. The `tput home` command moves the cursor to the home position.

The `readf` Command

This command was originally intended to be the opposite of the `printf` command. Instead of printing formatted data, it was supposed to read formatted data. For now, though, `readf` is a minimal program that reads a specified number of characters and echoes them to the standard output. This command is intended to be used in the same manner as `prompt`, and its normal syntax is the following:

```
X='readf 6'
```

In this case, `readf` reads a maximum of six characters and echoes them to the standard output, which is placed in the environment variable X. The `readf` command is written in C, so it requires a C compiler. Because `readf` is central to the SCREEN package, a C compiler is required. The annotated source code for `readf.c` is as follows:

This program is used to gather a fixed number of characters. It is used in the SCREEN system, and so on, called from the shell.

```
#include <stdio.h>
char *cpyrit = "#@ Readf -- Copyright (C) 1992
S.R.Glines";
char x;
main(argc,argv)
int argc; char *argv[];
{
    int a,i;char w[80];
    system("stty raw");
```

Put the system in `raw` mode to get one character at a time.

```
    a=atoi(argv[1]);
```

Read the first and only parameter and convert it into an integer.

```
    for(i=0;i<a;i++){
        w[i]=0;
        x=getchar();
        if(x == 13 ) goto end;
```

If a carriage return is detected, go to the end.

```
        w[i]=x;
        if(x == 8 ) {w[i]=0;i=i-2}
```

A backspace character is treated as such.

```
        if(x == 127 ) {system("stty
cooked");exit(-1);}
```

A delete character means abort. The terminal was reset to `cooked` mode and exited with an error so the shell knows what happened.

```
    }
    end:
    system("stty cooked");
    printf("%s\n",w);
    exit(0);
}
```

Everything has worked out. Set the terminal back to `cooked`, print the string, then use `exit(0)` so the shell knows that everything is OK.

Inside a Compiled Screen

 The `ccsc` command compiles SCREEN scripts into executable Bourne shell scripts. If the original script is named *File*, the compiled script is named `S`.*File*. The syntax for compiling is `ccsc` *File*. The following sample SCREEN file is named `File`:

```
screen

Format and print (on the default printer)

Enter File Name [                    ]
}
cursor 10 8
pr -155 -o5 -f $1|lp
```

This SCREEN program asks the user to enter the name of a file. The entered file name is placed in $1. The pr command forwards the file and the lp command prints it.

When executed, this script appears on the terminal as the following:

```
Format and print (on the default printer)

Enter File Name [                    ]
```

The Compiled Output of S.File

The annotated compiled output is as follows:

```
:
#SCREEN V2.2 (C) 1992 by S.R.Glines
set -f;hash tput readf
```

First of all, it helps to know what version of SCREEN did the compiling. The set -f command turns off file-name expansion, in case one of the passed parameters happens to be *. Next, use the hash command to make tput and readf run a little faster.

 The hash command looks up the disk address of a program using the PATH variable so that the full path name is known when the program is called. Whenever a new program is called, its path is placed in the hash table. If you use hash when a program is called for the first time, the program executes a little faster than it would otherwise.

```
clear>/dev/tty
echo "
Format and print (on the default printer)

Enter File Name [                    ]
">/dev/tty
```

First clear the screen and then paint an image of the screen on the terminal.

```
if [ -n "$*" ]
  then
if [ -n "$1" ];then tput cup 3 17;echo $1;
Y1=$1;fi
fi
```

Here, you discover if there are any positional parameters. If there are, paint the screen in the right place, and then set Y1=$1, Y2=$2, and so on, for as many parameters as were passed.

```
tput cup 3 17
X1='readf 17';
if [ $? -ne 0 ];then exit;fi
X1=${X1:-$Y1}
```

Here, position the cursor with tput, read the right number of characters with readf, and place the values in X1, X2, then test for the exit value of the last command run, which happens to be readf. If the user presses Del in a field, readf returns an exit - 1, otherwise it returns an exit 0. If the exit value is not 0, then exit. Otherwise, replace X1 with the default if X1 was not set. Remember that the default was passed as a parameter. Note that the same is true with X2.

```
set "$X1"
set +f
```

Here, all the data collected in the screen ais placed in the environment with the set command. If there were more than one data-entry field, the command would have been the following: set "$X1" "$X2".... The "X1" values are placed in quotation marks, so that fields like "John Doe" are placed in one parameter, not two. The last command of the display section is set +f. This enables file-name expansion again so that commands in the command section execute like normal Bourne shell commands and sends it to the printer.

```
cursor 10 8
pr -l55 -o5 -f $1|lp
```

These last two lines of code constitute the command section. The cursor command positions the cursor so that any output can be read, and the `pr` line formats the file defined in the screen.

Inside the ccsc **Compiler**

Conceptually, the `ccsc` command was very difficult to create. The first few attempts were aimed at generating C code. These were marginally successful, but they did not meet the requirement of being easily integrated into the Bourne shell.

The only difference between the first release of SCREEN and the one incorporated in this book is the addition of the `respawn` command and the use of `readf`. In future releases, manipulating the data-entry screens will be better, but the current release of SCREEN performs almost as well as a CICS screen, and it is a lot faster.

The `readf` command is a bit primitive and will be updated in future releases.

Although the SCREEN system was conceptually more difficult than MSH, the actual compiler for SCREEN is a lot simpler. The `ccsc` command is a mere 1300 bytes; the CC compiler for MSH is almost 3700 bytes. (Both, by modern standards, are tiny.) The reader should recognize a similarity in design between the MSH and SCREEN compilers. This is because the SCREEN scripting language is a language that must be parsed first, and then the parsed script is reassembled in executable form.

The ccsc SCREEN Compiler

The following is the annotated ccsc SCREEN compiler:

```
:
if [ -r "$1" ]
then
```

First, test for the existence of the file to be compiled.

```
trap "rm X[123] " 0 1 2 3 4 5
```

If anything goes wrong (or at the end of the program), remove the debris.

```
echo "SCREEN Compiler V2.2-Copyright (c) 1992 by S.R.Glines"
echo "Compiling..."
```

Print a banner to occupy the programmer while the compiling takes place.

```
nawk '/^screen/, $1 == "}" {print;next}
{print >"X3"}' $1|
```

Here, the display section is separated from the command section of the screen script. The display portion is passed on to the next stage through a pipe, while the command section is saved for later processing.

```
sed 's/\[/</g; s/\]/>/g'|
```

This preprocessing of the display section changes the square brackets into corner brackets. This is necessary because the square brackets have a special meaning in nawk and cannot be escaped. The output is again passed through a pipe.

```
nawk '
BEGIN{k=0;j=0;printf(":\n#SCREEN    V2.2    (c)    1992    by
S.R.Glines\n")>"X1"
print "set -f
hash tput readf">>"X1"
printf("clear@/dev/tty\necho \"") >"X1"}
```

Here, the header is printed; all screens have the same header. Also, k is set to 0 and j is set to 0; k is just a switch, but j is incremented to keep track of the number of data-entry fields that are discovered:

```
NR > 1    {if($1 == "}"){k=1;next}
    if( k == 0) {print> "X1";Q[NR-1]=$0;next}
    else {next};
}
```

Here, the first line containing screen is ignored, and the program bypasses the last line that contains a }. All other lines are placed in a nawk array for parsing. Also, the image of the screen is placed in the "X1" file.

```
function pos(s,b,l){
```

Next, a function called pos is defined; pos performs the parsing of the screen. This function is *recursive* (it calls itself as it looks for matched pairs of corner brackets). Whenever it finds them, a data-entry field is defined.

Arguments to pos are the string being searched, the starting position in the string, and the length of the string. On each new row of the screen image, the starting position is 1.

```
a=substr(s,b,l)
x=match(a,"<");
y=match(a,">");
```

The substring to be tested is placed in a, which is from starting position b for a length of l. Then the program finds the x and y positions, that is, the locations of matching brackets. You cannot use [here, even if escaped. The `match` command returns a 0 if no match is found.

```
if (y != 0 ) {
X=X+x
```

If the program gets this far, you know a matched pair was found and the starting position of the field is *x* characters away from the ending position of the previous field. On each new line, X is reset to 0.

```
print "if [ -n \"$"++j"\" ];then tput cup "i-1" "X"
echo $"j";">>"X1"
print "Y"j"=$"j";fi">>"X1"
```

Note the use of the variable i. Because this is a function, any variables used before this function is called are available for use (i is the row number on the screen). Note also the discrete incrementing of the j variable to keep count of the number of fields.

For each new field discovered, it is assumed that there might be a default. The program checks to see if there is any length to the positional parameter. If so, the program positions the cursor using the `tput` command, echoes its value to the screen, and places "$1" in "Y1" and so on. so that it can be restored if nothing was entered in the field. All "default" logic is placed in the "X1" file. so that all default values are displayed before any data entry takes place. To prevent intermingling of logic, the screen read logic that follows is placed in a separate file.

```
print "tput cup "i-1" "X";X"j"=\`readf
"y-x-1"\`;">>"X2"
print "if [ $? -ne 0 ];then
exit;fi;X"j"=${X"j":-$Y"j"}">>"X2"
```

The program inserts the logic that positions the cursor for reading and tests the results. The `tput` command used in "cursor" is used raw. The `readf` command reads only the number of characters that will fit in the field, "y-x-1", and returns a non-zero exit if the user presses Del. The next step replaces a null value with any default (if the user presses Enter instead of entering a string). This logic is placed in "X2" and is merged later with "cat".

```
X=X+y-x
```

X is updated and set to the end of the current field.

```
pos(a,y+1,length(a))
}
```

The previous line demonstrates recursion in nawk. An ever-smaller string is passed to pos. The parameters are the substring searched in the last pass, the position of the end of the field found in the last pass, and the length of the substring found in the last pass.

```
}
```

This is the end of the function pos. The function is defined, but it has not yet been called.

```
END{ printf("\"@/dev/tty\n") > "X1";
```

None of the parsing in the pos function has yet taken place and only the screen image has been placed in "X1". Because this is the nawk END section, you know that the screen is complete, so you may end it. Do so by closing the quote that began the echo statement. Redirect output to "/dev/tty". Instead of using the redirection symbol (>), use an "at" sign (@). The] character was changed to a > symbol so that nawk could search for it. Use @ to represent the redirection sign so the sed script that converts everything back does not get confused.

NOTE /dev/tty is a pseudodevice that points to whatever device the user is logged in to. By directing output to /dev/tty, you can use the command inside command substitution because anything directed to /dev/tty does not show up on the standard output.

```
printf("if [ -n \"$*\" ]\n then\n") > "X1";
```

`pos` is still not yet called, so the logic that checks for default values has not been printed. Here, the program inserts logic that checks to see if there are any positional parameters.

```
for(i=1;i<=NR;i++)
{X=0;pos(Q[i],1,length(Q[i]))}
```

An image of the screen has been placed in the array `Q`, and a `for` loop is used to pass one row of the screen at a time to `pos`. At the beginning of each pass, the program sets `X` to zero and passes the entire array with starting position 1.

 The difference between C and `awk` arrays is that with `awk`, arrays begin with 1, as in `X[1]`. In contrast, C begins all arrays with the "zeroth" position, or `X[0]`.

The home position on a terminal for `tput` is 0,0; this loop generates 1,1. That is why 1 is subtracted from the positions in the `pos` function.

```
print "fi">"X1"
```

All data has been parsed. The screen image and all the logic for detecting and printing the defaults are now in the "X1" file. All that remains is to end the if command that detected whether there were any positional parameters.

```
printf("set ")> "X2"
for(i=1;i<=j;i++)
{printf("\"$X%-d\" ",i)>"X2"}
```

These two lines create the code to set the data collected into the variables `$1`, `$2`, ... Because any field can contain strings with embedded spaces, each of the fields must be quoted (thus, the convoluted logic). The output of this code looks like this: `set "$X1" "$X2" ...`

```
printf("\nset +f\n")>"X2"
}'
```

Finally, the program ends the `nawk` program by appending `"set +f"` to the end of the "X2" file. At the beginning, `set f` was used to prevent any wild-card expansion. The program turns back on wild-card expansion so that the "command section" behaves like normal Bourne shell script.

```
sed 's/>/]/g;s/</[/g;s/@/>/g' X1 >S.$1
```

The `>` is changed back to `]` and `<` back to `[`. The program also converts `@` into `>`. The ordering of the `sed` commands is very important. If `@` had been converted into `>` before `>` was converted into `]`, the intentional redirection would have been destroyed because all `>` would have been converted to `]`. The program is now building the executable file `"S.File"`.

```
cat X2>>S.$1
```

The program appends the remaining code that reads the fields to the executable file. Next, the program tests to see if there is a command section.

```
if [ -s "X3" ]
then
sed '
s/respawn/set -f; X="exec $0 "
for i do X=$X" \\\""$i"\\\" ";\
done;eval $X/' X3 >>S.$1
fi
```

The raw command section is passed through a `sed` filter to insert the code that performs the respawn. The code is easier to read if untangled. This is what it looks like after it has been inserted:.

```
set -f;
X="exec $0 ";
```

```
for i do
X=$X" \""$i"\" ";
done;
eval $X
```

The program uses set f again to prevent wild-card expansion. Next, the program builds up the string "X" by setting it initially to "exec $0". The "$0" variable is the name the command was called by and is generic. The for loop sets i to each positional parameter, so X eventually becomes the equivalent of exec $0 "$1" "$2".... In other words, the screen program is called again with positional parameters intact. eval is used to cause two passes of shell substitution.

```
chmod +x S.$1
```

The SCREEN program has been built. All that remains is to make it executable and close the initial "if" statement.

```
else
echo "SCREEN - file not found: "$1
fi
```

Summary

In this chapter, the SCREEN program was introduced. This program facilitates data entry by providing a standard data-input screen that can be coupled with any application or DBMS. Any programmer can set up a screen-based data-entry system using the ccsc SCREEN compiler provided in this chapter.

The next chapter covers various methods for controlling and scheduling jobs on a UNIX system.

## Chapter 12

Program Spooling (Batch Spooling)

N ovice users often confuse program spooling with print spooling. They do not understand the strategic benefits of program spooling. The concept of spooling is nothing more than the rationing of scarce system resources. Printers, obviously, are a scarce resource. After all, printers can only print one file at a time. Print jobs are placed in line to wait their turn at the printer.

Other resources on the system are just as scarce. Every system has a limited amount of random-access memory (RAM), a limited number of CPU cycles every second, and a limited amount of space on a disk. UNIX masks many of these limitations by using various techniques. None slows down the UNIX system like demand paged virtual memory or paging, however.

Chapter 5 was devoted to the limitations of system resources. Chief among these limitations is the danger of a UNIX system thrashing.

Thrashing occurs when all RAM is used up and the system begins to use demand paging to make up the deficit. It also occurs when so many programs are running that the kernel spends an inordinate amount of time switching programs.

Program spooling can easily overburden a system by queuing low-priority jobs for one-at-a-time execution. The process of spooling programs is exactly the same as for spooling print jobs to a printer.

 This chapter refers to program spooling as *batch spooling* because the procedure mimics the process of mainframe batch programming.

Using Batch Spooling

The most valuable resources of any organization are its staff members, and anything that prevents them from doing their jobs in the most efficient manner costs the organization money. In an information-system environment, therefore, users must have the highest priority, and interactive applications must take precedence over long-running reports.

Without guidance, UNIX treats all running programs more or less equally. In theory, the `nice` command enables a user to control the priority of a task. Other factors, however, share control over the task priority. As a result, on-line users are generally left to compete, on an equal basis, with any *hogs* (applications that use a lot of system resources) that happen to be running on the system.

Consider the kinds of applications that run in an MIS environment, such as data-entry applications. If the data-entry program is part of a DBMS, it can require large amounts of memory. These applications are not very demanding, however; the time it takes an average UNIX system to swap pages of memory in and out is very fast, compared to the DBMS user's data-entry speed. DBMS systems, therefore, are well-suited to paging environments. At some point, paging slows down the system enough to be noticeable. Even then, using more memory is cheaper than the price of aggravation experienced by users if batch spooling is not applied.

Unfortunately, data entry does not exist in a vacuum. Sooner or later, managers want reports or complex database queries. Some systems also support scientific or engineering applications. Both types of applications—database queries and engineering applications—are resource hogs on any system. Reports and complex database queries tax a disk system; engineering applications can use up most of the CPU's available power. In addition, a database application can create enormous temporary files as it sorts data. These files not only increase the need to access the disk, but also can use up much of the available free space on a disk.

 Data-entry applications can coexist with other types of applications, but UNIX runs these hogs on an equal footing with data-entry applications. The application that makes the most demand on the system is given most of the resources; the others must wait until those resources are free again.

Users (and management) cannot afford to wait for a long-running report program to end. Time is inefficiently used, and patience runs short very quickly. Fortunately, two mechanisms are available within UNIX that can resolve the problem by running tasks in the background, free from the state of a user's login.

The first mechanism is the nohup command, which renders a command free to run, regardless of whether a user is logged in or not. The syntax of nohup is: nohup *command* &. The nohup command frees the task from the user's terminal; the & places it in the background. Unfortunately, you cannot place any controls on the number of tasks placed in the background this way, so using this mechanism for hog programs can quickly and radically slow a UNIX system by inducing thrashing. If the programs are database-related, UNIX might create huge volumes of temporary storage, even to the point of running out of free space on a disk.

The second mechanism UNIX provides to run tasks in the background is the `batch` command. The `batch` command is, in fact, a Bourne shell script with a single command: `at -bq`. Like the `at` command, `batch` runs only Bourne shell scripts and takes its input from the standard input, not from the command line. The `batch` command enables you to limit the number of tasks it runs; however, it still treats all submitted tasks as equals.

Although both the `batch` and `at` commands only run Bourne shell scripts, you can make a Bourne shell execute any other shell. To run a `csh` script through `batch` or `at`, add the following line to the head of your `csh` script:

```
exec /bin/csh <<!
```

As a general rule, if a program does not require user intervention, you should run it through a batch spooler instead of using the `nohup` command and `&` operator. For small systems, the simple `batch` command is probably adequate. The `batch` command provides only one queue, which can easily become clogged with long-running hogs. Larger systems, however, require more control than `batch` can provide.

Because batch spooling is a necessity in the MIS world, this chapter introduces two batch spoolers that offer greater control over background tasks than is found in normal UNIX. The first batch spooler, EBATCH, is a simple modification and enhancement of the `batch` command, suitable for small installations. The second, BATCHQ, is a more comprehensive treatment of the problem. You can find these two programs on the disk that accompanies this book.

Both EBATCH and BATCHQ arose from the same environment. One of the author's first clients was a new private bank that specialized in equipment leases. From humble beginnings, the bank's MIS quickly grew into an Intel 286-based XENIX system. Data-entry applications ran in the foreground and reports in the background using the `nohup` & construct. With 16M of RAM, this system worked adequately until about the fifteenth user was added.

At peak periods, the system normally had 70 to 100 tasks running at any one time. As soon as the system reached its thrash point—about 120 tasks—normal additions to the run queue quickly pushed the number of running tasks to more than 200.

A report program that normally required two or three minutes to complete might take fifteen to twenty minutes. A limit on the number of running tasks had to be imposed. This limit implied the use of the batch program. To control the batch command more effectively, however, the EBATCH system was created. As the bank continued to grow, more severe restrictions were imposed and a prioritized system created. This lead to the BATCHQ system.

Examining the EBATCH Batch-Spooling System

The `batch` command is essentially a single-queue system. Using `batch` allows a two-priority system for batch programs—those run with `nohup` and those run with `batch`. The UNIX manual claims that `batch` allows programs to run as the system load permits, but this statement is not completely accurate. Only a fixed number of `batch` programs are allowed to run at any one time. This fixed number bears no relation to the actual load on the system. To make the `batch` command effective, the number of tasks `batch` is allowed to run must dynamically change to reflect the actual load on the system. Thus, the origin of EBATCH (*enhanced batch*).

An Improved `batch` Command

The standard `batch` command is a Bourne shell script that contains the command `at -qb`. The standard `at` command expects the execution time on the command line and accepts the program to run from the standard input.

You can use the `at` command in a pipe, as in `echo "command string" | at now + 1 day`, or from the terminal.

Because the `at` command behaves like a shell, you must terminate any command submitted to `at` with an end-of-file signal. If you input the command directly from a terminal, you must terminate it by pressing Ctrl-D (or whatever is defined). The standard `batch` command does not expect switches on the command line, but still requires input from the standard input. Because the standard `batch` command is difficult to use, nobody uses it. The following syntax may be an improvement:

```
batch command-string
```

Any new `batch` command must behave like the standard version in order to accommodate those programs that use the standard syntax. You can modify `batch` to replace the standard version by using the following program:

```
:
New batch command Copyright (c) 1992 S.R.Glines
set -f
```

Use the `set -f` command to prevent file-name expansion of any wild cards—leave that task to `cron`. Next, test to see if the new or the old syntax is used. If the old syntax is used, you can expect nothing on the command line.

```
if [ "$*" ]
then
at -qb << END_OF_BATCH
echo batch job \""$*"\" "submitted @" `date`
$*
echo batch job \""$*"\" ended with exit \$?
END_OF_BATCH
```

The new syntax has been detected. Use the `at` command's inline form, so that you can easily insert the echo messages. These echo messages, together with any command output, are mailed to you. The message's first line tells you when you submitted the job. The mail date tells you when the job actually finished. Note that you also return the job's exit status ($?) by mail. If you do not want this default output sent to you by mail, comment out the echo lines:

```
else
at -qb
fi
```

If nothing was found on the command line (by virtue of the null $* string), revert to the old syntax and accept input from the standard input.

Listing the at Queues' Contents

The command to list the contents of all the at queues is at -l. In true UNIX form, this command delivers the following cryptic output:

```
user = root   710976211.b  Sun Jul 12 17:23:31 1992
user = root   710976227.b  Sun Jul 12 17:23:47 1992
```

This output matches the report produced by the at command or its options. Whenever you submit a job to at or batch, it issues a report that resembles this syntax:

```
job 710976227.b at Sun Jul 12 17:23:47 1992
```

In the preceding output, the job ID is based on the number of seconds since the beginning of the UNIX epoch on January 1, 1970, with the queue identifier appended (.b). Thus, this example was submitted 710976227 seconds after midnight on January 1, 1970.

The at -l command discloses the job's owner. The jobs listed have not yet been run. After the job has started, it disappears from the queue listing. Although this information is nice to know, it does not tell you much about the queues' status. You do not know their nice level, the number of tasks allowed in any of the queues, or the system's waiting period between jobs. You can, however, get this information from a file called queuedefs, which is usually found in /usr/lib/cron in Release 3 and in /usr/sbin/cron.d in Release 4.

The following lines are an example of the `queuedefs` file:

```
a.10j10n10w
b.10j10n10w
c.10j10n10w
```

The first field is the queue name, delimited by a period: `a.` is for the `at` queue, `b.` is for the `batch` queue, and so on. The field `10j` means that only ten jobs can execute at any one time. The field `10n` indicates the jobs run at the `nice` level 10. The field `10w` defines how many seconds `cron` waits if the queue is full before it attempts to run another job.

As part of a status report, you can use `aq` to see what the `queuedefs` have to say about the `batch` queue, in addition to a list of pending jobs.

 On most Release 3 machines, the `at -l` or `atq` command lists all the jobs in the queue. Release 4 systems only list the jobs initiated by the user (unless the person issuing the command is the superuser). In this case, the `aq` command is not as useful.

Listing of the `aq` Command

The `aq` command gives you the queues' status, just as `at -l` or `atq` does. In addition, it offers the parameters for the `batch` queue in particular. It also tells you if the *load adjustment feature* is on, which continually adjusts the `batch` queue to reflect the actual load on the system. The output of `aq` looks like this:

```
At Queue Status
user = root  710976211.b  Sun Jul 12 17:23:31 1992
```

```
user = root   710976227.b  Sun Jul 12 17:23:47 1992
Batch Jobs:6  Nice:19  Wait:30
load adjustment is On
```

The source for aq is:

```
echo "At Queue Status\n"
at -l>/tmp/atq$$
```

Provide a header and save the output of ls -l to a temporary file so that you can test the output:

```
if [ ! -s "/tmp/atq$$" ];then echo "No jobs in the
queue";
else cat /tmp/atq$$;fi
```

If the file exists and its size is not greater than 0 (in other words, the file size is 0), tell the user that no jobs are in the queue. Otherwise, issue the cat command to view the temporary file on the screen:

```
set 'grep "^b" /usr/lib/cron/queuedefs|sed 's/
[a-z\.]/ /g''
```

The following statement places the number of jobs, the nice level, and the wait period into the positional parameters, $1, $2, and so on. You can use both grep and sed instead of a more convoluted sed statement.

```
echo "\nBatch Jobs:"$1"  Nice:"$2"  Wait:"$3"      "
```

Now that you have the queuedefs file contents in the environment, print it out in a less cryptic form.

```
if [ -r "/usr/lib/cron/lock" ]
then
echo "load adjustment is Off";
else
```

```
echo "load adjustment is On ";
fi
rm /tmp/atq$$
```

This step illustrates using a file's existence as a semaphore for the shell. If the `lock` file exists, no updates are made to the number of batch jobs that can run at a given time; therefore, continuous load adjustment is `Off`. Finally, remove the temporary file.

Adjusting `batch` to the Actual Load on the System

UNIX system administration can be very tedious. You must police dozens of files; examine, truncate, or purge log files; and maintain lots of little tables. If you perform these tasks manually, it takes you many hours. Because most of the administrative tasks are simple and repetitious, however, they are well-suited to automation.

The `queuedefs` table is one of those tables that you must change several times a day as the system load varies. The `queuedefs` file structure is easy to edit, but you have to decide what constitutes the load on the system and how that affects the queue definitions.

Preferably, you should base your strategy on total resource use. Unfortunately, no simple way exists to learn this information. You can easily count tasks, however, and you can reasonably assume that total system resource use increases linearly with the number of tasks. Thrashing is usually caused by one of two problems: a few programs using too many resources, or too many tasks running at once. If you can estimate the number of tasks running when thrashing begins, you can limit the system to that number. Because you cannot police the number of foreground tasks or tasks launched with the &-operator, you must take up the slack with a batch program. Thus, the thrash number, minus the actual number of tasks currently running, should yield the total number of batch programs allowed to run. This number obviously varies minute by minute, so you must frequently modify the batch queue definitions on systems that operate near their thrash point. This suggests a daemon.

To implement this strategy: run a daemon program, /usr/lib/cron/qadj (*queue adj*ust), on a periodic basis using cron. The frequency with which cron runs qadj varies from system to system. The smallest unit of time that you can define in a cronfile is one minute, so you can allow cron to adjust every minute the number of tasks that batch runs. Such a cronfile entry might resemble the following example:

```
* * * * * /usr/lib/cron/qadj
```

This syntax tells UNIX to run the qadj daemon every minute of every day, which might be overkill unless you have a large 24-hour operation.

A more rational approach might be to run the daemon every five minutes between 9 a.m. and 5 p.m., and once per hour the rest of the time. This could be accomplished with two cronfile entries:

```
5,10,15,20,25,30,35,40,45,50,55 9-17 * * * /usr/
lib/cron/qadj
0 * * * * /usr/lib/cron/qadj
```

The owner of this cronfile must have read and write permission to the /usr/lib/cron directory and the queuedefs file it contains.

The code that performs the queuedefs updates is /usr/lib/cron/qadj:

```
MAX=400
MAXQ=10
```

Set the variable MAX, the expected thrash point, to the maximum number of tasks the system can run. The variable MAXQ sets an upper limit on the number of batch tasks to run at any one time. The remainder of this program varies the number of batch tasks between 0 and MAXQ.

```
cd /usr/lib/cron
```

Go to the appropriate directory so that you do not have to specify full path names.

```
if [ -r "lock" -o -r "Qlock" ];then exit;fi
```

Look for the two shell semaphores. The lock file is an external semaphore that stops the program's continued execution. The Qlock semaphore is used internally to prevent multiple executions of this program.

```
>Qlock
```

Set the internal semaphore.

```
cp queuedefs old.queuedefs
x='ps -e|wc -l'
x='expr $MAX \- $x \+ 3 '
if [ "$x" -le "0" ]
then
x=0
fi
if [ "$x" -gt "$MAXQ" ]; then x=$MAXQ;fi
```

Make a copy of queuedefs, then count the number of processes running. Next, subtract the current number of running tasks from MAX and add three back to the total for the gadj program overhead. Check to see if the new total is less than 0, which means that the system is operating over the thrash point. At the other extreme, if the system is free, put a cap on the number of tasks that can run in batch.

```
sed "s/[0-9]*j/${x}j/" queuedefs >qdfs
```

Use `sed` to apply the new values. The quotation marks are used so that the value `${x}` is substituted first:

```
mv qdfs queuedefs
rm Qlock
```

Finally, copy the edited file back to `queuedefs` and remove the shell semaphore.

Controlling the `qadj` Program Administration

The three programs (the modified `batch` command, the new `aq` status report, and the daemon `qadj`) form the basis of the original EBATCH system. They form what the military likes to call a "fire and forget" system—after you launch it, you can forget about it. You can, however use an editor to make any changes to the queue definitions. Still, a simple front-end administration program can make your job even easier.

 The EBATCH administration program `agadmin` has changed its form dozens of times. The version presented here was completely rewritten for this book, using SCREEN. In fact, the present version began as a demonstration program for SCREEN.

Only the system administrator should run the `aqadmin` command, so you must apply restricted permissions. If the installation program does not do this correctly, change the permissions with the `chmod 700 aqadmin` command. The `aqadmin` command normally resides in `/bin` and calls the SCREEN program `/usr/lib/cron/S.Qstat`. When it runs, `aqadmin` presents a screen that looks like figure 12.1.

```
   Adjust AT batch queue definition

Stop Continuous Queue adjustments [n] ("n" restarts adjustments)

   Number of jobs [300 ] in the system, max
      There are 175 tasks currently running
   Number of jobs [0  ] in queue, max
Execute jobs with nice [19 ] priority
        Wait [20 ] seconds if the queue is full
At Queue Status
user = root    710976211.b    Sun Jul 12 17:23:31 1992
user = root    710976227.b    Sun Jul 12 17:23:47 1992
Batch Jobs:0  Nice:19  Wait:20
load adjustment is On
```

Figure 12.1:
A typical aqadmin *display.*

This display shows the $MAX variable's current value in qadj as 300 and the current value of $MAXQ (also in qadj) as 0. This last value also matches the current number of jobs in the queuedefs file.

Using the aqadmin Command

The only thing aqadmin does is to define the defaults for the S.Qstat screen. It does this by using the following code:

```
:
trap "cursor 23 0;if [ -w \"Qlock\" ];then rm
Qlock;fi" 0
```

Use the `trap` command to position the cursor so that the shell prompt does not reappear in the middle of the screen output when the program is finished. Then remove the `Qlock` semaphore.

```
cd /usr/lib/cron
```

The preceding line changes directories to avoid using full path names.

```
PATH=.:$PATH;export PATH
```

This line has the same function as the preceding example, but is used for executable programs.

```
while [ -r "Qlock" ]; do sleep 1;done
>Qlock
```

You want to prevent `qadj` from changing anything while you are looking at the screen, so the shell semaphore is `Qlock`. If `qadj` is already running, wait for it to finish.

```
CJOBS='expr \'ps -ed|wc -l\' \- 3';export CJOBS
```

You can pass data to a SCREEN program in several ways. One way is to set shell variables. Because SCREEN is a shell script, it can use these shell variables.

```
S.Qstat "n" \
'sed '/^MAX=/,/^MAXQ=/ {s/MAX=//;s/MAXQ=//;p;}
d' qadj' \
'grep "^b" queuedefs|
sed 's/b\.[0-9]*j//;s/[a-z\.]/ /g'`
```

Finally, the preceding lines call the SCREEN program with the desired positional parameters. The first parameter is n, which tells the screen that the default is to run the `qadj` program. The `sed` program, which follows, extracts the current values of MAX and MAXQ from the `qadj` shell script. The next command uses both `grep` and `sed` to extract the `nice` and `wait` fields' values from the `queuedefs` file.

The `S.Qstat` **Data-Entry Screen**

In the interests of simplicity, this section presents only the SCREEN source script, `Qstat`, instead of the more massive `S.Qstat` program. Both `Qstat` and `S.Qstat`, however, are included in the EBATCH package. The `Qstat` program follows:

```
screen
        Adjust AT batch queue definition

Stop Continuous Queue adjustments [ ] (\"n\" re-
starts adjustments)

        Number of jobs [ ] in the system, max
            There are $CJOBS tasks currently running
        Number of jobs [ ] in queue, max
Execute jobs with nice [ ] priority
            Wait [ ] seconds if the queue is full
    'aq'
        }
```

The quotation marks displayed on the screen must be escaped or else they accidently terminate the screen. Notice the use of the `$CJOBS` environment variable, which was set in `aqadmin` and exported to this program. Also note the use of command substitution on the screen's last line.

```
cd /usr/lib/cron
umask 0
cursor 12 0
```

Make sure you are in the right directory, in case you are called by a program other than `aqadmin`. After you create some temporary files, you want to be able to read and write them, regardless of the user's umask setting; therefore, impose your own settings. The cursor is positioned so that you can overwrite the on-screen data by running aq again when you are finished.

```
X=${1:-"N"}
M=${2:-"200"}
J=${3:-"20"}
N=${4:-"10"}
W=${5:-"20"}
```

If no data was passed and no fields were changed, set everything back to the standard defaults.

```
if [ "$N" -ge "19" ];then N=19;fi
```

Normal users—even the superuser—run at nice level 20, so the maximum level for anyone is nice 19.

```
sed "s/[0-9]*j/${J}j/ ; s/[0-9]*n/${N}n/ ; s/
[0-9]*w/${W}w/ " queuedefs>/tmp/QDF$$
```

Patch the queuedefs file with whatever you have done. Notice that shell-parameter substitution takes place on the sed commands before sed gets a chance to do anything.

```
mv /tmp/QDF$$ queuedefs
case $X in
[Yy] ) >lock;;
 * ) if [ -r "lock" ]; then rm lock;fi;;
esac
cp qadj /tmp/QDF$$
```

Set the shell semaphore to run or stop adjusting the queue.

```
sed "s/MAX=[0-9]*/MAX=${M}/ ;s/MAXQ=[0-9]*/
MAXQ=${J}/ " /tmp/QDF$$ >qadj
rm /tmp/QDF$$
```

Patch the program `qadj` with the new values.

```
qadj
aq
```

Now that you have everything set, run `qadj` to put everything into effect, and then run `aq` to see the results.

Examining the BATCHQ Batch-Spooling System

In UNIX, as in life, you can usually accomplish the same task using many different methods. The EBATCH system is good, but it offers no way to prioritize tasks. The `batch` command treats all jobs as equals and executes them on a first-come, first-served basis. This treatment is sufficient on relatively small systems, in which normal background processing and the `batch` system constitute a two-class priority system.

Larger systems, however, have a wider variety of programs, from quick-running reports to superhogs that might take hours to run. In these circumstances, a two-tiered priority system is inadequate because the smaller programs compete head-to-head with the superhogs. Larger systems require the same kind of batch spooling found on mainframes.

Mainframe batch spoolers have multiple queues that run at different priorities. The system administrator can easily move jobs from queue to queue or change the status of an individual queue without changing the others. These features also are characteristic of the BATCHQ system.

In the BATCHQ system, new jobs are submitted into a particular queue with the `sub` command, are listed with the `bq` command, have their priority changed with the `bump` command, and are removed with the `brm` command. Individual queues are locked and unlocked with the `lbq` and `rlbq` commands, respectively, and, like the `batch` command, each queue is controlled by a daemon—in this case the `batdaemon`.

The BATCHQ Environment

In its original form, the BATCHQ system contains four active queues: A, B, C, and D. Each has a declining priority imposed by the `nice` command. The system also has two inactive queues, H (*hold*) and M (*mount*), and two pseudo-queues named X and Y. The X queue runs commands with the `nohup &` syntax; the Y queue runs commands through the EBATCH system. You can move any job that has not yet started to the bottom of any other queue. In addition, you can kill any job, whether or not it is running.

Jobs are submitted with the `sub` command, using `sub -a command`, in which *a* is any of the queues A, B, C, D, H, M, X, or Y. In the absence of a command, UNIX takes input from the standard input. If no queue or an invalid queue ID is placed on the command line, `sub` defaults to the D queue.

You can use uppercase or lowercase letters when specifying a queue.

After `sub` has successfully inserted a command into a queue, it reports the task's queue ID, which looks like the following example:

    D92196115522

Like the `batch` or `at` identifier, the BATCHQ ID is a time stamp. Unlike the `at` identifier, however, the BATCHQ ID consists of two major fields: the batch queue identifier (D in the preceding example) and a time stamp. The time stamp includes the year in YY format, the three-digit Julian date (the number of days since the beginning of the year), and a time stamp in HHMMSS format. Thus, D92196115522 translates to queue D, year 1992, Julian day 196 (July 14) at 11:55 and 22 seconds. The BATCHQ ID, like its at counterpart, sorts correctly for first-come, first-served processing. Output from any command run through BATCHQ is placed in a file named batchout in the user's home directory. Any error messages are copied to the BATCHQ log file, /usr/spool/batch/ .logfile.

Like the EBATCH system, the BATCHQ system has a status command. The EBATCH status command is aq; the BATCHQ status command is bq. The bq command is run with no parameters and produces the following output:

```
#    Batch ID        Owner  Start Date
1    D92196115522    root   Tue Jul 14 11:55:22 EDT  *
2    D92196115719    root   Tue Jul 14 11:57:19 EDT
3    H92196115922    root   Tue Jul 14 11:59:22 EDT
The following Batch Queues are locked: A B C D
```

The asterisk (*) indicates what job is running or is eligible to run if the queue is locked.

The system administrator uses this report to move jobs to a different queue or to remove them with the brm command. The bump command syntax is as follows:

```
bump -q job_#
```

In the preceding line, q is the target queue identifier A, B, C, and so on, and job_# is the job number as listed in the first column of the bq report you saw a moment ago. Thus, you can move the second job in the preceding queue to queue A by entering **bump -a 2**.

NOTE You cannot bump a job that is currently running.

The `bump` command assigns a new batch ID to the job and places it at the bottom of the new queue. You can bump jobs up or down in priority, place them on hold in the H queue, or move them to any other valid queue.

Similarly, you can remove a job from the queue by using the `brm` command. The `brm` command takes the form: `brm n`, in which *n* is the job number as listed by `bq`. You can remove the second job in the preceding queue by using the command `brm 2`.

Beneath the surface are the `batdaemon` programs, one for each operating queue. The BATCHQ daemons are run by the `/etc/rc2` startup script, which calls `S00batchq`. The `/etc/rc1` script calls `K00batchq` to stop the daemons. These two programs are, in fact, links to the actual startup program, `sbatchq`, which is located in the `/etc/init.d` directory. This pattern is normal for commands run by the `rc` scripts from within `init`, the system-initialization program.

Running the `batdaemon` Programs

At the heart of the BATCHQ system is the `batdaemon`. This daemon is a free-standing shell script located in `/usr/lib`. The `batdaemon` daemon is a Bourne shell script owned and run by `root`. (The `setuid` bit has no effect on shell scripts.)

 You can launch the daemon manually by using the command `nohup batdaemon D&`, but you might opt to use `init` to automate repetitive tasks like this one.

Recall that the `init` program switches the system between operating modes or `init` states. After `init` changes states, it scans the

/etc/inittab table for commands to run. When init first enters state 2 (multiuser mode), it runs the /etc/rc2 shell script. This script, in turn, runs every shell script in the /etc/rc2.d directory that begins with the letter K to halt tasks that should be killed. It then runs every shell script beginning with the letter S to start up tasks. When entering states 1 (single-user) and 0 (shutdown), init does the same to the /etc/rc1.d and /etc/rc0.d directories, respectively. Thus, start BATCHQ in state 2, and kill BATCHQ in state 1 and state 0.

Traditionally, all startup scripts are kept in the /etc/init.d directory, with links to the appropriate /etc/rc.d directories. Thus, the startup script for the batdaemons is /etc/init.d/sbatchq, which is linked to entries in the /etc/rc0.d and /etc/rc1.d directories as a shell script named K00batchq to kill the batch daemons. The batdaemon startup script also is linked to an entry in the /etc/rc2.d directory as a shell script named S00batchq.

The following lines show the /etc/init.d/sbatchq script:

```
BATCHQ V3.0 (c) S.R.Glines 1992
case $1 in
'start')
   set 'who -r'
   case $9 in
   [23])   exit ;;
   esac
   echo "Starting batdaemons"
   /etc/startbq ;;
'stop')
   /etc/stopbq ;;
*)
   echo "usage: /etc/init.d/sbatchq {start|stop}"
   ;;
esac
```

Obviously, the real work is performed by /etc/startbq and /etc/stopbq. The /etc/startbq program code is simple:

```
su root -c "PATH=.:$PATH;export PATH
umask 0
>/usr/spool/batch/lock
cd /usr/lib
nice -5 nohup batdaemon A  2>&1 /dev/null &
nice -5 nohup batdaemon B  2>&1 /dev/null &
nice -5 nohup batdaemon C  2>&1 /dev/null &
nice -5 nohup batdaemon D  2>&1 /dev/null & " >/
dev/null
```

Anyone can run this command to start up the batch daemons, but the daemons are then run as if owned by root. The lock file that is created contains a list of queues to be locked. This startup script clears the locks away and resets the BATCHQ system state. If you do not want to unlock the queues, you can comment or delete the line creating the lock file.

Stop the daemons by using /etc/stopbq:

```
:
X=
for i in A B C D
do
if [ -f "/usr/spool/batch/${i}lock" ]
```

This program defines four active queues named A, B, C, and D. Each active daemon has an associated file: Alock for the A queue, Block for the B queue, and so on. These files serve as semaphores that prevent more than one daemon from being active on any one queue. The files also serve another purpose. When a daemon first runs, it creates the lock file by inserting its process ID in the file with the command echo $$>${PRI}lock, in which $PRI is the name of the queue the daemon is servicing.

```
then
X=${X}" "`cat /usr/spool/batch/${i}lock`
fi
done
```

Extract the process ID from the lock file and place it in X.

```
if [ -n "$X" ]
then
X="kill -15 "$X";sleep 5"
```

Test $X to see if it contains anything. If it does, create a string resembling kill -15 2234 1123 4432;sleep 5. The daemons respond to signal 15 by gracefully shutting down. The program waits five seconds to be sure.

```
su root -c "$X">/dev/null
fi
```

Finally, let the su command do the dirty work.

The Batch Daemon

The batch daemon, /usr/lib/batdaemon, is nothing more than a simple clockwork mechanism. It runs down a list of jobs in its queue and executes them one at a time. Some commercial programs on the market do exactly the same thing, but they cost thousands of dollars, employ expensive DBMSs, and occupy hundreds of thousands of bytes of RAM.

What is the point? A clockwork mechanism does not have to be very fast, it does not have to be written in C, and it does not have to employ a database manager. If a batch spooler's job is to run time-consuming programs (anywhere from a few seconds to several hours), does it really matter if the spooler takes a tenth of a second or a half-second to load and run a program? Of course not. For that reason, this program was written in Bourne shell script rather than in C.

When the `batdaemon` first runs, it looks for the locking semaphore file for its queue. The semaphore file for the D queue is `Dlock`. If the file exists, the daemon gracefully exits—you do not want more than one daemon running on the same queue. If the `lockfile` does not exist, UNIX immediately creates one with the daemon's process ID inside. After this housekeeping is complete, the daemon is ready to begin work.

The `sub` command creates a Bourne shell script that encapsulates the commands to be run, then places the script in the `/usr/spool/batch` directory with a file name that matches the batch ID. The daemon searches this directory for any files that match its queue. If it finds any, it executes the first one on the list. After the job runs, the daemon searches the directory again. It repeats this process until the queue is exhausted. Finding no more jobs to run, the daemon goes to sleep for ten seconds, wakes up, and repeats the entire procedure. This loop continues until the daemon receives a signal 15 from the `stopbq` program, when it locks its queue and exits.

The `batdaemon` program is not very complex:

```
BATCHQ V3.0 - batdaemon (c) by S.R.Glines 1992
set -h
exitloop()
{
```

The `set` command used in this line uses `hash` to recompute the command-name hash table for the shell functions listed on the following lines, which makes them a little faster. After the daemon receives a signal 15, the `trap` command calls the `exitloop` function that follows.

Because you must define the functions before the program calls them, the logic appears to be out of order.

```
wait
```

Wait for any job to complete. One of the next commands in the shutdown script kills it anyway and leaves the batch queue dangling.

```
sleep 'random 5'
```

Because all the daemons receive their kill signals at the same time, and each is required to lock its queue, use `sleep 'random 5'` to add a little "noise" to discourage any file contention. Because `sleep 10` follows and because of the randomizing influence of running jobs, you only need to use `random` if the BATCHQ system is rarely used.

```
echo $PRI>>lock
rm -f $1
rm -f ${PRI}lock
```

Remove the last running job, if any, and the queue `lockfile` semaphore.

```
echo "daemon $PRI halted on "`date`>>.logfile
exit 0
}
```

Note the daemon's demise in the BATCHQ log, then exit.

```
loop()
```

Find the clockwork mechanism that looks for and runs one queued job at a time.

```
{
while :
do
if test -n "`grep $PRI lock`"
```

Test for a lock on the queue. If the `lock` file contains the queue name, the queue is locked. Exit the loop.

```
then
return
fi
set ${PRI}[0-9]*
```

An interesting trick: the variable $PRI is set to the queue name that the daemon is working on, so the `set $PRI[0-9]*` command generates a list of files in the queue and places them in the positional parameters, $1, $2, and so on. If no files match, $1 is set to something like D[0-9]*, for which you can test.

```
echo $#>.$PRI
if [ "$1" = ${PRI}'[0-9]*' ]
then
return
```

If no files need to be run, exit the loop.

```
else
NAME='grep LOGNAME $1|sed 's/LOGNAME=//''
echo $1" run on "`date`>>.logfile
nice $ni su $NAME -c \"\./${1}\"&
DPID=$!
echo $PID>${PRI}run
wait $PRI
>${PRI}run
echo $1", completed on "`date`>>.logfile
rm -f $1
fi
done
}
```

The `sub` command creates a shell script using a clone of the caller's environment. This script includes the user's LOGNAME, which is extracted from the file using `grep`. The `su` command uses this script to run the batch file under the user's login. Thus, root must own the daemon. Otherwise, the `su` command wants to know a password. The batch file is actually executed by the line that begins with `nice`. The value for `nice` is found later. After the job is running, store the task's process ID in `DPID`, descendent `PID`, and write the number to `${PRI}run`. If you are managing queue D, the current job's process ID is stored in `Drun`. (You can use this later if you need to kill it.)

Up to now, you have only loaded functions into the environment. Now you are ready to actually execute something.

```
trap "exitloop" 15
```

Set a `trap` for signal 15. If you get it, execute the `exitloop` function.

```
cd /usr/spool/batch
PRI=$1
export PRI
case $PRI in
```

Change directories so you do not need to use path names, then set `PRI` to $1, which is set to one of the queue identifiers.

```
A) ni=-5;;
B) ni=-10;;
C) ni=-15;;
D) ni=-19;;
*) exit 255;;
esac
```

Permanently set the `nice` levels for each queue. Because the daemon only knows which queue is serviced at execution time, you must recalculate when the daemon is launched.

```
lockfile=${PRI}lock
if [ -r $lockfile ]
then
exit 255
fi
```

Establish the semaphore lock's file name, then test to see if it already exists. If it does, a daemon is already running for this queue or the system crashed, so exit.

```
echo "daemon $PRI started on "`date`>>.logfile
```

Sign on to duty in the `logfile`.

```
umask 0
echo $$>$lockfile
```

Create the semaphore lock to prevent more than one daemon from running. You also fill the lockfile with your present process ID so that UNIX can signal you to stop using `stopbq`.

```
while loop
do
sleep 10
done
```

These four lines of code is where the daemon spends most of its time. The `loop` command runs anything it can find. If it cannot find anything, it exits. This `while` loop goes to sleep for ten seconds to conserve CPU cycles.

Controlling the Batch Queues

So far, the BATCHQ system works about as well as a severely restricted batch system with only four concurrent jobs and slightly differing prioritie, such those are affected by using `nice`. To be as effective as a mainframe batch-queueing system, far more control is needed. You can use the following programs to provide such control:

❖ `rsbq`. Restarts the BATCHQ system after a panic or power failure

❖ `lbq` and `rlbq`. Locks and unlocks specific queues, respectively

- ❖ brm and bump. Delete items from the queues and change the target queue of a batch job
- ❖ bq. Reports the BATCHQ system's status

Begin with the system-administration utilities that lock and unlock the queues.

Locking a Queue

When a queue is locked, you prevent the daemon from executing any jobs in its queue. To lock a queue, simply place the queue name in the file /usr/spool/batch/lock. If queue D is locked, the lock file contains the letter D. Append the queue name to the lock file:

```
:
BATCHQ V3.0 - lbq (c) 1992 by S.R.Glines
#
if [ "$*" ]
then
for A
do
case $A in
[aA] )
echo A >>/usr/spool/batch/lock;echo Batch Queue A
Locked! ;;
[bB] )
echo B >>/usr/spool/batch/lock;echo Batch Queue B
Locked! ;;
[cC] )
echo C >>/usr/spool/batch/lock;echo Batch Queue C
Locked! ;;
[dD] )
echo D >>/usr/spool/batch/lock;echo Batch Queue D
Locked! ;;
esac
done
fi
```

Unlocking a Batch Queue

To unlock a queue, remove the queue name from the `/usr/spool/batch/lock` file. The `rlbq` removes a lock from a batch queue. Because locking adds characters to the file, also take an opportunity to reduce its size and delete any duplicates.

```
:
cd /usr/spool/batch
umask 0
```

Use `cd` so that you do not have to use full path names. Set `umask` 0 so that everyone can read and write the files. You also might want restrict access to the programs.

```
for A
do
sort -u lock|sed 's/ //g'>/usr/tmp/bq$$
case $A in
[aA] ) sed "s/A//g" /usr/tmp/bq$$>lock;
    echo "Locks removed from batch queue A";;
[bB] ) sed "s/B//g" /usr/tmp/bq$$>lock;
    echo "Locks removed from batch queue B";;
[cC] ) sed "s/C//g" /usr/tmp/bq$$>lock;
    echo "Locks removed from batch queue C";;
[dD] ) sed "s/D//g" /usr/tmp/bq$$>lock;
    echo "Locks removed from batch queue D";;
esac
    done
```

Order the contents of the lock file and remove any duplicates. Also remove any extra spaces that might have snuck in from other sources. Then strip the temp file of the queue name you want to release and replace the lock file.

If you have more than one system administrator, make sure that this command is only run one at a time. Running multiple `rlbq` commands simultaneously can corrupt the `lock` file.

Listing the Batch Queue's Contents and Status

You might have trouble manipulating the batch queues unless you know more about them. Fortunately, you can use the `bq` command to get some of this information. The `bq` command output lists any running or pending jobs in the queue. It also tells you which queues, if any, are locked.

The `bq` program's output depends on the jobs having been submitted by `sub`. The `sub` command encapsulates the job in a Bourne shell script, which the `batdaemon` program actually runs. Both the `bq` command and the `batdaemon` program are dependent on the jobs having been properly presented by the `sub` command.

The `sub` command should include a line in the shell script that contains the characters (`#@`), which `bq` searches for, and the environment setting `LOGNAME=`, which `batdaemon` searches for. The absence of either line in the encapsulating shell script causes the system to fail.

The line in a job script that contains (`#@`) has the ownership information that `bq` displays. The full rendering of a sample line containing `#@` follows:

```
(#@) D92197172354  Owner: srg  Date: Wed Jul 15
17:23:54 EDT 1992
```

The `bq` command uses this data to display the queues' status:

```
:
```

The colon ensures that if the bq command is run from the C shell, it performs properly.

```
BATCHQ V3.0 (c) 1992 S.R.Glines
echo "\n    #  Batch ID       Owner   Start date"
X='sort -u /usr/spool/batch/lock'
```

First, display the header. This program takes up to a second to run on a heavily burdened system. By displaying the header, the program appears to run faster and appeases impatient users. Next, place any queue locks in the variable X by sorting and outputting them using command substitution.

```
grep '#@' /usr/spool/batch/* |
```

Extract the status line from any and all files in the directory. Then send these lines into a pipe so that the next command can pick them up and process them. One virtue of using the * wildcard is that it gives a list of files in alphabetical order, which is useful later.

```
awk 'BEGIN{x="X"}
{z=" ";y=substr($3,1,1);if (x != y && y < "E")
z="*";x=y}
```

If the contents of the status line and the file name are synchronized as they should be, the data piped into this awk program is in the correct order. All the jobs are in the proper queues and ordered as they arrived. This means that you can detect a queue change if the first character of the third field (the batch ID) changes. The variable x contains the previous record's queue ID, which is compared against the current record's queue ID. If a queue was changed, the current record represents the job that is running or eligible to run in the queue. If so, x is set to an asterisk, otherwise to a space.

```
{printf("%6d  %12s",NR,$3);
print "     "$5" "$7" "$8" "$9" "$10" "$11" "z}
```

Print out the status line with an asterisk or blank at the end of the line, depending on whether you have determined that the job is eligible to run.

```
echo  "\n\n\n\t\c"
if [ -z "$X" ]
then
echo There are no Batch Queues locked.
else
echo The following Batch Queues are locked:$X
fi
```

Remember that you set X just after displaying the header. Now you are ready to use it. If X is the null string, no batch queues are locked. If X is not the null string, you want to display the list of locked queues.

Deleting a Job from the Queue

Deleting jobs from the batch queue by using the brm command, which uses the syntax brm *n*, in which *n* is the line number, as listed by the bq command. In other words, if the bq command lists something like the following output, you can remove the first item on the list using the command brm 1, the second item on the list with brm 2, and so on:

```
#    Batch ID        Owner   Start Date
1    D92196115522    root    Tue Jul 14 11:55:22 EDT *
2    D92196115719    root    Tue Jul 14 11:57:19 EDT
3    H92196115922    root    Tue Jul 14 11:59:22 EDT
```

Keep in mind that if you delete item one, item two becomes item one the next time you run it. If you are removing more than one item, begin with the highest number and work down. Alternatively, you can avoid this problem altogether by using the command's interactive form. In this case, brm is called without parameters. The `bq` status report is automatically displayed and you are prompted for a job number. If no jobs need to be deleted, `brm` reports the fact and exits.

The initial letter of the job ID also tells you the queue ID. If the job has not yet run, you can delete it by simply deleting the file that contains the job. If the job is already running, you must delete the file and kill the running process. In fact, you must kill any child processes as well, or run the risk of creating zombies. As you learned in Chapter 4, *zombies* are tasks whose run status is complete but which are not purged from the run queue because they are still in the grips of an imaginary parent. They cannot be killed, purged, or otherwise manipulated except by a system shutdown. Thus, you must kill all the children of a background task, beginning with the highest process ID.

The `batch` daemon knows the new job's process ID and has placed it in a file known as `${QUE}run`. The daemon managing queue D, for example, places the current job's process ID in `/usr/spool/batch/Drun`. You must kill this parent process, together with its children, using the `brm` command:

```
cd /usr/spool/batch
X=$1
```

Change directories to avoid path names. Then save `$1` as `X` because you are going to use the `set` command.

```
set " " `grep -s -e '#@' * `
shift
```

Use `grep` to extract any status lines from any and all files in the directory. Set `$1` equal to `" "` with the `set " "` command in the event `grep` finds nothing. Without the added parameter, the `set` command displays the environment if no status lines were found. Because the initial parameter is a throwaway, use `shift` to get rid of it.

```
if [ $# -eq 0 ];
then echo "nothing to kill";exit; fi
if [ -z "$X" ]
then
```

If grep did not find anything, you do not need to kill anything. Next, test to see if anything was placed on the command line; if not, enter interactive mode.

```
bq
echo "\n\tEnter item number to remove  >\c"
X='read x;echo $x'
if [ -z "$X" ];then exit;fi
fi
```

Display the batch queue status with the bq command and prompt the user for a job number. If the user enters a carriage return, then exit.

```
set " " `grep -s -e '#@' * |
awk 'BEGIN{x="X"}\
{z=" ";y=substr($3,1,1);if (x != y && y < "E")
   {print NR,$3" "$5" "y;x=y}
else print NR,$3" "$5" Y" }' |grep "^$X"`
shift
```

This code is substantially the same as the code used to create the output for bq except that you output it differently. The first field is the line number, the second field is the job ID, the third field is the user, the fourth field is the queue identifier if the job is running or eligible to run, or a Y otherwise. Finally, pass the output through grep to filter out only the line that matches the request. Place the filtered line in the environment using set, together with a bogus initial parameter, which is then removed using shift. Again, this prevents set from merely listing the current environment if no match is found.

```
if [ $# -eq 0 ];
then echo "nothing to kill";exit; fi
```

If no match was found, exit.

```
if [ "$4" != "Y" ]
```

If the fourth field contains a Y, the task selected is not running or eligible to run so all you have to do is delete the file.

```
then
if [ -s "${4}run" ]
then
PID='cat ${4}run'
PID='kids $PID'
kill -9 $PID
fi
fi
```

The job is running or eligible to run, so check if the ${QUE}run file is empty. If so, the job is not running so you can, again, just delete the file. If the ${QUE}run file is not empty, it contains the process ID of the target job. The running job's process ID is extracted using cat and placed in the variable PID. Then update the PID variable with all the child tasks using the kids command.

```
if [ -f "$2" ];then rm $2;fi
```

Finally, delete the file if it still exists. The batch daemon already has deleted the running job files, and you do not want to generate any error messages.

Finding all the Children of a Running Process

If you must kill a task for some reason, you usually run the ps command to learn its process ID, and then use the kill command to kill it.

The `kill` command is short for "signal," but its primary purpose is unambiguous given its name. The `kill -9` *pid* command is a sure hit on all process except zombies, which are immune to all signals.

Unfortunately, killing a parent without killing the child first can sometimes create zombies or force `init` to take over the parentage of orphaned tasks. For example, if you run a command that then calls `sleep`, and you kill the parent process while the `sleep` command is running, the parent dies. The `sleep` command, however, which has not been killed, is orphaned and its parentage is taken over by `init`. Thus, you must kill all of the child tasks as well as the parent task.

You can manually find the descendants of a task by using the `ps -edf` command, which lists not only every process's PID (*process ID*) but also each process's PPID (*predecessor PID*). Although you can accomplish this task manually, you can easily automate it. Use the `kids` command to find all of a process's lineal descendants.

The `kids` command syntax is `kids` *pid*, in which *pid* is the process ID of the command whose children are to be located. Because the primary purpose of `kids` is to aid in killing processes, the `kids` command lists the process and all its descendants in reverse numerical order. Thus, the `kill` command signals all the processes in the chain from the most recently born back to the original process, so that `kill` does not kill parent tasks before child tasks. To kill an entire line of processes, use the syntax: `kill -9 'kids` *pid*`'`, in which *pid* is the process ID whose line you want to kill:

```
    :
if [ -n "$1" ]
then
```

First, check to see if you need to kill any processes.

```
ps -edf|sort +3 -4 |awk " BEGIN {l=1;c[1]=$1 }
```

Use `ps -edf` to list all processes currently running, sort them in descending process ID order, and pipe them into an `awk` program. Notice that you use quotation marks instead of an apostrophe, so that variable substitution takes place before the `awk` program takes over. The variable `l` is used as an index to the number of `kids` you find, which are placed in the array `c[]`.

```
{P[NR]=\$2;PP[NR]=\$3}
```

Place the `PID` field in the `P[]` array and the `PPID` field in the `PP[]` array. Notice that you had to escape the `$`, so that it is not interpreted by the shell.

```
END {for (k=1;k<= l;k++) {
    for (i=1;i<= NR ; i++ ) {
        if (PP[i] == c[k] ) { l++;c[l]=P[i] }
      }
   }
for (k=1;k<= l;k++) { print c[k]}
}"|sort -r
fi
```

Perform an exhaustive search for each generation of children. K is an index to the children you have found, and `l` is the total number of children you have found. When you have looked at all possibilities, print the list out in reverse order.

Changing the Assigned Queue

After a job has been submitted, but before it runs, the user or system administrator can change the assigned queue by using the `bump` command. The syntax is very similar to the `brm` command, but you must specify a target queue. The syntax is the following:

bump -q job#, in which q is any valid queue identifier, and job#
is the row number listed with the bq command. In the absence of
any command-line parameters, bump enters an interactive mode
similar to the brm command. You must, however, specify a target
queue:

```
:
cd /usr/spool/batch
umask 0
```

Change to the operating directory to avoid using path names, and
then set umask 0 so that others can read the created files.

```
X='grep '#@' *'
if [ -z "$X" ];then echo "nothing to bump";exit;fi
if [ "$#" -lt "2" ]
   then
   bq
```

Look for the special marker. If nothing turns up, you do not need
to continue. Next, check to see if both parameters were supplied. If
not, enter the bq command's interactive mode.

```
    X='prompt "   Enter target queue (a-d,h,m,x,y)"'
    Y='prompt "   Enter Job #"'
    echo "\n\n\n"
    set -$X $Y
    shift
    if [ "$#" -lt "2" ];then exit;fi
fi
```

Display the batch queue status, then prompt for the new queue ID
and job number, which is different from the job ID. If the user has
supplied both required inputs, you can continue.

```
case $1 in
-[aA] ) PRI=A;shift;;
-[bB] ) PRI=B;shift;;
-[cC] ) PRI=C;shift;;
```

```
-[dD] ) PRI=D;shift;;
-[hH] ) PRI=H;shift;;
-[mM] ) PRI=M;shift;;
-[xX] ) PRI=X;shift;;
-[yY] ) PRI=Y;shift;;
  * ) echo invalid queue;exit;;
esac
```

Check the user's queue ID validity and set PRI if the queue is valid. If not, exit and tell the user why. After you know the desired queue, throw that away with the shift command.

```
xxx=$1
set 'date '+%y%j%H%M%S''
```

Save the batch job's line number (the job number) in xxx. Then place the formatted date in the environment. This time stamp forms part of the job ID. Also provide an alternate.

```
#set 'echo $$|awk '{ printf "%6.6d\n",$1} ''
NEW=$PRI$1
```

Form the new batch ID from the queue name and time stamp.

```
set " " `grep '#@' * |awk 'BEGIN{x="X"}\
{z=" ";y=substr($3,1,1);if (x != y && y < "E" )
{print NR,$3" "y;x=y}\
else print NR,$3" Y" }'|grep "^$xxx"`
shift
```

This code is similar to bq and brm. The final grep command gives you the unique match. Use shift to remove the place holder.

```
if [ -z "$*" ];then echo "no such job";exit;fi
```

If you do not have anything after shifting, you do not need to continue because the job number does not exist. If you pass the test, three fields are present in the environment, $1, $2, and $3. They are, respectively, the job number, the batch ID, and the queue ID.

Only the job that is eligible to run gets a queue ID in this field; all pending jobs get a Y in this field.

```
if [ -w "$2" ]
then

if [ "$3" = "[A-D]" ]
    then
    if [ -n "`cat ${PRI}run`" ]; then
    echo "Job currently running";exit;fi
fi
```

Check the batch ID and $2's file name. If they are identical, the file still exists, and you can proceed.

If the file exists and the job is eligible to run, check the ${PRI}run file to see if the job is running. If the file is not empty, the job is running, and you cannot bump it, so exit. If the job has not started to run, continue.

```
mv $2 .$2
```

Quickly move the file to a hidden file so it cannot run while you modify it.

```
sed "/#@/ s/$2/$NEW/" .$2 > .$NEW
rm .$2
chmod +x .$NEW
mv .$NEW $NEW
echo "Batch file $2 resubmitted as $NEW"
```

Patch the status line in the shell script with the new batch ID and place the output in another hidden file with the new batch ID so that the daemons do not pick up the job while sed is still working. When finished, delete the hidden copy of the old job and rename the hidden new file to the new batch ID.

Because you are finished, you can allow the daemon to pick it up and run it. Finally, announce to the user that the job has been re-submitted with a new name. Next, you have to deal with the special case of jobs being sent to the X and Y queues.

```
case $PRI in
"X" ) echo "trap \"/usr/tmp/$NEW\" 0">/usr/tmp/$NEW
    cat $NEW >>/usr/tmp/$NEW
    chmod +x /usr/tmp/$NEW
```

Normally, the daemon deletes the job file; however, a job launched by nohup does not. Create a new file with the trap command to clean up.

```
rm $NEW
nohup  /usr/tmp/$NEW  &
;;
```

After you create the temp file with the trap command, append the standard batch file to the end of the new file. Remove the original file still in the batch directory. Now you are ready to run it with the nohup command, confident that it deletes itself after it is finished.

```
"Y" ) cat $NEW|batch;rm $NEW;;
esac
else
echo "Job has run";exit
fi
```

In the case of the Y queue, concatenate the shell script into the batch command, which makes a copy of it anyway. Then simply delete it from the batch directory and manage the rest of the job using the EBATCH system.

Submitting a BATCHQ Job

Now that you understand the BATCHQ system's underlying structure, take a look at the sub command. The key to the BATCHQ system lies in every BATCHQ job having the same internal structure—specifically, the status line that is embedded in the job itself.

Without this key data record, the daemon and the system's other components do not recognize a file as a legitimate batch job. Like the `batch` command, `sub` copies the user's environment and embeds the command line to execute the job as though it were running in the shallow background.

In other words, if the user has permission to perform a job, the batch job also has permission to perform that job. If the user has become a superuser, the batch job still runs as the user's original `LOGNAME`, which cannot be altered. Like the `batch` command, a job run by the BATCHQ system must be a Bourne shell script.

Start a BATCHQ job, using the `sub` command in one of the following forms:

```
sub -q command
sub command
echo command|sub
cat file|sub
```

In the first example, the target queue, q, is specified. In the second example, the default queue D is implied. The default is also implied in the third and fourth examples, in which the *command* text is piped into `sub`. For example, the command `sub echo hello world` generates a shell script destined to run in the default queue D, and places it in the `/usr/spool/batch` directory with a name that matches its batch ID. As the `sub` command exits, it reports this batch ID so the user can monitor the job with the `bq` command. After the daemon runs the job, it places any data that is not explicitly redirected, along with a start and stop marker, in a file named `batchout` in the user's home directory.

The command `sub echo hello world` generates the following Bourne shell script:

```
:
# (#@) D92199084238  Owner: srg  Date: Fri Jul 17
08:42:38 EDT 1992
```

This status line generated by sub is used by bq, brm, and bump. You must include it for the system to work properly.

```
WD=/usr/srg
```

This variable, WD, is set by the sub command so that the script knows what directory it should be in when the job runs.

```
BATCHID=/usr/spool/batch/D92199084238
DBEDIT=vi
HOME=/usr/srg
IFS=
LOGNAME=srg
MAIL=/usr/spool/mail/srg
MAILCHECK=600
OPTIND=1
PATH=/usr/srg:/usr/srg/bin::/bin:/usr/bin:/usr/
local/bin:/usr/srg /bin
PLACE=/usr/spool/batch/.D92199084238
PRI=D
PRINTER=oki
SHELL=/bin/sh
TERM=altos3
TZ=EST5EDT
where=/usr/spool/batch
```

These environment settings are the result of using the set command redirected to this file. It includes some debris left by the sub environment.

```
cd $WD
PRI=D92199084238
JOBID='basename $0'
```

Use the `WD` variable to place you in the directory from which the job was run. The `PRI` variable is the original batch ID. The current batch ID is placed in the `JOBID` variable, just in case the job was bumped. If the job was not bumped, `PRI` and `JOBID` remain the same.

```
(echo $JOBID; echo "echo hello world ") >>$HOME/
batchout
(echo hello world) 2>&1 >>$HOME/batchout
echo $JOBID completed @ 'date' code $?>>$HOME/
batchout
if [ -x "$O_FILE" ];then rm $O_FILE;fi
exit $?
```

In the previous lines, the batch ID and the original command line are echoed to the user's output file `batchout` in the user's home directory. On the next line, the command is actually run. It runs from within a `sub` shell, in case the user placed multiple commands, as in `sub 'command;command'`, on the command line. Then place a completion marker in the user's output file and exit.

The command that produces this file is the `sub` command:

```
:
#
# BATCHQ V3.0 - sub(V3.1) Copyright (c) 1992 by S.R.Glines
#
PRI=D
if [ -z "$*" ]
then
```

Set the default queue. Next, check to see if the user placed anything on the command line. If nothing is found, assume piped input.

```
O_FILE="/tmp/xxx$$"
cat >/tmp/xxx$$
```

```
chmod +x /tmp/xxx$$
set "/tmp/xxx$$"
else
case $1 in
```

Define O_FILE as the target of the piped input, so that you can delete it later after the job has run. Then take input from the standard input and place it in temporary storage, change it to the executable mode, and set the file name to $1 so the command can proceed as if the command were sub file.

```
-[aA] ) PRI=A;shift;;
-[bB] ) PRI=B;shift;;
-[cC] ) PRI=C;shift;;
-[xX] ) PRI=X;shift;;
-[yY] ) PRI=Y;shift;;
-[hH] ) PRI=H;shift;;
-[mM] ) PRI=M;shift;;
-* ) PRI=D;shift;;
esac
fi
```

If the user specified a queue with a flag, check the queue's validity, then set the variable PRI to the requested queue. Use shift to remove the flag. Assume that what remains on the command line is what the user wanted to run.

```
if [ "$#" -eq 0 ];then echo "No command";exit;fi
```

If nothing else is on the command line, an error occurs.

```
XX=$*
set 'date '+%y%j%H%M%S''
```

In the preceding lines, save the command line in XX and place a formatted time stamp in the $1 position with set.

```
umask 0
BATCHID=/usr/spool/batch
```

```
where=$BATCHID
PLACE=$BATCHID/\.$PRI$1
BATCHID=$BATCHID/$PRI$1
echo ":">$PLACE
```

Unmask the file-creation mask so that the file is readable by all (this is necessary for bq). Place the target directory in the variable BATCHID. Save this in the where variable, in case it is needed later by the application. Set PLACE to the name of the file you are creating and BATCHID to the file name that the daemon is looking for. PLACE contains the name of a hidden file so that the daemon does not accidentally pick it up while you are still creating it. Next, begin to create the file.

```
echo "# (#@) $PRI$1  Owner: "$LOGNAME"  Date:
"`date`>>$PLACE
```

Insert the batch status line.

```
echo "WD="`pwd`>>$PLACE
```

Set the variable WD to the current working directory. Use this to get back home after the daemon runs this job.

```
set|sed '/^XX/d
/^SYS/d'>>$PLACE
echo 'cd $WD'>>$PLACE
```

The set command without arguments lists the current environment. Pipe the output through sed to remove some debris and put it in the file. You can pass environment variables to your batch command; however, the variables are set at submission time, not at runtime.

```
echo "PRI=$PRI$1">>$PLACE
echo 'JOBID=`basename $0`'>>$PLACE
```

```
echo '(echo $JOBID; echo'" \"$XX \")"' >>$HOME/
batchout' >>$PLACE
echo "($XX) 2>&1"' >>$HOME/batchout' >>$PLACE
echo 'echo $JOBID completed @ `date` code
$?>>$HOME/batchout'>>$PLACE
```

Insert the standard command strings to set PRI to the original batch ID and JOBID to the job's batch ID when it was run. This method helps the user determine if the job was bumped by anyone. Insert the code to run the job and note its start and stop times in the user's batchout file, together with any output that is not redirected.

```
echo 'if [ -x "$O_FILE" ];then rm
$O_FILE;fi'>>$PLACE
```

If the job was submitted through a pipe, the daemon does not know it, so include code to delete the temporary file you created after the job has been run. If O_FILE is not defined, this line of code has no effect.

```
echo 'exit $?'>>$PLACE
chmod +x $PLACE
case $PRI in
"X" )
```

Now that the file is complete, place an exit command at the file's end and make it executable.

Remember, so far the file is still a hidden file. Now you can make it visible to the daemon or send it to the X or Y queues.

```
echo 'trap "rm '"/usr/tmp/$PRI$1"'" 0'>/usr/tmp/
$PRI$1
cat $PLACE >> /usr/tmp/$PRI$1
rm $PLACE
chmod +x /usr/tmp/$PRI$1
exec nohup /usr/tmp/$PRI$1 >>$HOME/batchout& ;;
```

If you want the job to go to the X queue, you must force it to clean up after itself. Use the `trap` command, which leads off the new shell script. Then combine the original file with the new file and make it visible. Delete the file from the `batch` directory, make the new file executable and run it with `nohup`.

```
"Y" )
cat $PLACE|batch
rm $PLACE ;;
* )
```

If the job is going to the Y queue, all you have to do is pipe it into the `batch` command and delete it from the batch directory.

```
mv $PLACE $BATCHID
echo $PRI$1
read zzz ;;
esac
```

If all else fails, you know that the job is an ordinary BATCHQ job. The file you have created is still hidden, so you can make it visible by changing its name. Finally, print the batch ID and pause, waiting for a carriage return, so that the user can make note of the batch ID.

Using the BATCHQ System

The BATCHQ system is designed to be easy to use. The standard interface enables full and free access to all modes of unattended background processing. The system administrator can lock the queues herself, or place the lbq and rlbq commands in a cronfile to automatically lock and unlock specific queues as the day's processing burden varies.

In general, the queues' processing priority (and hence the burden on the system) is X, Y, A, B, C, and D. The H queue is designed as a "holding pen" for jobs that the operator must release. The M queue, although similar to the H queue, is designed to signal the operator that he must "mount" the magnetic tape or other medium before the queue can release the job. The user should send instructions to the operator by electronic mail or other means for how to dispose of the job.

In general, the BATCHQ system provides most, if not all, of the batch-queueing system functionality. Instead of an arcane "Job Control Language," however, the user or programmer has full access to the UNIX tool kit.

Summary

The previous three chapters illustrated the use of software tools that generate menus, generate data-entry screens, and control jobs that run in the background.

This chapter discussed batch spooling—specifically, the EBATCH batch-spooling system and the BATCHQ batch-spooling system.

The next chapter illustrates and documents the use of several tools that are crucial in the management of large UNIX installations.

Chapter 13

System Administration Commands and Utilities

When MSH, BATCHQ, EBATCH, and SCREEN were first packaged as commercial products, they were installed on many of the author's client's systems. This was done to create uniformity among the systems, as well as to make sure the programs worked on the wide variety of UNIX systems supported. One of the last systems, BATCHQ, was installed manually on an Amdahl 390 running UTS, which is Amdahl's version of UNIX System V for IBM mainframes and clones. BATCHQ was intended to solve the problem of operators who had little or no control over processes run in the background (or in the foreground).

BATCHQ helped with the control issue, but the real problem was that some old programs would occasionally spin out of control and consume CPU cycles. The only way to deal with these programs was to "kill" them. This was done by locating the offending tasks' process IDs, using the `ps` command, and then killing the tasks.

There were a couple of disadvantages to this procedure, however. Operators did not always know that about the problem until users began complaining. Also, running the ps command took twenty minutes and listed thousands of processes.

Obviously, any system that supports 1500 users and runs UNIX creates a lot of processes—thousands of them. When one in ten thousand spins out of control, it is a lot easier to shut down and reboot than it is to find one process that has consumed fifty seconds of CPU time in the last five minutes.

The ps -l command lists the total CPU time accrued for a process to date, and you can determine the change in elapsed CPU time by comparing two ps -l listings taken at known intervals. Using the same technique and data, you can also determine any changes in memory usage.

The output of the ps -l command (on one version of UNIX System V Release 3.2) looks like this:

```
F S P    UID    PID  PPID  C PRI NI  SZ    WCHAN TTY   TIME CMD
10 S 0    203    104     1  0  30 20  72 c0105e7c con  0:01 sh
10 S 0      0   9449   104  0  30 20  72 c010677c con  0:04 sh
10 P 0      0  13825  9449 17  71 20  60          con  0:00 ps
```

The most interesting fields are the following:

❖ S (process status) field. Indicates the run status of the field.

❖ PID (process ID) field. Serves as a tag for internal manipulation.

❖ SZ field. Indicates the amount of RAM used.

❖ TIME field. Indicated the total elapsed time in which the process has been running.

❖ CMD field. Carries with it the name of the command.

By taking "snapshots" of the process status every few minutes, and then looking for any changes, you can eliminate searching through dozens, hundreds, or thousands of lines of output for an offending task. This is the job of the following three programs: dps, dpsn, and dpscron.

Using the dps, dpsn, and dpscron Commands

The dpscron program is intended to be run by the cron daemon on a periodic basis, every five minutes, for example.

The first time dpsn runs, it places a parsed and reformatted output version of the ps -edl command in a file called /tmp/Cstatus. Subsequently, the reformatted data is placed in a file named /tmp/Ostatus, and the Ostatus and Cstatus files are joined on the process ID by using the join command. The output of this process is used to generate reports that show changes in RAM size, changes in CPU time used, and programs stopped for any reason. This output is placed in /tmp/PSTATUS for all to see.

The dps command performs the same function, but does it interactively by using the existing Ostatus file for input and then creating a new Ostatus file as a result.

The dpsn command is the same as the dps command, but it does not update the Ostatus file.

 These commands process can be confusing, so it is useful to describe it another way. To detect any change, you always need two data points. The first set of data points is contained in the file Ostatus; the most recent set of data points is contained in the file Cstatus. By using the UNIX join operator, only those processes that exist in both files are listed and can be compared. If there are any changes in process status (shown by the Greek symbol Delta), they can then be determined.

It is the operator's preference for which command to use: dps or dpsn.

The output of all three programs looks like this:

```
PID   dt   sT    dR   R    N    S    cmd

23    1    3:18  0    72   29   S    sh Time Change
24    2    4:04  0    72   29   S    sh Time Change
25    1    3:41  0    72   29   S    sh Time Change
26    1    3:18  0    72   29   S    sh Time Change
```

These columns can be read as follows:

- ❖ PID. The process ID.
- ❖ dt. (Delta time). The change in CPU time used since the last invocation of dpscron or dps.
- ❖ sT. The sum of the CPU time to date.
- ❖ dR. (Delta RAM). The change in RAM use since the last snapshot.
- ❖ R. The RAM currently being used by the process
- ❖ N. The nice level of the command.
- ❖ S. The process status.
- ❖ cmd. The command that changed and a comment as to why the process is listed.

Just one of the `dps` commands is discussed in depth because they differ only in where they place their output and whether or not they reset the clock by creating a new `Cstatus` file. The package on the disk is called DPS and includes `dpscron`, `dpsn`, `dps`, and another program called `ko`, which is used to "knock out" a user and all his associated processes. More about `ko` later.

Inside the dps Command

Many versions of UNIX are currently available, and although most of them behave more or less the same (at least at the shell level), there are always minor incompatibilities between them, especially among the minor and more obscure commands. One irritating incompatibility is in the output format of the `ps - l` command.

 The following program is offered with a caveat. It probably will not work on your machine at first, but with minor changes it will.

The (annotated) `dps` source is as follows:

```
:
# dpscron - © 1992 by S.R.Glines
NEW="/tmp/Cstatus"
OLD="/tmp/Ostatus"
```

In the preceding lines, the program defines the two outputs, rather than hard wires them. It is assumed that this code will not work and that the user will want to direct the output elsewhere while testing.

```
ps -el|awk 'NR > 1 {
```

In the preceding lines, the program uses `ps -el` to generate a process status of all running programs and to throw away the header line in the `awk` program.

```
time=$12;cmd=$13
if(NF==14){time=$13;cmd=$14}
```

In this version of UNIX, the `ps -el` command normally produces 14 fields. You also notice that running programs have blanks in the WCHAN column, which means that these records only have 13 fields. There are versions of the `ps -el` command that have as many as 17 fields, so adjust the positional parameters accordingly.

```
split(time,ft,":");
ftime=(60*ft[1])+ft[2];
```

In the preceding lines, the program parses the time field and converts it into seconds from the minute:second format.

```
PID=$5
S=$2
NI=$9
SZ=$10
print PID"    "S"    "NI"    "SZ"    "ftime"    "cmd}'|
```

The preceding lines define the variables to be the same as the column head generated by the `ps -l` command. Change the positional parameters to match your local system (this should take about two minutes).

```
sort -n>$NEW
```

The preceding line sorts the output in numerical order (in PID order) because PID is the first field of your output and takes precedence. Next, the program joins the new and old snapshot files on the first field, which is the PID. To keep it straight, list the field number and their meanings of the output of the `join` command are listed, as follows:

```
    1    2    3    4    5    6    7    8
   pid  S    N    R1   R2   T1   T2   CMD
if [ -w "$OLD" ];then
join -o 1.1 1.2 2.3 1.4 1.4 1.5 2.5 1.6 $NEW $OLD |
awk ´ BEGIN {
print "PID   dt    sT    dR    sR    N    S   cmd"
print ""
}
```

If the old file exists, this command has already run at# least once,
so there is something to compare against. If the old file is not
found, all exit (depending on which dps command this is). If the
program passes the test, it performs the join and prints the#
header for your report.

```
{
dt=$6-$7;dr=$4-$5;text=""
```

The program calculates your "deltas" dt and dr.

```
if($4 != $5 ) text="RAM changed size"
if($6 != $7 ) text="Time Change";
if($2 == "Z") text=" ZOMBIE"
if($2 == "W") text=" Waiting for IO"
if($2 == "T") text=" Stopped"
if($2 == "X") text=" Waiting for Memory"
```

The preceding lines show the conditions that the program will
report on.

```
if (text != "")
print $1"   "dt"   "$6"   "dr"   "$4"   "$3\
"   "$2"   "$8"    "text}'|pg
fi
mv $NEW $OLD
```

If any of the preceding conditions have been met, the text field is not a blank, so the program prints it out. If this program is `dps` or `dpsn`, the program pipes the output through `pg`. Otherwise, the program places the output in `/tmp/PSTATUS`. Having made its report, the program moves the "`NEW`" file to "`OLD`" to be ready for the next request. If the command were `dpsn`, the program would not move the new to the old.

Killing Users with the `ko` Command

An alternate way to deal with users' programs is the `ko` command. Other ways that this command is used is up to the individual system administrator.

If a user's program gets lost or hangs up for any reason, the only way to free the terminal is to "kill" the offending program. This involves running the `ps` command and searching for the problem, which can be both time-consuming and inconvenient. Instead of shutting down and rebooting if the offending program cannot be located, it is better to simply "kill" the user's primary and dependant tasks. This is the function of the `ko` command.

The syntax of the `ko` command is `ko` *logname tty* in which *logname* is the user's login name, and *tty* is the name of the device associated with the login. This last is necessary only if the user is logged in more than once. Like many of the commands listed in this book, the absence of any parameters on the command line sends the program into interactive mode, in which the system administrator is prompted for the login name after a list of logged-in users is displayed. The system administrator is forced to enter the full login name of the user to be "killed."

In interactive mode, the output of the who -H -u -T command is displayed and piped through more, in case more than 22 users are logged in. The output of the who -H -u -T command looks like this:

```
NAME    LINE      TIME            IDLE  PID    COMMENTS
srg     +console  Jul 18 09:24    .     203
guest   -tty05    Jul 18 10:49    2:20  20413
```

 This application used more instead of pg because more only pauses if there is more than one screen full of data. The default for pg is to pause at the end of the data.

The user whose login name is "guest" is a candidate for being "ko'd" because the terminal has been rendered immune to messages, and the user has been idle for two hours and twenty minutes. The dash (-) next to the user's device indicates that either the user has deliberately used the mesg -n command or that the terminal is hopelessly lost.

The ko command prompts the system administrator for the user name, which must be entered exactly as shown. In this example, the system administrator enters **guest**. A prompt appears for the line ID. If only one user is logged in under that name, the login name is unique. Otherwise, the line ID is needed. The line ID may be entered as **tty05**, or simply as **05**. If the user to be ko'd is on the console, then any of the following valid substitutes are permitted: **console, cons, 00**.

The annotated ko program is as follows:

```
:
# This pgm kills the named person
if [ ! "$*" ]
```

If there is nothing on the command line, the program goes into interactive mode.

```
then
echo "Remove a user and all associated processes\n"
who -u -T -H|more
echo ""
X='prompt "Enter NAME"'
if [ ! "$X" ];then exit;fi
Y='prompt "Enter LINE id"'
set " " $X $Y
shift
fi
```

In interactive mode, the program displays a header announcing its intentions and displays the output of the who command. Then the program prompts for the NAME field and exits if nothing is typed. The program then prompts for the LINE ID and places both NAME and LINE in the environment.

```
if [ -n "$2" ]
then
xxx='echo $2|sed "s/tty//"'
if [ $2 = "00" -o $2 = "cons" -o $2 = "console" ]
    then
    xxx="console"
    else
    xxx=tty$xxx
    fi
fi
```

The program normalizes the name of the device line so that the user can enter a wide variety of device names, and the program can still recognize it.

```
if [ "$#" = "1" ]
   then
   X='who|grep "$1"|wc -l'
   if [ "$X" -gt "1" ]
      then
      echo "Multiple logins "
      exec ko
   fi
fi
```

If the user only gives us a login name and no device, then the program must check to see if more than one user is logged in under that name. If so, the program informs the user and executes the ko program again. This is a "poorman's loop."

```
set " " `who -u|grep "$1"|grep " $xxx"`
shift
```

The preceding lines extract a unique user and places the output in the environment. If there is no match, the 'set " "' command prevents set from simply dumping the environment to us. The shift command removes this bogus field.

```
if [ ! "$*" ]; then echo "no match";exit;fi
```

The program already knows that there are no duplicates. Now it checks to see if there is even one match. If not, it exits.

```
xxx="/dev/"$2
```

If there is a unique match, the program knows the login name, the device name, and the shell process ID.

```
mytty='tty'
mytty='basename $mytty'
if [ "$2" = "$mytty" ];then
echo "You cannot KO yourself";exit;fi
```

The preceding lines prevent the system administrator from "shooting himself in the foot."

```
echo "
#      #
#   #        #     #       #        ######  #####
#  #         #     #       #        #       #    #
###          #     #       #        #####   #    #
#  #         #     #       #        #       #    #
#   #        #     #       #        #       #    #
#     #      #     ######  ######   ######  #####
"|write $1 $xxx 2>&1 >/dev/null
```

These lines inform the victim of what is about to happen.

```
kill -9 'kids $7'
```

The program performs the deed before the victim can appeal. It is justice swift and sure.

Using Private Cryptography with the pcrypt Command

This command evolved because a client wanted to use electronic mail to communicate with his sales agents in this country and in Europe. The standard UNIX crypt command cannot legally be exported, and the client wanted his communications kept private. Besides, the client had read that the UNIX crypt command was not very secure. No reason was offered as to why the NSA, the CIA, or the KGB might want to read his mail, but he wanted it encrypted. Because the client was something of a spy novel buff, all the different espionage schemes that he had read about were incorporated in the pcrypt system.

The `pcrypt` command uses a scheme that only correctly encrypts seven-bit ASCII characters. Thus, binary programs and data cannot be encrypted and transmitted.

The `pcrypt` system relies on two principles. First, any character exclusively OR'd with another is rendered unrecognizable, but when exclusively OR'd with the same character again, the first character magically reappears. The second principle is that of using a random number generator to create the XOR mask.

Random Number Generators

Random number generators do not really generate random numbers (they do not create an endless series of numbers that never repeat) They eventually repeat themselves (which is why they are called pseudo-random number generators. Only a small fraction of the entire series is ever used, and the starting place in the series provides the key to their use.

The fact that random-generated numbers repeat is what makes them useful in cryptography. The random number generator creates an even dispersion of numbers over any range in the series. With any given series of numbers, the chance of any one number coming up is exactly the same as any other number. In other words, the encrypted text has been completely randomized when XOR'd with the random mask. Thus, the only key to unlocking the encrypted data is knowing the starting place in the series and knowing the program used to generate the pseudo-random numbers.

 The four basic commands all computers must execute are AND, OR, XOR, and NOT. Figure 13.1 shows these commands.

	AND	
DATA	0	1
MASK	1	1
RESULT	0	1

	NOT	
DATA	0	1
RESULT	1	0

	OR	
DATA	0	1
MASK	1	1
RESULT	1	1

	XOR (Exclusive OR)	
DATA	0	1
MASK	1	1
RESULT	1	0

Figure 13.1:
Logic tables showing the four basic commands.

If the pseudo-random algorithm is known and the "seed" or key is not known, a supercomputer can be used to try all possible keys. To guard against this, you must use a number generator that has the largest possible number of keys. Some public key-encryption systems use two 64-bit private keys and a single 128-bit public key. In this scheme, anyone knowing the public key can encrypt a message, but only the person knowing the two private keys can decrypt it.

Because this scheme seemed a bit excessive, given the content of the messages, this book uses a 64-bit key. Still, this gives the number 2 raised to the 64th power or 18,446,744,073,709,551,616 possible keys, which should be sufficient. The algorithm that was used recycles after 2 to the 48th power or 281,474,976,710,656 iterations. Because most of the messages are under 10,000 characters, only a very small fragment of the entire series—fewer than 1/17,179,869,184th—is utilized.

The following output shows how it is done:

```
#include <stdio.h>
main(argc,argv)
int argc;
char *argv[];
{
    long i;
    char c;
    union {
        long j[2];
        double k;
        unsigned short l[4];
    } x;
```

For FORTRAN programmers, a union is the way C creates equivalences. In other words, all three variables occupy the same memory, and the program will use all the variations.

```
    x.k=0;
```

Here, the program sets the whole union to 0.

```
    if(argc>1){
        x.j[0]=a641(argv[1]);
    }
    if(argc>2){
        x.j[1]=a641(argv[2]);
    }
```

It was important that the keys used be normal, printable characters. The keys in the preceding output consist of one or two six-character strings. Thus, a key can be "hello world." To convert the keys to something more useful, the program uses the a641 function, which converts from a radix 64 number to a long integer.

The radix 64 number scheme that is described for this function is perfect for this problem. In the `a641` version of a base-64 number, a period (.) represents a zero, a slash (/) represents a one, the numbers 0 through 9 represent 2 through 11, A through Z represent 12 through 37, and a through z represent 38 through 63.

Thus, any word up to six characters long that is found in a dictionary, together with the numbers 0 through 9, as well as slashes and periods, can be used as keys. If two keys are given, they are loaded into the two halves of the double k variable.

```
seed48(x.1);
```

Two random functions exist in the UNIX math library. One is found under `rand` in the manual pages, and it yields random numbers with a period of 2^31. The other random number generator is listed under `drand48` and yields both a longer period between repetitions and a better distribution of numbers than the former does.

The seeding of the generator is done with the first 48 bits of an array of two long integers. Thus, the two ASCII strings are converted into the seed for the random number generator. Notice that the program loaded the high-order word of the seed first to frustrate anyone trying an exhaustive search.

```
while((c=getchar())!=EOF){
    i=((lrand48() ^ x.1[4]) & 127);
    c=c ^ i;
    printf("%c",c);
    }
}
```

The key to the encryption lies in the central two lines of the `while` loop of the above output. The `irand48` function generates a random number, which is rearranged by XORing with the last (and so far unused) member of the long integer array. This does not change the periodicity of the function but it changes the apparent sequence. At the end of the line, the program uses an AND mask to filter out all but the low order seven bits.

On the next line, the program XORs the character it got from the standard input without random mask and prints it to the standard output. This creates only seven-bit data, so binary programs cannot be transmitted accurately. Note that an almost infinite number of different encryption programs can be created by varying these two lines. For example, the program only uses the first seven bits of the lowest order byte for the XOR mask. The program could have been designed to use any of the eight bytes in the long integer, or it could have shifted the long integer any number of bits to the right. It also could have rotated the high order long integer with the low as in the following:

```
i=((lrand48() ^ x.l[4]) & 127);x.l[4]=i & 127;
```

Practical Use of Private Encryption

The `pcrypt` program is intended to be used within a pipe because encrypting the data is only part of the problem. Most mail systems, including the standard UNIX mailers, only transmit printable ASCII characters. Because the `pcrypt` program limits itself to seven bits, many of the characters are control characters which are not permitted.

Two public-domain programs are included in the PCRYPT package. These two programs, `btoa` and `atob`, translate binary code into ASCII and vice versa. The `atob` program only translates files back to binary that were converted to ASCII by `btoa`. These programs are included in the package, in case your system does not already have them. The other program needed is `compress`. This also is a public-domain program that is now included in most UNIX systems.

The `pcrypt` program is used both in encrypting and in decrypting. The key that locks data also unlocks data. When used in conjunction with `compress`, `btoa`, and `atob`, however, the encryption and decryption programs are different.

As an exercise in the use of `pcrypt`, suppose you have a secret message that you want to send to your special agent hidden someplace in the East. The secret message reads:

```
Clean up "dirty laundry" and report back ASAP. HQ
```

Although a bit cryptic, you do not want the code words "`dirty laundry`" to be seen by prying eyes. Back at headquarters, you place the text of your message in a file named X. To encrypt it, issue the following command:

encrypt X

You are next prompted for the first key, which is **hello**, then the second key, which is **world**. Your encrypted file is placed in X.X. The text of X.X looks like this:

```
xbtoa Begin
"8oD41LIT(.WZYV3af$p9Ci3c&.6m_HiZ&`712+ja<Meb::2K:&\A3F82uo.,O\/
J3a#-h"]]OB
xbtoa End N 59 3b E fa S 15ec R 89083e83
```

Because this message is Top Secret, you immediately delete your plain text file X. You then mail the file by using the following command:

```
mail -s "top secret" bustah <X.X
```

Some hours later (the International Internet is not always fast), the secret agent is notified that he has mail. After reading the mail and saving the message in a file that he has called X.XXX, he looks at it a second time. The following is what the secret agent sees:

```
From boss-x Sat Jul 18 18:13:13 1992
To: bustah
Subject: top secret
Date: Sat Jul 18 18:13:13 1992

xbtoa Begin
"8oD4lLIT(.WZYV3af$p9Ci3c&.6m_HiZ&`712+ja<Meb::2K:&\A3F82uo.,O\/
J3a#-h"]]OB
xbtoa End N 59 3b E fa S 15ec R 89083e83
```

Using whatever editor he chooses, the agent deletes all text down to the line that begins `xbtoa` and saves the file again. To decrypt the message he uses the command:

decrypt XXX

After entering the correct keys, the decrypted output is piped through `pg`. At this point, the agent has the option of saving the plain text.

This secret preserving service is performed by two very small commands, `encrypt` and `decrypt`. Both require `btoa`, `atob`, and `compress` in addition to `pcrypt` to function. The source code for `encrypt` is as follows:

```
CMPRS="compress"
BTOA="btoa"
K1='prompt Enter First key'
K2='prompt Enter Second key'
( $CMPRS | pcrypt $K1 $K2 | $BTOA )< $1 > X.$1
```

The source code for the `decrypt` command is:

```
CMPRS="uncompress"
ATOB="atob"
K1='prompt Enter First key'
K2='prompt Enter Second key'
( $ATOB | pcrypt $K1 $K2 | $CMPRS )< X.$1 |pg
```

Another problem is that of keeping secrets. If you repeat something often enough, and the "other side" is interested enough, eventually they catch on. Thus, if the secret agent really wants to encrypt the plain text above, the scheme of coding should be changed often or the encoding scheme made more complex. This can be done in two ways.

One way is to use double encryption; that is, to take the output of one pass of the encrypt program, and to run it through again with different keys. In other words, you utilize a new program with a line that looks like this:

```
( $CMPRS | pcrypt $K1 $K2 |pcrypt $K3 $K4| $BTOA )< $1 > X.$1
```

This technique prevents the "other side" from knowing when it has hit on half the keys.

The other way to increase system security is to never use ordinary words as keys and to never use the same keys twice. One of traditional way to do this is to keep two identical copies of a list of words to be used as keys, and as the keys are used, tear them up and throw them away.

Generating a list of randomly created keys is easy; the key-generation program must generate a different sequence of numbers from any given input, however. This is the service performed by the kgen program and the shell script keygen.

The kgen program is as follows (the annotations are the differences between kgen and pcrypt):

```
#include <stdio.h>
main(argc,argv)
int argc;
char *argv[];
{
```

```
long i,m;
char c[6];
union {
    long j[2];
    double k;
    unsigned short l[4];
} x;
x.k=0;
x.j[0]=a64l(argv[1]);
x.j[1]=a64l(argv[2]);
seed48(x.l);
for(m=1;m<=atoi(argv[3]);m++){
    i=lrand48() ^ x.l[4];
    printf("%s\n",l64a(i));
}
}
```

In the preceding output, you use exactly the same line of code (without the AND 127) to generate a long integer. This time, however, you are using the entire number generated and not just one byte. To show the kind of variety possible, here is an alternative code generator:

```
i=irand48() ^ x.l[4] ^ i;
```

This generates an entirely different sequence of random numbers from the preceding example, as does the following:

```
i=irand48() ^x.l[4];x.l[4]^=i;
```

The possibilities arc endless, and electronic mail can be made as safe from prying eyes as it needs to be.

The last command encapsulates the use of kgen. The keygen program is as follows:

```
kgen $1 $2 $3|paste - - - -
```

The command-line arguments for `keygen` (and `kgen`) are key1, key2, and the number of keys to generate. Thus, `keygen`, called as `keygen hello world 64`, generates 64 randomly-generated keys in radix 64 (base 64) notation and prints them on the standard output in four columns. This is the PCRYPT package.

Summary

This chapter discussed helpful system-administration commands and utilities. You learned how to use `dps`, `dpsn`, and `dpscron` commands, as well as how to kill by using the `ko` command. The chapter also discussed using cryptography with the `pcrypt` command.

The following final chapter gives you an idea about what will happen when downsizing is a thing of the past.

Index

C

E

F

M

O

P

New Riders Covers
All Your Operating System's Needs!

Maximizing MS-DOS 5

Through DOS 5

1-56205-013-3, 700 pp., 7³/₈ x 9¹/₄
$34.95 USA

Maximizing Windows 3.1

Windows 3.0 & 3.1

1-56205-044-3, 800 pp., 7³/₈ x 9¹/₄
$39.95 USA

More Titles from New Riders!

Inside OS/2, Release 2.0

Version 2.0

1-56205-045-1, 850 pp., 7³/₈ x 9¹/₄
$34.95 USA

Inside SCO UNIX

SCO Xenix 286, SCO Xenix 386, SCO UNIX/System V 386

1-56205-028-1, 600 pp., 7³/₈ x 9¹/₄
$29.95 USA

Inside Solaris SunOS

SunOS, Sun's version of UNIX for the SPARC workstation

1-56205-032-X, 750 pp., 7³/₈ x 9¹/₄
$29.95 USA

Inside Windows 3.1

Windows 3.0 & 3.1

1-56205-038-9, 750 pp., 7³/₈ x 9¹/₄
$29.95 USA

Maximizing Windows 3

Windows 3.0

1-56205-002-8, 704 pp., 7³/₈ x 9¹/₄
$39.95 USA

UNIX On Command

SCO UNIX, AT&T System V, & BSD 4.X

1-56205-027-3, 140 pp., 6³/₄ x 8¹/₂
$19.95 USA

Windows 3.1 Networking

Windows 3.0 & 3.1

1-56205-053-2, 350 pp., 7³/₈ x 9¹/₄
$22.95 USA

Windows 3.1 On Command

Windows 3.0 & 3.1

1-56205-047-8, 140 pp., 6³/₄ x 8¹/₂
$19.95 USA

Windows 3 On Command

Windows 3.0

1-56205-016-8, 140 pp., 6³/₄ x 8¹/₂
$19.95 USA

To Order, Call: (800) 428-5331
OR (317) 573-2500

NRP
NEW RIDERS PUBLISHING